NEWMAN AND LIFE IN THE SPIRIT

NEWMAN AND LIFE IN THE SPIRIT

THEOLOGICAL REFLECTIONS ON SPIRITUALITY FOR TODAY

JOHN R. CONNOLLY AND BRIAN W. HUGHES, EDITORS

Fortress Press
Minneapolis

NEWMAN AND LIFE IN THE SPIRIT
Theological Reflections on Spirituality for Today

Copyright © 2014 Fortress Press. All rights reserved. Except for brief quotations in critical articles or reviews, no part of this book may be reproduced in any manner without prior written permission from the publisher. Visit http://www.augsburgfortress.org/copyrights/ or write to Permissions, Augsburg Fortress, Box 1209, Minneapolis, MN 55440.

Cover image: John Henry Newman/The Fathers of Birmingham Oratory/PA
Cover design: Laurie Ingram

Library of Congress Cataloging-in-Publication Data
Print ISBN: 978-1-4514-7253-0

eBook ISBN: 978-1-4514-8438-0

The paper used in this publication meets the minimum requirements of American National Standard for Information Sciences — Permanence of Paper for Printed Library Materials, ANSI Z329.48-1984.

Manufactured in the U.S.A.

This book was produced using PressBooks.com, and PDF rendering was done by PrinceXML.

To
Rosemary, Alex, Elizabeth,
and
to
The Sisters of Charity of Leavenworth, Kansas

CONTENTS

Acknowledgments   ix
Abbreviations of Newman's Works   xi
Introduction   1
   John R. Connolly and Brian W. Hughes

1. John Henry Newman's Apologia as a Journal of His Conversions   13
   John T. Ford, CSC

2. The Indwelling of the Holy Spirit   31
   The Foundation of Newman's Spirituality
   John R. Connolly

3. Coming to Terms with the Past   51
   The Role of History in the Spirituality of John Henry Newman
   Kenneth L. Parker

4. Sympathy in the Spiritual Theology of John Henry Newman   75
   Donald G. Graham

5. Trinity, Imagination, and Belief in the Spirituality of John Henry Newman   97
   Theodore J. Whapham

6. Marked by Christ's Presence   113
   Newman's Incarnational Spirituality
   Danielle Nussberger

7. Newman's Mariology   129
   A Model for a Spirituality of Reception
   Ryan Marr

8. Newman's Vision of Holiness in This World   145
   John R. Connolly

9. John Henry Newman and the Communion of Saints   167
   Brian W. Hughes

10. Newman and the Spirituality of the Oratory   187
   Embracing the Presence of the Indwelling Spirit
   Kevin Mongrain

Bibliography   201
List of Authors   223
Index   227

Acknowledgments

The authors would like to thank the members of the board of the Catholic Theological Society of America (CTSA) for giving us the opportunity to convene an interest group on the spirituality of John Henry Newman at the 2011, 2012, and 2013 national conferences. Special thanks to Mary Ann Hinsdale, IHM, Ph.D. for her gracious advice in the preparation of the proposal for the interest group. In addition, we are grateful to all those members of the CTSA who participated in the Spirituality of John Henry Newman interest group. This includes those who have authored chapters in this book, as well as those who participated by attending the sessions and contributing through questions and discussion.

In a most special way John wishes to thank Rosemary, his wife, who allowed him to take time from their retirement to work on this book. She supported and encouraged him throughout the whole process. John would like to thank his colleagues and friends in the Newman Association of America, NAA, who have supported his research and writing over the years. Chapter 8, "Newman's Vision of Holiness in This World," was first presented as a paper at the 2012 national NAA conference. Their comments and suggestions have been most helpful. John also would like to thank the editors of the *Newman Studies Journal*, particularly John T. Ford, CSC, the editor in chief, and Lisa M. Goetz, the managing editor, for granting him permission to republish his article on the indwelling of the Holy Spirit as chapter 2.

Brian would like to thank his wife Rosario for her support and encouragement. He is also grateful for the support and review of his chapter by members of the Newman Association of America (NAA) in 2010 and by Dr. Grant Kaplan. In addition, he would like to thank Sr. Diane Steele and Dr. Bryan LeBeau for granting him sabbatical leave in fall of 2013 which provided time for this project. For their help with the editorial process, he is grateful to Diana Mera, and Steeli Norton.

Together we would like to give special thanks to those at Fortress Press who have assisted us in a very kind and professional way throughout the process of publishing this book. These include, Michael Gibson, Acquisitions Editor, Esther Diley, Rights Coordinator, David Cottingham, Copyeditor, and Lisa

Gruenisen, Development Editor. Without their assistance this book would not have been possible.

John R. Connolly and Brian W. Hughes

Abbreviations of Newman's Works

Apo	*Apologia Pro Vita Sua*
Ari	*The Arians of the Fourth Century*
AW	*John Henry Newman: Autobiographical Writings*
Cons	*On Consulting the Faithful in Matters of Doctrine*
Dev	*An Essay on the Development of Christian Doctrine*
Diff	*Certain Difficulties Felt by Anglicans in Church Teaching Considered*
GA	*An Essay in Aid of a Grammar of Assent*
HS	*Historical Sketches*
Idea	*The Idea of a University*
LD	*Letters and Diaries of John Henry Newman*
Lfc	*Lectures on the Doctrine of Justification*
MD	*Meditations and Devotions of the Late Cardinal Newman*
OS	*Sermons Preached on Various Occasions*
PPS	*Parochial and Plain Sermons*
TT	*Tracts Theological and Ecclesiastical*
US	*Fifteen Sermons Preached Before the University of Oxford (1826–1843)*
VM	*The Via Media of the Anglican Church* Vol. 1: *Lectures on the Prophetical Office of the Church* Vol. 2: *Occasional Letters and Tracts*
VV	*Verses on Various Occasions*

Introduction

John R. Connolly and Brian W. Hughes

The second precept then of the religious guides to whom I have alluded is this: that if we would aim at perfection, we must perform well the duties of the day. I do not know anything more difficult, more sobering, so strengthening than the constant aim to go through the ordinary day's work well.[1]

John Henry Newman (1801–1890) is a nineteenth-century British Catholic theologian and religious leader who converted from the Anglican Church to the Roman Catholic Church in 1845. He is a rich source of theological and spiritual wisdom. His views are relevant for the twenty-first century, and he is a reform-minded theological and spiritual leader, open to necessary changes in thought and practice essential for a vital church and spiritual life. For over two hundred years, he has been a major source of theological and spiritual wisdom for Catholic thinkers, church leaders, educators, pastoral ministers, and the laity, as well as for many outside the Catholic Church. He has been referred to as the Father of the Second Vatican Council.

His works on the notion of faith, the *University Sermons* (1826–43) and the *Grammar of Assent* (1870), introduced a nonscholastic and a more historical view of faith and reason that has and continues to influence philosophers and theologians.[2] Written in 1845, Newman's *Essay on the Development of*

---

1. John Henry Newman, "The second precept then of the religious guides to whom I have alluded is this: that, if we would aim at perfection, we must perform well the duties of the day. I do not know anything more difficult, more sobering, so strengthening than the constant aim to go through the ordinary day's work well." Oratory Paper, no. 10, 11 December 1850. Placid Murray, *Newman the Oratorian: His Unpublished Oratory Papers* (Dublin: Gill & Macmillan, 1969), 235.

2. Bernard Lonergan penned the well-known statement attesting to Newman's influence. "My fundamental mentor and guide has been John Henry Newman's *Grammar of Assent*. I read that in my third year philosophy (at least the analytic parts) about five times and found solutions for my problems. I was not at all satisfied with the philosophy that was being taught and found Newman's presentation to be something that fitted in with the way I knew things. It was from that kernel that I went on to different authors." "Reality, Myth, Symbol," in *Myth, Symbol, and Reality*, ed. Alan M. Olson (Notre Dame: University of Notre Dame Press, 1980), 32–33. See Philip A. Egan, "John Henry Newman and Bernard Lonergan: A Note on the Development of Christian Doctrine," *Revista Portuguesa de Filosofia* 63 (2007):

Doctrine remains an essential source for anyone who wishes to understand the role of change and development in the Church and doctrine. His *Idea of a University* (1852–59) is still a classic, and is referenced by educators today in discussions of liberal education. Any analysis of the role of the laity in the church today must consider Newman's essay, *On Consulting the Faithful in Matters of Doctrine* (1859). Before his election as pope, Cardinal Joseph Ratzinger praised Newman's concept of development, describing it as one of the "decisive and fundamental concepts of Catholicism."[3] His *Apologia Pro Vita Sua* (1864) is not only a vital resource for understanding Newman's religious development, but is a literary masterpiece studied by scholars in a wide variety of disciplines such as history and English. Those wishing to further understand the intricate relationships between authority, infallibility, and conscience in the Catholic Church still refer to his *Letter to the Duke of Norfolk* (1875).

Another area in which Newman has been a perennial source, but to many still remains a hidden treasure, is Christian holiness and spirituality. Newman's personal holiness has long been recognized. Recently, the Catholic Church and the papacy of Benedict XVI made progress in establishing this conviction formally. At the beatification of John Henry Newman at Cofton Park, Birmingham, England, on September 19, 2010, Pope Benedict XVI delivered an inspiring homily in which he celebrated Newman's holiness and sanctity before the whole world. The pope spoke of Newman's understanding of Christian life as a call to holiness and of his faithfulness to prayer. He concluded with a brief reflection on Newman's life as a priest and a pastor of souls.[4]

NEWMAN'S NOTION OF SPIRITUALITY

What remains challenging about interpreting Newman's view of spirituality is that he blends the emphases of two spiritual traditions: Tractarian Anglican and Roman Catholic. There are certainly features of traditional Anglican spirituality one notices throughout the *Parochial and Plain Sermons* and that one can glimpse in this book's chapters. Gordon Wakefield describes many aspects of Anglican piety and life that appear in Newman's Anglican period: the centrality of

---

1103–23. Avery Cardinal Dulles, SJ, also mentions the influence of Newman on Michael Polanyi. *John Henry Newman* (New York: Continuum, 2002), 45.

3. Joseph Ratzinger, "The Ecclesiology of the Second Vatican Council," *Communio* 13 (1986): 241–42. We are grateful for Professor Ken Parker for alerting us to this reference.

4. Benedict XVI, "Homily for Beatification of Cardinal Newman," accessed, August 14, 2013, at http://www.speroforum.com/a/40077/Pope-Benedicts-homily-for-beatification-of-Cardinal-Newman.

common worship, prayer, the preached Word as expressed in Old and New Testaments, the pursuit of personal holiness through ecclesial sacraments, liturgy, and moral discipline consonant with the Evangelical tone of Anglicanism.[5] Nevertheless, such emphases are common to a variety of Catholic spiritualities too. One can find overlap, for instance, on Newman's treatment of the patristic notion of deification or *theosis* that aligns with the teachings of the Cambridge Platonists such as John Smith, Benjamin Whichcote, and Henry More.[6] Consequently, one will be frustrated by trying to identify hard distinctions in Newman's writing between an Anglican and a Catholic spirituality *per se*. Indeed, the Oxford Movement aimed to recover more patristic, doctrinal, and liturgical elements from its own Catholic heritage, making the effort at identifying denominational features of Newman's spirituality more difficult.

Bearing in mind the commonalities between Anglican and Catholic spiritualities, there are three major characteristics at work in Newman's spirituality. At one and the same time, it is personal, social, and rooted in the Catholic tradition. Newman's notion of spirituality, being grounded in the believer's experience of the triune God though the indwelling of the Holy Spirit, is God-centered and deeply personal. Here we are at the heart of the theological basis of Newman's understanding of spirituality. It is a transformation of the interior life of the believer through the experience of the triune God in the very depths of one's being. This relationship with God begins with the Christian's acceptance of the presence of the indwelling of the Holy Spirit conferred at baptism. It is important to stress that, for Newman, this faith acceptance of the indwelling Spirit occurs at the level of a real assent. As a real assent, faith is a response of the whole person in the totality of one's being. This affirmation results in personal transformation, a new awareness of self; it engages the imagination, stirs the affections, and moves one to action. Holiness at the personal level is communion with God.

Newman's focus on the interior life and the personal experience of the indwelling of the Holy Spirit might give the impression that his spirituality is exclusively individualistic and isolated from involvement in the world. A certain

---

5. See Gordon S. Wakefield, "Anglican Spirituality," in *Christianity Spirituality: Post-Reformation and Modern*, ed. Louis Dupré and Don E. Saliers (New York: Crossroad, 1993), 257–93. Also see A. M. Allchin, "Anglican Spirituality," in *The Study of Anglicanism*, ed. Stephen Sykes and John Booty (Philadelphia: Fortress Press, 1988), 313–24. It should be noted that Newman did not claim to experience strong passions and violent emotions indicative of Evangelical conversions. See Ian Ker, *John Henry Newman: A Biography* (Oxford: Oxford University Press, 2009 [1988]), 5.

6. Wakefield, "Anglican Spirituality," 269–71.

view of Oratorian life and spirituality—with its emphasis on the individual in community—might suggest this. Such a view would be false. To begin with, the acceptance of the indwelling Spirit places one in a communal relationship of love, the love of the three divine persons in relation to one another and to the world, which, in turn, places the believer in a relationship with others and the world. So, by its very nature, a spirituality based upon the indwelling of the Holy Spirit establishes a relationship with and a responsibility to others and the world. It is communal and social as well as personal.

Further evidence supporting this social dimension of Newman's spirituality can be found in his life. Newman was far from being a self-absorbed recluse, concerned only with his interior life, separated from others and world events. For him, holiness is a process of making the indwelling Spirit present and operative in one's daily life. Newman was actively involved in this world, working to make the Spirit present in his relationships with others, and in educational, political, and ecclesial matters of the Church and society of his day. Newman's notion of spirituality as realizing the presence of the Holy Spirit in one's life and in the world is a reform-minded spirituality. It does have, therefore, implications for the Christian's participation in the transformation of the structures and institutions of the Church and the world.

Newman's spirituality is also firmly grounded in the Catholic tradition. It is based upon the revelation of God in Jesus Christ, rooted in the Hebrew and Christian Scriptures, the early Christian writers, the history of Christianity, and nineteenth-century Anglican and Catholic theology. Illustrated throughout this book, Newman's spirituality is shaped by the basic doctrines of Christian faith: the Trinity, the indwelling of the Holy Spirit, the Christ event, the Church and its sacraments, the doctrines of sin and salvation, devotion to Mary and the saints. Doctrines and dogmas are essential aspects of Newman's spirituality, but they are not ends in themselves. They are prior communal and individual experiences of the indwelling Spirit articulated in propositional forms. For Newman, doctrines have a twofold purpose. Apprehended as notions, they ascertain and clarify for the believer "the truths on which the religious imagination has to rest."[7] Notional assent to doctrines is necessary to ensure that one's understanding of revelation is accurate. Apprehended and accepted through real assent, doctrines personally transform the believer and become objects of devotion. But, Newman cautions, if doctrines are viewed only as abstract notions—accepted through notional assent only—they can present problems for personal faith and devotion.[8] The experience of the triune God

---

7. John Henry Newman, *An Essay in Aid of a Grammar of Assent* (Notre Dame: University of Notre Dame Press, 1979), 120.

through the indwelling Spirit is realized fully as a source of spirituality if it is concretely realized through real assent.

Definition of Spirituality

A work on spirituality can be obtuse and confusing if the term is not defined and placed in some context. Newman's spirituality can be understood better if we turn to two scholars' views insofar as they express the contextual and suggestive aspects of holiness in the modern world. Michael J. Buckley distinguishes two historical types of Western Christian spirituality: ascent and descent.[9] As the terms imply, ascent and descent correspond to directions, to how and where one perceives God's activity within daily life. In the ascent tradition, God is discovered above and beyond the material word, through detachment, and often characterized by contemplative prayer, asceticism, and seclusion. One ascends through prayer and ascetical practices up and beyond this world to the mystical darkness that is the reality of God. Ascent spirituality would be typical of cloistered or monastic spirituality. Conversely, descent spirituality locates the experience of God within and through created realities, people, things, events, actions, and such, that form the matrix of a living engagement with the world. This approach to life in the indwelling Spirit of the Trinitarian God corresponds nicely to Sandra Schneiders's definition of spirituality as "the experience of consciously striving to integrate one's life in terms not of isolation and self-absorption but of self-transcendence toward the ultimate value that one perceives."[10]

Relevance for Today

Today the Catholic Church needs a personal approach to Christian spirituality wedded to social concern. Newman's spirituality offers hopeful direction and guidance for an integrated, holy life. Presently, the Church is blessed with an educated laity, the type of laity that Newman so elegantly wrote about and for which he hoped. However, many traditional ways of presenting the

---

8. *GA*, 120.

9. Michael J. Buckley, SJ, "Spirituality and the Incarnate God," *Spirituality for the 21st Century: Experiencing God in the Catholic Tradition*, ed. Richard W. Miller III (Ligouri, MO: Ligouri, 2006), 23–38; 26–30.

10. Sandra M. Schneiders, "Theology and Spirituality: Strangers, Rivals, or Partners?," *Horizons: Journal of the College Theology Society* 13 (1986): 266. Schneiders narrows this definition to specify Christian spirituality as referring to Christian religious experience that is "affective as well as cognitive, social as well as personal, God-centered and other directed all at the same time" (267).

gospel and guiding Christians to live meaningful spiritual lives are no longer working. Current efforts to bring back older devotional forms such as novenas and Eucharistic adoration, emphases on traditional confession, and so forth, may stimulate small, traditional populations within the church. Still, they are not speaking to the greater numbers of Catholics who leave and the growing number who subscribe to no religious affiliation at all. Further, all the Church's efforts to restore faith through a notional evangelization seem ineffective. Authentic and serious evangelization requires more than repetition of well-known and sometimes controversial doctrines.

The pontificate of Francis I offers signs that the Church is aware of the inadequacy of its traditional ways of evangelizing. In a speech to the Latin American Bishops, Francis warned against dealing with the Church's problems with "a purely disciplinary solution" and against a "restoration of outdated manners and forms which, even on the cultural level, are no longer meaningful." He warns against "exaggerated tendencies toward doctrinal or disciplinary safety."

Even more important for a Christian spirituality and contemporary evangelization, Pope Francis continues: "Responding to the existential issues of people today, especially the young, listening to the language they speak, can lead to a fruitful change, which must take place with the help of the Gospel, the magisterium, and the church's social doctrine. . . . If we remain within the parameters of our 'traditional culture' . . . we will end up nullifying the power of the Holy Spirit."[11] Certainly, the spirituality of John Henry Newman, which is grounded in the presence of the Holy Spirit and the continual realization of this presence in one's life and in the life of the Church, has much to teach and guide Christians and the Church in the twenty-first century. Based upon his belief in the universal presence of the Holy Spirit, individual discernment, prayer, and personal engagement with the world, Newman's view of spirituality has significance for all denominations of Christians, peoples of faith, and those who feel alienated by it, as well as for our relationship with the natural world.

Reform Minded

Newman also is an innovative and reform-minded thinker. He supported change and development in the Church. As a leader of the Oxford Movement

---

11. "Apostolic Journey to Rio de Janeiro on the Occasion of the XXVIII World Youth Day," Address to the Leadership of the Episcopal Conferences of Latin America during the General Coordination Meeting, Sunday, July 28, 2013, accessed September 4, 2013 at http://www.vatican.va/holy_father/francesco/speeches/2013/july/documents/papa-francesco_20130728_gmg-celam-rio_en.html.

(1833–41), he prophetically called for a reform of the Anglican Church. As a reformer in education, he founded a Catholic University in Ireland (1851–58). During the nineteenth century, when the bishops wanted a laity that would "obey, hunt, and shoot,"[12] Newman called for an educated and informed laity—far ahead of his time. Recognizing the role of the laity in the reception and development of doctrine, Newman supported the notion of the *sensus fidelium* that the Second Vatican Council incorporated as a key doctrine.[13] Toward the end of the reign of Pius IX, Newman called for a new pope and, perhaps, the need for a new council.[14] Newman's notion of spirituality as realizing the presence of the Holy Spirit in one's life and in the world is a reform-minded spirituality. What could be a more powerful agent in the transformation of the Church and Christians in the twenty-first century than the universal and all-inclusive presence of the indwelling of the Holy Spirit?

Rationale for the Book

Newman's beatification reminds Christians of the deep spirituality possessed by this great nineteenth-century religious thinker and pastoral minister. His spirituality and the awareness of its enduring significance for Christians living in the twenty-first century is the inspiration for this book. Indeed, a book on Newman's spirituality is certainly both intellectually and practically relevant for today.

Although Newman's holiness and deep spiritual life have long been recognized, works on his notion of spirituality are few compared with the scholarship treating his other contributions and biography. One of the reasons for the relative lack of works on Newman's notion of spirituality is that he never wrote a systematic treatise specifically on that topic.[15] Another difficulty is that Newman's views on spirituality are so scattered throughout his works that one has to read a great number of them to discover patterns to his insights regarding a holy life.[16] However, his works are full of theological descriptions of what it

---

12. The statement was made by Msgr. Talbot to Archbishop Manning. Wilfred Ward, *The Life of John Henry Newman: Based on His Private Journals and Correspondence*, vol. 2 (New York: Longmans, Green & Co., 1921), 147.

13. Second Vatican Council, *Lumen Gentium*, par. 12, accessed September 3, 2013 at http://www.vatican.va/archive/hist_councils/ii_vatican_council/documents/vat-ii_const_19641121_lumen-gentium_en.html.

14. John Henry Newman, *LD*, 25:310.

15. See William R. Lamm, SM, *The Spiritual Legacy of Newman* (Milwaukee: Bruce, 1934), ix–x; Hilda Graef, *God and Myself*, 9; and Vincent F. Blehl, SJ, *The White Stone: The Spiritual Theology of John Henry Newman* (Petersham, MA: St. Bede's, 1993), x.

means to be a Christian, filled with guidelines, spiritual advice, and illustrations of concrete, Christian holiness. It is precisely part of this book's aim to develop and highlight various themes and insights and theological principles that inform his spirituality.

Relationship to Other Works

There are a few works in English that treat John Henry Newman's spirituality. Unfortunately, most of those are quite outdated.[17] In the last decade, for example, only one book was published on the topic and that work explored Mary's role within Newman's spirituality.[18] Despite a renewed interest in John Henry Newman due in part to his recent beatification, there is a serious lack of scholarship on Newman's spirituality that this volume seeks to fill. What distinguishes this book is the scope and diversity of the aspects of Newman's spirituality that it addresses. Further, each chapter relates Newman's spirituality to contemporary issues and shows how his spiritual and theological insights apply to Christian daily life in the twenty-first century.

A further objective of this book is to make Newman's view of spirituality available and accessible to contemporary theologians, scholars, believers, and seekers.

Chapter Summaries

The chapters in this book represent the research of the participants in a Catholic Theological Society of America (CTSA) Interest Group on the Spirituality of John Henry Newman that convened at the CTSA conferences between the years 2011 and 2013.

John Ford, in chapter one, drawing upon Newman's chronicle of his spiritual journey in the *Apologia Pro Vita Sua* (1864), discusses Newman's understanding of conversion and its significance for Christian spirituality. After summarizing Newman's four major conversions, 1) Evangelical; 2) Noetic; 3) Tractarian; and 4) Roman Catholic, Ford highlights and provides nuance to some of the characteristics of his conversions. Six major characteristics are

---

16. Graef, *God and Myself*, 9.

17. Louis Bouyer, *Cardinal Newman: His Life and Spirituality* (New York: P. Kennedy, 1958); C. S. Dessain, *The Spirituality of John Henry Newman* (Minneapolis: Winston, 1980); Graef, *God and Myself*; Ian Ker, *Healing the Wound of Humanity: The Spirituality of John Henry Newman* (London: Darton, Longman & Todd, 1993); Blehl, *The White Stone*.

18. Nicholas Gregoris, *"The Daughter of Eve Unfallen": Mary in the Theology and Spirituality of John Henry Newman* (Mount Pocono, PA: Newman House, 2003).

discussed: 1, Conversion as a process; 2, Conversion as complementary; 3, Conversions as defining moments; 4, Newman's conversion as revelations of his personal approach to apologetics; 5, Conversion as an exercise of the illative sense; and 6, Conversions as requiring duration. In the conclusion, Ford demonstrates how these characteristics are spiritually insightful and applicable to the spiritual life of all Christians. Newman's spiritual journey shows that at the heart of every spirituality, there is some type of conversion that results in a fundamental life change, and that the spiritual life is gradual and progressive, involving change and development.

In chapter two, John Connolly presents a summary of Newman's understanding of the Christian notion of the indwelling of the Holy Spirit and demonstrates its significance for his understanding of spirituality. After presenting a critical analysis of Newman's notion of the indwelling of the Holy Spirit in the *Parochial and Plain Sermons*, Connolly maintains that this Christian doctrine is the foundation of Newman's understanding of spirituality. Newman views the spiritual life as a lifelong process of realizing the presence of the Holy Spirit in oneself, in the Church, and in the world. One of the major implications of Newman's notion of spirituality for Christians today—indicated in this chapter—is its personal nature. Spirituality is rooted in a personal relationship with God and not in a notional assent to the external expressions of Christianity. Other implications for Christian's today include: the gifts of the Holy Spirit as a source of spiritual direction, the universal presence of the Holy Spirit, and his insight that the quest for holiness is an ongoing process, a process ones moves toward but does not perfectly achieve.

In chapter three, Kenneth Parker traces the connection between Newman's spirituality of conversion—his journey of faith—and his evolving thought regarding historical consciousness that led to his famous theology of doctrinal development. He outlines the personal, spiritual movement from his early evangelical period to his conversion to Roman Catholicism by marking Newman's intellectual struggles with the Christian past. These struggles, reflecting upon different points of view from his study of historical events and friends, kept prodding Newman to reexamine critically his assumptions about a rigid view of history. Parker recounts diverse elements involved in Newman's change from a static view of history. This change was influenced by his love of the Church Fathers and the recognition that different periods within Church history manifest purity, decline, and reform. He explores the changes, for Newman, in that model's adequacy as a support for his ecclesial commitments and spirituality.

In chapter four, Donald Graham brings together Newman's doctrinal theology regarding sympathy and shows how it links to Newman's spiritual theology—his spirituality. For instance, he tells how a connection between Trinitarian sympathy can speak to youth who feel alienated from religion; how Newman's view of sympathy—drawing upon creation and incarnation—connects to environmental concern and a practical spirituality of caring; and how the sympathy of Jesus' human-divine nature lifts up and points to genuine human experience as occasions of grace. Indeed, Graham demonstrates that Newman's theology of sympathy helps Christians better see that "our yearnings for life, love, justice, goodness, beauty, and wholeness" have a purposeful meaning and do not end with natural death. In such ways, Graham argues that Newman's understanding of "sympathy" is powerfully relevant for a contemporary spirituality.

In chapter five, Ted Whapham explores Newman's thought about making a real assent to the Trinity through the imagination for a contemporary spirituality. Using the *Grammar of Assent*, Whapham argues that Newman seeks to make relevant the ordinary experience of Christians to the teaching on the Trinity especially through the Bible, the church's liturgical life, individual and communal prayer and devotions. What is of crucial importance here concerns the integration of patterns of thought and action, doctrine and daily prayer, that connect theological teaching with the lived practice of faith—its "affective, rational, and volitional dimensions." Theologically expressed, Whapham argues that Newman's link between a real assent, the imagination, and the Trinity is another way of understanding "deification, revelation, sanctification." For Newman, a real assent to the Trinity through the imagination comes alive in and is enriched by the diverse images of the Trinity that the imagination can integrate as well as the experiences of relationship and community that shape daily life informed by the Spirit.

In chapter six, Danielle Nussberger's analysis of Newman's incarnational spirituality reaffirms the personal nature of Newman's spirituality. Describing Newman's notion as being marked by Christ's presence, the author sees a bond between Newman's understandings of the incarnation, Mary, and the Eucharist that explains how Christ's presence in the world through the incarnation continues as a dynamic, current presence in the lives of Christians today. Newman's view of holiness is described as being marked by the presence of Christ. Through the incarnation, all humanity and everything in the world are marked by the presence of Christ. In Mary, Newman finds an exemplar for what it means to live in the restored bond between God and humanity that occurs in the incarnation. She lived in the presence of Christ. Through participation in the Eucharist, Christians today are continually being marked by the presence of Christ. In homiletic fashion, Nussberger urges Christians today to embrace Newman's incarnational spirituality and become contemporary exemplars of those who live in the presence of Christ.

Ryan Marr, in chapter seven, sees Newman's Mariology as a model for a spirituality of reception for interpreting church teachings. Drawing upon Newman's fifteenth Oxford University Sermon, the chapter begins with an analysis of Newman's notion of Mary as the pattern of faith. From Newman's description of Mary as the pattern of faith, Marr develops some principles of interpretation that constitute what he refers to as the Marian mode of interpretation. Describing the different roles of theologians and laity, the author explains how this Marian mode of interpretation can assist both in their efforts to contribute to the process of Church teachings. Applying the Marian mode of interpretation specifically to the teachings of the Second Vatican Council, Marr admits that it will not end all disputes, because the reception of Church teaching is an ongoing process. However, it will provide theologians and the laity with a specific spirituality of reception adequate to their respective vocations.

In chapter eight, John Connolly describes the development and characteristics of Newman's vision of "holiness in this world." As an Evangelical, Newman tended to emphasize the unseen world, embracing what can be described as an "other-worldly holiness." By 1845, his view of holiness had shifted toward a more "this-worldly" form of holiness. Through his readings of the early Christian writers, his deepening consciousness of the sacramental principle, and his sermons on the indwelling of the Holy Spirit, Newman begins to emphasize the visible signs of God's presence in this world. Holiness becomes a quest to discover and encounter the invisible world in the visible world. The primary objective of Newman's "this-worldly holiness" is to live daily life in the presence of the indwelling Spirit and to work to make the Spirit present in all things in this world. After analyzing Newman's vision of this-worldly holiness, this chapter discusses the significance of Newman's view of holiness for a Catholic lay spirituality today.

In chapter nine, Brian W. Hughes focuses on showing how John Henry Newman's own relationship with St. Philip Neri provides a case study in Christian spirituality. In this way, Newman's example is a rich resource in understanding how the communion of saints can be understood and experienced today. He develops Newman's theology of the communion of saints through particular sermons and treatises, highlighting Newman's theological and pastoral principle of "personal influence." He then enriches this interpretation by incorporating the insights of Elizabeth Johnson's seminal work on the communion of saints, using the categories of "patron" and "friend" to interpret and texture Newman's own thoughts and experiences of St. Philip's activity in his own life. Finally, he develops important dimensions of Newman's thought and his own personal spiritual practice to highlight how the reality of the communion of saints can function in a contemporary Christian spirituality.

Kevin Mongrain in chapter ten, drawing upon Newman's *Oratory Papers*, presents a critical analysis of Newman's Oratorian Spirituality. After reviewing Newman's reasons for choosing the Oratorian Congregation over other possibilities, the author maintains that Newman's Oratorian Spirituality is grounded in the "primitive Church," in the *Disciplina Arcani*, the secret esoteric wisdom of Alexandrian Christianity and its notion of salvation as deification. According to Mongrain, the major teaching that Newman receives from this early Christian tradition—and that becomes the basis of his Oratorian Spirituality—is the belief in the indwelling Trinity. Spirituality for Oratorians is a lifelong process of embracing the indwelling of the triune God in the depths of one's heart, and allowing it to rule the actions of one's life in the performance of ordinary duties. Oratorian Spirituality is at once both mystical and practical. In the conclusion, the author shows how the spirituality of the Oratory is relevant to the life of Christians and the Church today.

September, 2013

1

John Henry Newman's Apologia as a Journal of His Conversions

John T. Ford, CSC

INTRODUCTION

For twenty centuries, "conversion stories" have had tremendous appeal for both Christians and observers interested in Christianity. Mention the word "conversion" and what immediately comes to mind are people like Paul and Cornelius in the New Testament, people like Augustine and Francis in Christian history—people whose lives were headed in one direction, before their minds and hearts were changed, before their lives were redirected and transformed—not only in a uniquely personal way, but also in ways that have continued to enlighten and inspire the spiritual search of numerous people throughout the centuries.[1]

Although a fundamental life-change is an essential component of all conversions, there is considerable variety in the "timing" of conversions. Christian history offers examples of converts like Saul, whose conversion was sudden and totally unexpected;[2] yet there are other people, whose "conversion" was years in coming, as in the case of Augustine, whose mother's "prayers indeed and tears" were only answered after a protracted period of time.[3]

---

1. "Conversion" (from the Latin *convertere*, to turn around, to turn back) in a religious context commonly means a redirection or transformation of a person's life—for example, a change from a life of sin to one of virtue, a change from one church to another, etc.

2. See Newman's sermon, "St. Paul's Conversion Viewed in Reference to His Office" (preached on 25 January 1831), *Parochial and Plain Sermons* (San Francisco: Ignatius, 1997), 2:287–94.

3. See Newman's sermon, "Intellect, the Instrument of Religious Training" (preached on St. Monica's Feast, 4 May 1856), *Sermons Preached on Various Occasions* (Notre Dame: Gracewing, 2007), 1. Insofar as conversion can be considered a type of "informal inference," a person examines and evaluates the arguments pro and contra; in this process, some people will find the arguments unconvincing and remain

Obviously, we would know little or nothing about such conversions had not these converts shared their experiences. The publication of such "conversion stories" is not surprising. Most converts want to share their conversion experiences: first of all, converts want, even need, to justify their conversion not only to themselves and their new co-religionists, but also to those who consider their conversion incredible or insincere; in this respect, "conversion stories" tend to fall somewhere between "a true confession" and "a profile in courage"—perhaps a bit of both. Given the highly personal nature of conversion stories, readers may justifiably have some hermeneutical suspicion about these accounts: Is this story really a record of what actually happened? Or is this story what the author remembers as happening? Or is this story what the author would like us to think happened? Conversion accounts seem to mix the factual, the memorable, and the apologetical.

Whatever their historical accuracy, conversion stories inevitably include—sometimes explicitly, sometimes implicitly—an invitation to readers to follow the example of their authors. Readers today are still fascinated by the conversion narrative of Saul in Acts 9: How could a persecutor of Christians suddenly be transformed into a preacher of Christianity? Readers are similarly engaged by the account of Augustine's conversion in his *Confessions*: Why did a pagan philosopher suddenly become a proponent of Christianity? For non-Christians, the conversions of Paul and Augustine pose the question: Should I become a Christian? For Christians, conversion stories prompt the question: Should I become a better Christian? Such questions are perennial: conversions are not limited to biblical and patristic times; conversions are an ongoing necessity for Christianity. Without conversions—both of non-Christians to Christianity and of Christians to a fuller practice of Christian spirituality—Christianity would wither, if not die.

Every list of nineteenth-century conversion stories almost invariably includes Newman's *Apologia Pro Vita Sua* (1845)—which has long been considered a classic of Victorian autobiography, and deservedly so, in spite of the fact that the book was written on short notice and under intense pressure. Unlike those authors who have had ample leisure to assemble materials and record their recollections for their autobiographies in the quiet of their study, Newman found himself unexpectedly drawn into a controversy that prompted him to write his life history in a matter of weeks. At the end of December

---

where they were—such was the case with Newman's fellow Tractarians, Keble and Pusey, who remained members of the Church of England; other people will examine the arguments and—sometimes quickly, sometimes gradually—come to the decision to convert. For Newman's description of "informal inference," see his *An Essay in Aid of a Grammar of Assent*, Chapter 8.2.

1863, he received by mail a copy of the January (1864) issue of *Macmillan's Magazine*, which contained a book review of James Anthony Froude's two-volume *History of England*. The reviewer, identified by the initials C. K., commented in passing:

"Truth, for its own sake, had never been a virtue with the Roman clergy. Father Newman informs us that it need not, and on the whole ought not to be; that cunning is the weapon which Heaven has given to the saints wherewith to withstand the brute male force of the wicked world which marries and is given in marriage. Whether his notion be doctrinally correct or not, it is at least historically so."[4]

Although Newman was reticent by nature and initially reluctant to engage in controversy, such a slur on both his personal integrity and the truthfulness of the Roman Catholic clergy prompted him to demand an apology. The editors of *Macmillan's* forwarded his request to the review author, Charles Kingsley (1819–1875), an Anglican clergyman and Regius Professor of Modern History at Cambridge (1860–1869)—perhaps best known to generations of youngsters as the author of *Westward Ho!* (1855). When a satisfactory apology from Kingsley was not forthcoming, Newman realized that the only way to refute these allegations was by providing a detailed history of his "religious opinions" during the years (1801–45) when he was a member of the Church of England. Literally working day and night, his *Apologia* appeared in "seven Parts, which were published in series on consecutive Thursdays, between April 21 and June 2," 1864.[5]

As a literary work, Newman's *Apologia* includes personal recollections of Oxford—which contrast sharply with the now-all-but-forgotten *Reminiscences* of his brother-in-law, Thomas Mozley (1806–1893).[6] Instead of criticizing the Oxford Movement, however, Newman seized the opportunity to acknowledge his indebtedness to the Church of England in general and Oxford University in particular for both the educational opportunities and the spiritual enrichment that he had been accorded as an Anglican. He also expressed his gratitude to his former colleagues for their continuing friendship—which had obviously

---

4. John Henry Newman, *Apologia Pro Vita Sua*, ed. David J. Delaura (New York: W. W. Norton, 1968), 298; this edition is particularly useful because of its informative footnotes and interpretive essays (hereafter, *Apo*). Ironically, the author of the *History* reviewed by Kingsley was James Anthony Froude (1818–1894), a younger brother of Richard Hurrell Froude (1803–1836), who along with Newman was one of the original leaders of the Oxford Movement.

5. *Apo*, 4.

6. Thomas Mozley (1806–1893), *Reminiscences: Chiefly of Oriel College and the Oxford Movement*, 2 vols. (London: Longmans, Green & Co., 1882).

been strained by his decision to become a Roman Catholic. In effect, while shooting arrows at Kingsley's accusations, Newman offered olive branches to his Anglican friends.

Newman's *Apologia* also has elements of an exposé—an art form that was highly enticing to Victorians who always wanted to know firsthand the "inside story": Why would any well-educated Anglican clergyman do such an unconventional—indeed preposterous—thing as become a Roman Catholic? Although Newman answered this question in a low key through his *Apologia*, his defense—even defensiveness—of his conversion to Roman Catholicism had previously appeared in his first novel, *Loss and Gain* (1848), where he somewhat playfully lampooned Victorians for their tendency to be excessively tolerant of the most bizarre religious idiosyncrasies—Roman Catholicism excepted.[7] Simultaneously, Newman's *Apologia* served as a counter-exposé to the sensationalistic anti-Catholic allegations of Maria Monk[8] and Giovanni Giacinto Achilli,[9] whose fabrications have fallen into the footnotes of history, while Newman's *Apologia*—readily available today both in paperback and on the Internet—continues to attract readers.

Seemingly for strategic reasons—as a rhetorical reply to Kingsley—Newman presented his *Apologia* as an autobiographical "history of my religious opinions"; in fact, his *Apologia* recorded not only the development of his theological views, but also chronicled his "spiritual journey" via a series of "conversions"—even though he seemingly had reservations about using this term.[10] Nonetheless, readers of Newman's *Apologia*, especially those interested

---

7. Although Newman lampooned Victorian religious idiosyncrasies throughout *Loss and Gain*, his chapter, "Irvingites and Other Visitors," is a particularly enjoyable example of his sense of humor. Newman, *Loss and Gain* (London: Longmans, Green, 1906), chs. 3–7.

8. Maria Monk (1816–1849) was the pseudonym of a Canadian woman whose *Awful Disclosures* (1836), subtitled, *The Hidden Secrets of a Nun's Life in a Convent Exposed*, were a fraudulent account of alleged immorality in Montreal convents.

9. Giovanni Giacinto Achilli (dates unknown), an Italian Dominican priest, who was defrocked for immorality, delivered a series of anti-Catholic lectures in England; after Newman accused Achilli of misconduct in *The Present Position of Catholics in England* (1851), Achilli sued him for libel; after a trial extending for nearly two years (1852–1853), Newman was found guilty of not proving all his allegations and was fined the then-not-insignificant sum of £100; in addition, he had to pay legal fees of £14,000, which were raised by worldwide subscription.

10. See Avery Dulles, "Newman: The Anatomy of a Conversion," in *Newman and Conversion*, ed. Ian Ker (Notre Dame: University of Notre Dame Press, 1997), 22. "Indeed it seemed problematic to Newman whether the term 'conversion' was appropriate to his own religious pilgrimage, since he had never undergone a violent change or reversal of views, such as was described in the writings of the Evangelicals."

in his personal development—both theological and spiritual—have long tended to focus on the two "bookend conversions" to his autobiographical narrative. At one end was his teenage conversion that spanned several months in the autumn of 1816, as he was in the process of leaving his adolescent security at Ealing School for the yet-unknown challenges of Oxford University. At the other was his midlife conversion, the painful and problematic process in which he gradually disassociated himself from the Church of England and eventually decided to enter the Roman Catholic Church.

Newman's Conversions

At the beginning of his *Apologia*, Newman memorialized his so-called "first" conversion as "confirming me in my mistrust of the reality of material phenomena, and making me rest in the thought of two and two only absolute and luminously self-evident beings, myself and my Creator."[11] In concluding his *Apologia*, he described his entrance into the Roman Catholic Church in similarly memorable terms: "From the time that I became a Catholic, of course, [I] have no further history of my religious opinions to narrate. . . . I have been in perfect peace and contentment; . . . it was like coming into port after a rough sea; and my happiness on that score remains to this day without interruptions."[12]

Although unforgettable summaries of his state of mind at two pivotal periods in his spiritual journey, these two succinct statements have a deceptive side-effect: both statements focus on the end result, the terminus of what was really a drawn-out process in both conversions; his teenage conversion extended over several months; his midlife conversion was drawn out over a half-dozen years. Indeed, if there had not been a "process" in these two conversions, it seems rather unlikely—given Newman's introspective personality and his illative epistemology—that either conversion would have taken place. Newman was not a person who made significant decisions swiftly; he examined and evaluated all the options available; he agonized about important decisions—reflecting at length about his options and then reconsidering his reflections—yet once he saw his course of action clearly, little or nothing could deter him.

---

11. *Apo*, 16.
12. *Apo*, 184. Although Newman claimed that his life as a Roman Catholic had been one of "perfect peace and contentment," in fact, during the two decades after his entrance into the Roman Catholic Church, he experienced a succession of difficulties with ecclesiastical authorities, including his less-than-harmonious relationship with the Irish bishops, while he was rector of the Catholic University in Ireland; his denunciation to Rome over his publication "On Consulting the Faithful in Matters of Doctrine"; etc.

To appreciate Newman's adolescent conversion, one should then look not only at its content—"myself and my Creator"—but also its context.[13] In retrospect, Newman's first conversion emerged from at least three quite different antecedent components—which incongruously played both complementary and conflicting roles in his adolescent conversion. The first was the conventional Anglicanism of his respectable middle-class family, which "observed the Sabbath" by attending church, having Sunday dinner at home, and passing much of the day in restful and sometimes religious pursuits.[14] The second was his adolescent flirtation with rationalism through reading Thomas Paine, David Hume, and Voltaire—whose allure he later recalled: "How dreadful but how plausible."[15] The third was his admiration for—as well as his indoctrination by—an Anglican clergyman, Walter Mayers (1790–1828), his classics teacher at Ealing School—certainly his *alter pater*, indeed his *almus pater*, whose paternal concern seems to have been more influential over the youthful Newman than that of his own father. These three quite different, yet interlocking, components—Anglicanism, Reasonableness, Evangelicalism—were interwoven in both his adolescent conversion and his spirituality as a young man.

A comparable set of components—though necessarily quite different in nature—formed the context of his "Roman Catholic Conversion" three decades later. In contrast to his adolescent conversion—when future opportunities seemed limitless and energies endless—his midlife conversion risked sacrificing a secure and comfortable university career as well as the fellowship of close friends and a circle of devoted students for an unknown future and a community of strangers—presumably kindly and well meaning—but strangers nonetheless. Although Newman's midlife conversion has occasionally been described rather triumphalistically by some Roman Catholics as an abjuration of Anglicanism, in retrospect it seems to have been more what his fellow Tractarian, Edward Bouverie Pusey (1800–1882), ecumenically characterized as Newman's being "transplanted to another part of the vineyard."[16] In fact, Newman carried the best of Anglican spirituality with him when he became a Roman Catholic: biblically based preaching and daily personal prayer.

---

13. *Apo*, 16.

14. In nineteenth-century England, Sunday devotions at home often included reading and discussing sermons and religious tracts. This practice provided a ready market for the eight volumes of Newman's *Parochial and Plain Sermons*.

15. *Apo*, 16.

16. Edward Pusey, *English Churchman* (1845), in *Annals of the Tractarian Movement, from 1842 to 1860*, ed. Edward George Kirwan Browne (London: Charles Dolman, 1863), 121–22.

Nonetheless, Newman's reception into the Roman Catholic Church in 1845—at least as far as externals were concerned—was anti-climactic; he was received without public fanfare by an itinerant Passionist missionary, Dominic Barberi (1792–1849) at Littlemore, a small village a couple miles south of Oxford.[17] There was no Pauline-like theophany prompting Newman's entrance into the Roman Catholic Church, nor was there the urging of an Augustinian voice. Newman's remarkably routine reception as a Roman Catholic paralleled his "first conversion"—which also lacked any landmark event. Like his adolescent conversion—which occurred over a span of several months—Newman's conversion to Roman Catholicism took time—a lot of time, extending over a half-dozen years—beginning in 1839 with his reading of Wiseman's article about St. Augustine's repudiation of Donatism via the thought-provoking phrase *Securus judicat orbis terrarum* ("the world judges with assurance")[18] and concluding with his "low key" entrance into the Roman Catholic Church in 1845.[19]

In fact, Newman's *Apologia* mentions a number of events between his reading of the Augustine article and his Littlemore reception that are equally if not more influential: his study of the Monophysite controversy; the creation of a joint Anglican-Protestant bishopric in Jerusalem;[20] his growing realization that his *Via Media* (his theory that Anglicanism was the "middle way" between Protestantism and Roman Catholicism) was a paper theory, not a reality; the popular rejection of *Tract 90*. While Newman's *Apologia* carefully chronicles the series of events that slowly diminished and eventually destroyed his faith in Anglicanism, readers may be puzzled about *how* and *why* such all-but-forgotten controversies of ecclesiastical history—like Donatism and Monophysitism, which generally aroused little interest either in mid-nineteenth-century England or today—could possibly facilitate his conversion.

The answer to *how* Newman managed to resuscitate the past was largely due to his literary power to describe historical events—which were customarily

---

17. See the "personal reminiscences" of Frederick Oakeley (1802–1880), a lifelong Anglican friend of Newman, in *The Letters and Diaries of John Henry Newman* (New York: Oxford University Press, 2008), 32:507–9 (hereafter, *LD*).

18. *Apo*, 98.

19. *Apo*, 183.

20. In 1840, King Frederick William IV of Prussia proposed to the British government that a Protestant bishopric be established in Jerusalem to minister both to German Protestants and to members of the Church of England; the episcopal office initially alternated between Anglicans and Germans; see: R. W. Greaves, "The Jerusalem Bishopric, 1841," *The English Historical Review* 64, no. 252 (July 1949): 328–52.

presented in dry accounts—in such an imaginative way that the dynamics of these long-forgotten controversies once again appeared as really vital issues. For example, even if one does not understand the details of the Monophysite controversy, what reader of Newman's *Apologia* fails to remember his dramatic statement: "I saw my face in that mirror and I was a Monophysite"?[21] Even readers who cannot explain what a Monophysite is can easily recognize Newman's candid confession of heresy; moreover, readers are nudged to ask themselves: Am I really a Christian? Or am I basically a heretic? In effect, Newman had the enviable talent of being able to describe ancient doctrinal controversies in such a way that people become vividly aware of how these past events really have importance today. In other words, Newman envisioned the past not as a notional set of persons, places, dates, and facts to be dutifully recorded in a dull ecclesiastical chronicle, but as an engaging narrative of real experiences: saints like Paul and Augustine, saints like Ambrose and Athanasius, were not simply theological writers of yesteryear, they are spiritual mentors for the present.

As to *why* Newman went to such pains to resurrect controversies of the past, he became convinced—particularly through his reading of the Fathers of the Church—that these usually forgotten and often-ignored controversies were essential for a true understanding of Christianity. Past controversies were not simply obscure occurrences for scholarly study on a notional level, but historical events that really had both theological importance and spiritual relevance—not only then but now. For Newman, the past was not simply a notional prelude to the present; the past has real importance for the present. Nonetheless, however vital and significant the doctrinal controversies of the past slowly took shape in his mind, he took his time in considering the past's implications for the present. Conversion, for Newman, was a process both gradual and careful.

During the half-dozen years (1839-45) prior to his entry into the Roman Catholic Church, Newman gave a number of indications of the direction that he was heading. Perhaps the most public and poignant indicator of his pending conversion to Roman Catholicism was his final sermon as an Anglican on 25 September 1843: "The Parting of Friends." At the conclusion of his sermon, "Newman took off his hood and threw it over the altar rails. No doubt he did this automatically, such being his custom whenever he was going to receive Holy Communion. But people knew that he had preached to them for the last time, and many of them interpreted this action as a sign that he was now renouncing all further right to address them as a minister of the Church

21. *Apo*, 96.

of England."[22] Newman's congregation at Littlemore seemingly foresaw his future more clearly than he did; it would be another two years before he finally decided to become a Roman Catholic. For the next two years, 1843–45, Newman became absorbed in a process of theological reflection that seemed at first sight extremely theoretical and essentially notional: Has Christian doctrine developed over the centuries since the time of the Apostles?

While such a question about the development of Christian doctrine was seemingly merely speculative, it was simultaneously both deeply personal and essentially spiritual: What Christian community offers *me* the best possibility of salvation? In tandem with this personal spiritual question was a practical ecclesiological one: Where do I find the Church of Jesus Christ today? Although his eventual answer to these questions was primarily personal, Newman organized his reflections in *An Essay on the Development of Christian Doctrine* (1845) as a "hypothesis to explain a difficulty"—a theological proposal to resolve an ecclesiological problem—and this is the way most people read his *Essay* today. As a theological investigation, his *Essay* was remarkably intuitive—a seminal study of doctrinal development that appeared a decade and a half before Darwin's provocative work on biological evolution—*On the Origin of Species* (1859). Similarly, Newman's *Essay* was a noteworthy theological landmark—that has effectively changed the history of modern theology—especially the understanding of doctrinal history.[23]

In spite of its obviously theological character, Newman's *Essay on Development* might also be described as a "hypothesis to explain a conversion"—he was writing not only to solve an ecclesiological conundrum, he was also writing to resolve a personal spiritual crisis. On the theological level, he attempted to validate his theological hypothesis by the application of seven "tests."[24] His theological testing began with a lengthy and detailed discussion of "preservation of type"; however, his hypothesis-testing was truncated in his subsequent discussion of the remaining six tests, so that the total amount of space given the remaining six tests barely equaled the amount of space given to his investigation of the first test.[25] One, of course, might conjecture that Newman realized that a book of a thousand pages was unrealistic—such would

---

22. Louis Bouyer, *Cardinal Newman: His Life and Spirituality* (New York: P. Kennedy, 1958), 231.

23. For a comprehensive study of Newman's *Essay on Development*, see Gerard McCarren, *"Tests" or "Notes"? A Critical Evaluation of the Criteria for Genuine Doctrinal Development in John Henry Newman's Essay on the Development of Christian Doctrine* (Ph.D. diss., Catholic University of America, 1998).

24. In the first edition of his *Essay on Development* (1845), Newman enumerated seven "tests" of development; in his extensively revised third edition (1878), he used the terminology "notes" instead of "tests."

have been the result had he given the other six tests the same amount of space as he gave the treatment of the first test.

One might also conclude that the first test convinced him that his hypothesis of development—both doctrinal and ecclesiastical—was true. If the first test provided the answer he was seeking—not only ecclesiologically but also spiritually—were additional tests really necessary? Seemingly convinced by his first test, he corroborated his conclusion by simply adding summary outlines and succinct examples as proofs for the other six tests. Subsequently, however, theologians have been prone to look more at his conclusion—Newman's purported "theory" of development—rather than the process of theological reflection that led him to the conviction that Christian doctrine has really developed. Yet, as Nicholas Lash has emphasized, Newman's *Essay* "undoubtedly contains, in rudimentary form, the seeds of a number of such theories" of development.[26] Such an emphasis on Newman's theological conclusions—as important as they are in themselves—runs the risk of ignoring his personal state of mind when he concluded his *Essay on Development*: his theological conclusion was the intellectual basis for his spiritual decision. In succinct terms, conversion involves both the head and the heart.

Characteristics of Conversion

In Newman's *Apologia*, one can find descriptions of at least four conversions.[27] The first, as already mentioned, was his Evangelical conversion as a teenager, when Newman both moved beyond the conventional Anglicanism of his family and turned away from his adolescent admiration for the rationalism of Paine and Voltaire. Newman's second conversion came as a young fellow of Oriel College in his twenties, when he came under the influence of the Oxford University Noetics: Richard Whately (1787–1863), later the Anglican Archbishop of Dublin, and Edward Hawkins (1789–1882), who served for over fifty years as Provost of Oriel. Whately and Hawkins convinced Newman to abandon the anti-dogmatic stance of Evangelicalism in favor of a greater respect for the Church and Tradition.

---

25. In the third edition (1878) of Newman's *Essay on Development*, the first "note" occupies 115 pages, while the other six notes are respectively treated (31, 27, 16, 18, 17, 7) in a total of 116 pages.

26. Nicholas Lash, *Newman on Development: The Search for an Explanation in History* (Shepherdstown, WV: Patmos, 1975), 56.

27. Dulles, "Newman: The Anatomy of a Conversion," 24–33, listed three "conversions": first: his Evangelical conversion as a teenager; second: his "transition" (28) to Anglo-Catholicism; third: his "submission" (33) to Roman Catholicism.

While gradually coming to acknowledge the importance of Tradition in the life of the Church, Newman was unwilling to accept the rationalistic views of the Noetics; as he later confessed in his *Apologia*: "The truth is, I was beginning to prefer intellectual excellence to moral; I was drifting in the direction of the Liberalism of the day."[28] In tandem with Newman's dalliance with Noeticism, another catalyst contributing to his waning Evangelicalism was his personal experience as curate of St. Clement's, Oxford, where he discovered that his parishioners did not really fit into his neat Calvinistic categories of "predestined" and "reprobate." In effect, his notional theology was tested and found wanting in the real world of his pastoral ministry;[29] in more general terms, spirituality is not only a matter of speculative theology, but necessarily relies on Christian experience.

Newman's Noetic allegiance was then quite temporary. To the apparent disappointment of Whately and Hawkins, Newman soon embraced the High Church views of three other Oriel fellows—John Keble (1792–1866), Edward Bouverie Pusey (1800–1882), and Richard Hurrell Froude (1803–1836)—who, along with Newman, eventually became the leaders of the Oxford Movement. Under the influence of Froude, Keble, and Pusey, Newman experienced a third conversion that led him not only to abandon Noetic rationalism but also to discard some typical Evangelical positions—the sufficiency of Scripture, justification by faith alone, and the indefectibility of grace—in favor of more "catholic" positions: the necessity of Tradition, the mediator-role of the Church and its sacraments, as well as the duty of continual spiritual renewal.

For the first half-dozen years of the Oxford Movement (1833–39), Tractarian Catholicism provided Newman with a satisfactory middle ground—a *via media* between what he considered the dogmatic diminutions of continental Protestantism and the doctrinal exaggerations of Roman Catholicism. However, his advocacy of the catholicity of Anglicanism in *Tract 90* (1841) quickly came under attack. With the widespread repudiation of his Anglo-catholic views, he reluctantly realized that he needed to look elsewhere for the Church Catholic. After four more years of personal soul-searching and with the encouragement *in distans* of Charles William Russell (1812–1880), president of Maynooth College (Ireland), who "had, perhaps, more to do with my conversion than any one else,"[30] Newman arrived at the conclusion that the

---

28. *Apo*, 24.

29. See John Henry Newman, *Autobiographical Writings*, ed. with Introduction by Henry Tristram (New York: Sheed & Ward, 1957), 72–84 (hereafter, *AW*).

30. *Apo*, 153.

Church of the Apostles was to be found at Rome, rather than at Canterbury—a conclusion that was basic to his fourth conversion.[31]

Although Newman's *Apologia* carefully chronicles these four conversions, it does not provide a "theology of conversion." However, his *Apologia* does suggest several characteristics of his conversions that seem to be spiritually insightful and, to some extent, broadly applicable to the spiritual life of all Christians. First, Newman's conversions were a *gradual* process in contrast to the sudden conversion of St. Paul or the instantaneous command to Augustine. Newman's conversions seem more like occasional rest stops on an exploratory journey—when he paused to consider the paths available and eventually decided on a route to follow. After examining this path and that, he eventually arrived at a destination that was initially unforeseen, yet a destination that again was only provisional and so a staging place for continuing on the next phase of his journey.[32] Similarly, while the spiritual life sometimes includes peak moments of special blessing, unexpected insight, and fervent devotion, more commonly the spiritual life involves frequent prayer, regular reception of the sacraments, and a continued effort to lead a Christian life—routine practices that *gradually* lead a Christian closer to God.

Second, Newman's conversions were *cumulative* insofar as some positions were abandoned—usually after a great deal of soul-searching—while others were enhanced and refined. For example, although Newman gradually relinquished the Evangelical emphasis on an individualistic relationship with Christ in favor of membership in a sacramental community, he never ceased to stress personal holiness and the importance of Scripture in general and the gospel in particular; thus, some decidedly Evangelical traits continued to play a dynamic role in Newman's Roman Catholic life. Similarly, while he eventually disowned Noetic rationalism, he was a lifelong defender of the reasonableness of faith. By way of a descriptive comparison, his conversions resemble a person, moving to a new home, who takes the valuable furniture along but leaves the

---

31. Many writers—emphasizing Newman's description of his entrance into the Roman Catholic Church as "coming into port after a rough sea"—have concluded their treatments of his conversions with his entrance into the Roman Catholic Church. In terms of church-membership, this was undoubtedly the case; however, insofar as conversion is a continual process, one can point to at least five options—and possible conversions—that Newman considered during the Roman Catholic half of his life: Italianate Catholicism (Faber); Liberal Catholicism (Acton); Ultramontane Catholicism (Manning); Historical Catholicism (Döllinger); Ecumenical Catholicism (Pusey), etc.

32. Sheridan Gilley, "Newman and the Convert Mind," in *Newman and Conversion*, ed. Ian Ker (Notre Dame: University of Notre Dame Press, 1997), 12, has commented: "[I]n conversion, there is push as well as pull, as a man moves to a more desirable house partly out of dissatisfaction with his own."

outmoded and dysfunctional behind.[33] Similarly, the spiritual life of a Christian can be envisioned as a growth process in which a person's basic identity remains the same lifelong, while the person discards vices and habits that are counterproductive and develops virtues and qualities that with the passage of time enable the person to grow closer to God.

Third, Newman's conversions included some events that he viewed at least retrospectively as *defining moments*—though this was not the case in his adolescent conversion, it was so in his midlife conversion. Yet, one of the most intriguing but unanswerable aspects of every autobiography is the extent to which events are later seen in a different light than the author saw them at the time they occurred. While Paul could point to his Damascus Road experience as the changing point in his life, while Augustine could describe the reading-command as his life-changing moment, Newman could only vaguely recall the details of his "first conversion"—the results were engraved on his memory, but the process and its details were not. Accordingly, Newman may have retrojected his later views on the past, his memory may have forgotten some details and enhanced others, and so forth. Similarly, in regard to the spiritual life, one person may have a Pauline experience that clearly defines the moment of conversion. Another person may only later come to realize that some events that may have seemed commonplace or problematic at the time of their occurrence were really "turning points" that helped the person grow closer to God; still other people may grow spiritually without being able to pinpoint a specific moment of conversion.

Fourth, as Terrance Merrigan has pointed out, Newman's conversion story and its collateral apologetics have continued to have a *postmodern* appeal in the twenty-first century for at least three reasons:[34] (a) "the valuation of the human experience": Newman's *Apologia*—unlike the conventional manuals of apologetics in the nineteenth century, which attempted to convert people by logical arguments—is an effective autobiographical apologetics that invited, and still invites, modern-day "spiritual seekers" to join him in his personal search for truth;[35] (b) "the demand to respect 'otherness'": unlike many other conversion stories in which a new convert repudiates and even condemns his previous religious affiliation, Newman went out of his way in his *Apologia* to show that "Catholics did not make us Catholics; Oxford made us Catholics";[36] (c) "the

33. Gilley, "Newman and the Convert Mind," 12.
34. See Terrance Merrigan, "The Anthropology of Conversion: Newman and the Contemporary Theology of Religions," in *Newman and Conversion*, 127.
35. This theme is emphasized by Juan R. Vélez, *Passion for Truth: The Life of John Henry Newman* (Charlotte, NC: Tan Books, 2012), reviewed in *Newman Studies Journal* 9, no. 2 (Fall 2012): 104–5.

recognition of the relative character of all cultural and religious traditions": in this regard, Newman's approach seems similar to that of Pope John Paul II in *Fides et Ratio*, who paid appropriate homage both to the unquenchable inquisitiveness of human reason and to the ultimate necessity of faith.[37] The enduring effectiveness of Newman's appeal was eloquently described by the Scottish author and convert, Muriel Spark (1918–2006): "It was by way of Newman that I turned Roman Catholic. Not all the beheaded martyrs of Christendom, the ecstatic nuns of Europe, the five proofs of Aquinas, or the pamphlets of my Catholic acquaintances, provided anything like the answers that Newman did."[38]

Fifth, Newman's conversions were *illative*. In his *Grammar of Assent*, he characterized the human process of decision making in real-life matters as "informal inference"—a process in which the mind selects, examines, and evaluates data in an essentially personal way in order to arrive at a decision. For Newman, such an epistemological process is "grammatically" operative not only in making everyday decisions, but also in spiritual decisions—especially in making an act of faith.

In effect, a prospective convert examines and evaluates the evidence available and eventually arrives at a decision—to change or not to change or to defer a decision. Similarly, the spiritual life is usually not a case of a person performing heroic deeds, but of faithfully fulfilling life's daily tasks—both mundane and spiritual—with consistency and constancy. Just as conversion can result from a series of apparently unconnected events, so too the spiritual life is often a cumulative process of fulfilling the tasks of daily life. Like the spiritual life, conversion can be regarded as an inferential or illative process.[39]

Finally, just as human decisions take varying amounts of time, so too faith-decisions—especially decisions as personally important as conversion. Newman's midlife conversion is a case in point: he carefully examined and evaluated the evidence for Roman Catholicism and while he found some aspects of the Roman Catholic Church that were uncongenial and even questionable,

---

36. Newman to E. E. Estcourt, The Oratory, 2 June 1860, *LD*, 19:352. Edgar Edmund Estcourt (1816–1884), an Oxford graduate and Anglican clergyman, who became a Roman Catholic in 1845, was ordained a Roman Catholic priest and became a canon of St. Chad's Cathedral, Birmingham.

37. An English translation of *Fides et Ratio*, which referenced Newman (§ 74), is available at http://www.vatican.va/holy_father/john_paul_ii/encyclicals/documents/hf_jp-ii_enc_15101998_fides-et-ratio_en.html.

38. Cited by Gilley, "Newman and the Convert Mind," 6.

39. For a discussion of the different types of inference at work in conversion, see John T. Ford, "John Henry Newman: Conversion as Inference," *Newman Studies Journal*, 10, no. 1 (Spring 2013): 41–55.

he eventually came to be convinced, even compelled, by the cumulative merits of the evidence to become a Roman Catholic. Simultaneously, he realized that his two closest colleagues in the Oxford Movement—Keble and Pusey—had examined and evaluated the same evidence that he had, but were not convinced that there were any compelling reasons for them to follow his example and move from the Church of England to the Church of Rome. Conversion is similar to the process of constructing a mosaic. While each artist has access to the same assortment of tesserae, the mosaic that each artist eventually constructs may vary widely. The design of the mosaic is not determined by the tesserae, but by each artist, who puts each tessera into place according to a preconceived design; even though the process of positioning each tessera is basically the same, the perspective of each artist may produce quite different results. Similarly, Newman, Keble, and Pusey all had access to the same evidence for Roman Catholicism; however, they viewed that evidence quite differently and so made different decisions.

Conversion then involves a change in the way a person views the evidence—not because of the meaning the evidence has in itself, but because of the meaning the evidence has for the individual. For Paul, that new perspective was the result of a dramatic experience; for Augustine, that new perspective resulted from a peremptory command; for Newman, that change in view, humanly speaking, came as the end product of a lengthy process of reflecting and interacting with the historical data—with the Church of the past, as presented in the writings of Scripture, the Fathers, and the Anglican Divines, and with the Church of the present, as exemplified in the Church of England and the Church of Rome. In Newman's case, that process extended over a half-dozen years (1839–45)—much longer than is currently customary in the *Rite of Christian Initiation for Adults*—years that Newman spent in carefully weighing the evidence, before deciding to enter the Roman Catholic Church. The amount of time required for conversion is inherently personal: different people need different amounts of time. Accordingly, Newman, as a spiritual director for prospective converts, did not rush people into conversion: he realized that conversion involves a growth process that takes time.

Concluding Reflections

The word *apologia*, which was used in ancient Greece to describe a defendant's speech at a trial and was adapted by early Christians to refer to the set of arguments they used to defend their belief, has a variety of interlocking meanings that are reflected in Newman's *Apologia*: self-defense, apology, accounting, narrative, encomium.

First, Newman's *Apologia* was obviously a *self-defense*, which probably would not have been written had Kingsley not cavalierly chosen Newman as a target for his gratuitous anti-Catholic allegations. Ironically, had Kingsley appropriately apologized, it is unlikely that Newman would have written his *Apologia*—at least in its present form; his *Apologia* was then the result of a set of contingent circumstances. Yet contingency is a common characteristic of conversion stories: would Saul have become a Christian had he not journeyed to Damascus to persecute his future co-religionists? Or would Augustine have remained a pagan philosopher had he not obeyed the commanding voice? Similarly, the Christian life, like conversions, is frequently one of contingent circumstance: a convert responds to a divine call in a specific place and time.

Second, when English-speakers see the word *apologia*, they instinctively think of *apology*. Although such a translation is incorrect, there is a sense in which Newman's *Apologia* was an "apology." Scattered through the book are incidents where he was less than the gentleman that he could and should have been. To some degree, his *Apologia* was an apology for such shortcomings and was accepted as such, insofar as it renewed his friendship with people like Keble and Pusey whom he had not seen for years; nonetheless, his *Apologia* was not universally effective in bridge-building with some former Anglican friends like Whately and Hawkins. Conversion, like the spiritual life in general, always involves reconciliation—with God and with others; while a Christian can always count on the former, the latter may be elusive.

Third, Newman's *Apologia* was obviously an *accounting* or "summing up" of his life. Yet an autobiographer is like a photographer who wants to take the picture from the subject's proverbial "best side." Like every historian, an autobiographer picks the events that he wants to discuss and glosses over others. While his *Apologia* brought to light Newman's unique perspective on the inner dynamics of the Oxford Movement, there were some notable omissions that only surfaced posthumously—perhaps because the work was written in haste, but perhaps because some incidents were still too sensitive to share.[40] In any case, no Christian ever has a completely accurate spiritual self-image.

---

40. For example, in his *Apologia*, Newman mentioned briefly that in 1826, he "became one of the Tutors of my College" (*Apo*, 26) and that in 1832, he "was disengaged from College duties" (*Apo*, 38); however, he did not mention in his *Apologia* that the reason for relinquishing his tutorship was an extended disagreement with Edward Hawkins, the Provost of Oriel; Newman recorded the details of this disagreement in his *Autobiographical Writings*, 86–107.

Fourth, as a *narrative*, Newman's *Apologia* provided what he called a "history of my religious opinions." That history was three-dimensional; it encompassed his theological development, his pastoral ministry, and his spiritual journey. In his *Apologia*, these three dimensions are so adroitly intertwined that readers may easily focus on one and overlook the others. Yet these three dimensions—theology, ministry, spirituality—were not only melded together in Newman's life in an inseparable way, they are essential dimensions of the Christian life: theology is notional without really being grounded in spirituality and implemented through ministry; ministry is mere activity unless it has a theological foundation and spiritual motivation; spirituality is elusive without theology and implausible without ministry.

Fifth, Newman's *Apologia* is an *encomium*—an expression of appreciation—first of all to the people who assisted him during his Anglican years. Sometimes this appreciation was positive; Newman made clear how indebted he was to Anglicans like Froude, Keble, and Pusey, for his catholicism. Yet, at times, Newman's appreciation was problematic—such was the case with his treatment of the opponents of *Tract 90*, who unintentionally convinced him that the Church of England was not the catholic community he wanted. But most of all, Newman's *Apologia* is an extensive hymn of thanksgiving to God for the divine guidance that he had experienced throughout his life. A convert, perhaps more than most Christians, usually has a keen personal sense of Divine Providence operative in his or her life.

Last but not least, Newman's *Apologia* provides its readers with both an *awareness* and an *agenda* for the spiritual life of every Christian. As a conversion story, his *Apologia* should heighten the awareness of readers that they too are—or should be—living a conversion story. In this respect, some Christians record their spiritual experiences and insights in a journal or diary to share with their spiritual director or spiritual friends or as a legacy for their religious community. Yet whether written or not, every Christian needs to recognize that their conversions are recorded in the book of life.

In addition, Newman's *Apologia* furnishes an *agenda* for every Christian. *Pace* the Evangelicals, then and now, the spiritual life is not simply a matter of a one-time extraordinary conversion—though such a conversion may be necessary to bring a particular person to recognize Christ. Rather the spiritual life is a series of conversions—occasionally dramatic, but more commonly small crossroads—where a Christian redirects the course of her or his spiritual life. *Pace* the Noetics—few in Newman's day but numerous in ours—who want a rational explanation for the spiritual. An important lesson from his *Apologia* is the need to recognize the working of Divine Providence in one's spiritual life. For Newman such a recognition is intuitively reasonable, though never rationally demonstrable. *Pace* the Catholics—both Tractarian and Roman—who overemphasize externals to the neglect of genuine sacramentality. Granted that a sacrament is an external sign of internal grace, externals—both liturgical and devotional—are necessary.[41] Newman was duly conscientious—both as an Anglican and as a Roman Catholic—in observing liturgical rubrics and in practicing a variety of private devotions; however, his focus was not on the externals as such, but on the grace channeled through the sacramental system.

Finally, Newman's conversion experiences—which he so eloquently described in his *Apologia Pro Vita Sua*—provided a basic paradigm for both his epistemology of faith in his *Grammar of Assent* and his advice to directees and potential converts that is found throughout his *Letters*.[42] Although Newman would not have disallowed unanticipated, instantaneous, overwhelming conversions—like those of Paul and Augustine—his personal experience was of conversions that were gradual, progressive, and eventually persuasive.[43] The spiritual journey that he described in his *Apologia* resonates well with his description of doctrinal change in his *Essay on Development*: ". . . here below to live is to change, and to be perfect is to have changed often."[44]

---

41. See John Henry Newman, *Meditations and Devotions*, ed. Rev. W. P. Neville (London: Longmans, Green, 1894).

42. See Peter C. Wilcox, *John Henry Newman: Spiritual Director, 1845-1890* (Eugene, OR: Pickwick Publications, 2013).

43. Although the conversions of Paul, Augustine, and many others seem instantaneous, conversions always have antecedents—even if these initially seem obstacles to conversion; for example, Paul, precisely because he was its fervent opponent, certainly knew much about Christianity; similarly, Newman in the process of attacking "Romanism," learned much about Roman Catholicism. Conversion is not an abrupt transition from the completely unknown to the new, but a new and positive view of what was previously viewed in a negative way.

44. Newman, *Dev*, 40.

2

The Indwelling of the Holy Spirit
The Foundation of Newman's Spirituality

John R. Connolly

INTRODUCTION

Any attempt to understand Newman's notion of spirituality must begin with an acknowledgment of the central role that the Christian doctrine of the indwelling of the Holy Spirit plays in his life and thought.[1] The purpose of this chapter is to present a summary of Newman's notion of the indwelling of the Holy Spirit and to demonstrate its significance for his understanding of spirituality. Newman's lifelong commitment to the presence of the Holy Spirit cannot be more eloquently expressed than in his work *Meditations and Devotions*: "When I was young, Thou [the Holy Spirit] didst put into my heart a special devotion to Thee. Thou hast taken me up in my youth, and in my age. Thou wilt not forsake me."[2] Although Newman maintained this special relationship with the Holy Spirit throughout his whole life, he developed his basic understanding of the indwelling of the Holy Spirit during his Anglican years in the *Parochial and Plain Sermons*, preached between 1825 and 1843.[3] These sermons span the period of Newman's life in which he moved from

---

1. This chapter is a revision of an article titled "Newman's Notion of the Indwelling of the Holy Spirit in the Parochial and Plain Sermons," which was originally published in the Newman Studies Journal 5, no.1 (Spring 2008): 5–18.

2. John Henry Newman, *Meditations and Devotions of the Late Cardinal Newman* (New York: Longmans, Green & Co., 1903), 398 (hereafter, *MD*). Newman's writings in this collection originally were intended to be part of a work that Newman proposed to call *Year-Book of Devotions*. Although Newman never completed this work, the volume *Meditations and Devotions* is based upon his meditation notes and was published after his death.

Evangelicalism to High Church Anglicanism and became the leader of the Oxford Movement. Although the *Tracts for the Times* were the major vehicles for disseminating the teachings of the Oxford Movement,[4] Newman's vision for the renewal of the Anglican Church is found also in the *Parochial and Plain Sermons*.[5] Ian Ker, however, reminds us that these sermons were written for Newman's parishioners and not for the members of the university; and, although these sermons are not "full of red-hot Tractarianism," it is "almost as hard to conceive of the Oxford Movement without the *Parochial and Plain Sermons* as without the *Tracts for the Times*."[6]

Before discussing the significance of the doctrine of the indwelling of the Holy Spirit for Newman's notion of spirituality, it is necessary to examine his understanding of this Christian doctrine. With this in mind, the chapter begins with a critical analysis of Newman's notion of the indwelling of the Holy Spirit as presented in the *Parochial and Plain Sermons*. Once this has been accomplished, the chapter will explain the significance of this doctrine for Newman's understanding of spirituality, and, finally, the chapter concludes by discussing some implications of Newman's notion of spirituality for Christians today.

Newman on the Indwelling of the Holy Spirit

When Newman speaks about the indwelling of the Holy Spirit he is speaking of the Christian belief that God the Trinity—Father, Son, and Holy Spirit—are present within the believer in a special, personal, and real sense. In his writings, he uses a number of different terms to describe this unique presence of God in the human person. Some of the most frequently used terms are the "Divine indwelling," "God's presence or indwelling," the "indwelling of the Trinity," the "indwelling of Christ," the "presence of Christ," the "indwelling of Christ through the Holy Spirit," the "indwelling of the three divine persons, Father, Son, and Holy Spirit," and, of course, the "indwelling of the Holy Spirit."[7] For Newman, the indwelling is the actual presence of God in God's Self, the actual

---

3. In Ian Ker, *John Henry Newman: A Biography* (Oxford/New York: Oxford University Press, 1988), 91. Ker observed that the notion of the indwelling of the Holy Spirit "is to be found prominently in these sermons."

4. John Henry Newman, *Tracts for the Times*, 3 vols. (New York: AMS, 1969). The *Tracts for the Times* that were written by Newman are available at http://www.newmanreader.org/works/times/index.html.

5. Vincent Ferrer Blehl describes these sermons as a "most effective means of renewing the spiritual life of the Church." *The White Stone: The Spiritual Theology of John Henry Newman* (Petersham, MA: St. Bede's, 1993), 21.

6. Ker, *Newman*, 90.

reality of the personal Trinitarian God. In his work, *Meditations and Devotions*, Newman writes, "Thou dwellest in me by Thy grace in an ineffable way. . . . Thou art present in me, not only by Thy grace, but by Thy eternal substance, as if, though I did not lose my own individuality, yet in some sense I was even here absorbed in God."[8] This special presence of God through the indwelling of the Holy Spirit has its source in the grace of God and is the foundation for the believer's personal quest for salvation. It is not a human work. In traditional theological terms, the indwelling of the Holy Spirit would be described as a supernatural presence.[9]

One of the first characteristics of the indwelling of the Holy Spirit is its highly personal nature. In a sermon titled "The Indwelling Spirit," preached at the end of 1834, Newman states that the Holy Spirit comes to us not as a mere "pledge," but, as Christ came, "by a real and personal visitation."[10] Christ is now present, both in the Church and in the individual Christian, not as a mere "gift," "but by the substitution of His Spirit for Himself."[11] Scriptural passages are cited to support this view: "But you are not in the flesh, you are in the Spirit, if the Spirit of God really dwells in you" (Rom. 8:9); "Do you not know that your body is a temple of the Holy Spirit within you . . ." (1 Cor. 6:19); "[The

---

7. William R. Lamm, SM, *The Spiritual Legacy of Newman* (Milwaukee: Bruce Publishing Company, 1934), 52–53. In an effort to explain this diversity in language, William Lamm draws upon a classical theological distinction. He points out that, in the indwelling, all three divine persons are present and that, as an ad extra operation, the indwelling is the work of the entire Trinity. However, it is attributed to the work of the Holy Spirit.

8. *MD*, XIV:401. Confirming this view, William Lamm maintains that, for Newman, God's presence in the indwelling is not merely the gift of the Spirit, but is the very presence of God in God's Self through a real, and not just a figurative presence. The grace of God and the divine presence are not one and the same thing. Lamm, *Spiritual Legacy*, 53.

9. Lamm, *Spiritual Legacy*, 207–8. Lamm distinguishes this presence of God through grace from God's presence in the human person through conscience. In God's presence through conscience God is present to all human persons, whether they are Christian or not. For the purposes of clarity, it is important to point out that this investigation is examining Newman's understanding of God's presence through grace, the special presence of God within the Christian believer, and not God's presence through conscience. It also is important to stress here that Newman's understanding of God's presence within the human person in the indwelling is not reduced to grace as the effect of God's saving work in the believer. It is Lamm's opinion that Newman does not consider the question of the precise relationship between these two modes of God's presence, conscience and grace, in the Christian believer. Adding to the ambiguity of this discussion, it is important to point out that, for Newman, God's presence through conscience, natural religion, also involves God's grace.

10. John Henry Newman, *Parochial and Plain Sermons* (San Francisco: Ignatius, 1997), vol. 2, 367 (hereafter, *PPS*).

11. *PPS*, 2:367.

Spirit] will give life to your mortal bodies also through his Spirit which dwells in you" (Rom. 8:11). Describing this presence, Newman writes that the Holy Spirit pervades our souls as a light pervades a building, or as a sweet perfume fills the folds of some honorable robe. We are in the Holy Spirit and the Holy Spirit is in us. Thus, the indwelling of the Holy Spirit "brings the Christian into a state altogether new and marvelous."[12]

Elaborating on the personal nature of the indwelling of the Holy Spirit, Newman describes how the presence of the Holy Spirit through grace is manifested through the regenerated person.[13] One of the first manifestations of the Spirit's presence is that the Holy Spirit establishes a relationship between the believer and God the Father. The Holy Spirit "impresses on us our Heavenly Father's image, which we lost when Adam fell, and disposes us to seek His presence by this very instinct of our new nature."[14] It is through the indwelling of the Spirit that we are able to cry "Abba Father."[15] The indwelling of the Holy Spirit also establishes a relationship between the believer and Jesus Christ. The Holy Spirit comes to "glorify" Christ and to make Christ known "in all His perfections, all His offices, [and] all his works," to the individual Christian.[16] The Holy Spirit came to unfold what remained hidden while Jesus Christ was on earth. Also, the Holy Spirit was involved in the formation of the Church, "superintending and overruling its human instruments."[17] It was through the indwelling of the Spirit that the Church was able to bring "out our Saviour's words and works, and the Apostles' illustrations of them, into acts of obedience and permanent Ordinances."[18]

This personal presence of the Holy Spirit is more than just an external gift; it brings about a change in the being of the person. The inhabitation of the Holy Spirit exalts the person in "the scale of beings and gives him a place and office which he did not have before."[19] One becomes a "partaker of the Divine Nature," a "son of God," a "new creation." "His rank is new; his parentage and service new."[20] This change, Newman said, is called "Regeneration" or the

---

12. *PPS*, 2:368.

13. *PPS*, 2:369. Newman expressed a reluctance to take up the subject of the manifestations of the presence of the Holy Spirit in the believer, because speaking about it might endanger his reverence toward God or his humility. Yet, because of certain errors and the tone of their advocates, he stated that the defense of truth obliged him to discuss this issue.

14. *PPS*, 2:369–70.

15. *PPS*, 2:370.

16. *PPS*, 2:371.

17. *PPS*, 2:371.

18. *PPS*, 2:371.

19. *PPS*, 2:368.

"New Birth," and it "is now conveyed to all men freely through the Sacrament of Baptism."[21] Through regeneration, the Holy Spirit impresses the divine image on us; however, the transformation of regeneration does not literally make us gods. The original nature of the person is not destroyed, but all forms of sin, original sin and actual sins, are pardoned once and forever.[22]

A further description of the transformation that the Holy Spirit effects in the person is found in his sermon, "Righteousness not of us, but in us," preached on 19 January 1840.[23] This sermon begins with a passage from 1 Cor. 1:30-31, in which Paul reminds the Corinthians that their righteousness and sanctification come from God and not from themselves. The Corinthians were acting as if the gifts of the Holy Spirit were the result of their own efforts. They had forgotten that their righteousness and sanctification were gifts of the Holy Spirit and did not belong to them.[24] Newman then pointed out: "God is in you for righteousness, for redemption, through the Spirit of His Son, and you must use His influences, His operations, not your own (God forbid!), not as you would use your own mind or your own limbs, irreverently, but as His presence in you."[25] We are not our own. Everything we do, our knowledge, good thoughts, prayers, baptism, our growth in holiness, comes from the Holy Spirit. On our own, we cannot do anything good but only evil, because, without grace, the nature of the human person is evil, and not good.[26] The good things that come from us are by exception, and are not in us by nature, but in us by grace. Newman quoted the Gospel of John, "Without Me you can do nothing" (John 25:5).[27]

---

20. *PPS*, 2:368.
21. *PPS*, 2:368.
22. *PPS*, 2:369.

23. *PPS*, 5:1041–49. Newman said that his overall purpose in this sermon was to reject two errors. The first maintains that righteousness and salvation are "of us." Those who hold this view forget that righteousness and salvation are inward gifts of the Holy Spirit. The other error denies that righteousness and salvation are "in us." Those who hold this error forget that righteousness (justification) must be in a person in order to be of spiritual profit. Newman said that it is hard to say which of these two errors is the greater. However, both errors deprive Christian life of its mysteriousness. Those who accept the first error think that righteousness can be achieved through their own efforts and, as a result, they have little awe, reverence, or wonder in their personal religion. Those who accept the second error find little mystery in prayer, Christian ordinances, and obedience because their righteousness is independent of these elements.

24. *PPS*, 5:1041–42.
25. *PPS*, 5:1043.
26. *PPS*, 5:1043–45.
27. *PPS*, 5:1045.

Although righteousness is not "of us," it is "in us," that is, the indwelling of the Holy Spirit and the regeneration that occurs through baptism result in a real change in the person. Righteousness, Newman stated, is certainly "in us," and is "not merely nominally given to us and imputed to us, but really implanted in us by the operation of the Blessed Spirit."[28] The gift of righteousness is a real appropriation within us of the life that comes through Jesus' event of salvation.

In the *Parochial and Plain Sermons*, it is clear that the appropriation of God's righteousness and the indwelling of the Holy Spirit come through baptism and the Church. Newman's understanding of the precise relationship between the Church, the Holy Spirit, baptism, and regeneration is presented in his sermon, "Regenerating Baptism" (15 November 1835).[29] At the beginning of this sermon, he states that there is one Holy Spirit, one Church, or visible body of Christians, and one baptism. The Holy Spirit is in the Church and it is through baptism that the Holy Spirit admits one into the Church. In fact, it is the Holy Spirit who baptizes.[30] As Newman expresses it, "[E]ach individual member receives the gift of the Holy Ghost as a preliminary step, a condition, or means of his being incorporated into the Church: or, in our Saviour's words, that no one can enter, except he be regenerated in order to enter it."[31] Unlike circumcision, which is a mere rite, Newman argues that baptism effects the indwelling of the Holy Spirit and confers the grace of regeneration.[32] From this sermon it is clear that, for Newman, the reception of the indwelling of the Holy Spirit through regenerating baptism within the Church is the normative way of receiving righteousness and God's grace of salvation.

The Holy Spirit in Salvation History

In the sermon, "The Law of the Spirit," preached on 12 January 1840, the feast of the Epiphany, Newman discusses the indwelling of the Holy Spirit within the context of salvation history.[33] The indwelling of the Holy Spirit began at creation with Adam. God "put His Spirit within him, and set up the Law in his [Adam's] heart; so that, what He [God] is in His infinite nature, such was man, such was Adam in a finite nature, —perfect after his kind."[34] As a result, when

---

28. *PPS*, 5:1046.
29. *PPS*, 3:655–64.
30. *PPS*, 3:655.
31. *PPS*, 3:655.
32. *PPS*, 3:657–64.
33. *PPS*, 5:1050–62. The principal scriptural text that Newman used for this sermon was "Christ is the end of the Law for Righteousness to every one that believeth" (Rom. 10:14), where Paul was arguing against the Jews who rejected the gospel (*PPS*, 5:1050).

Adam was created, he was righteous. God "called, accounted, dealt with him [Adam] as righteous, because he was righteous."[35] In this context, righteousness means following the Law and being acceptable to God who gave the law.[36]

After the Fall, Adam lost both the indwelling of the Holy Spirit and righteousness.[37] As a result of sin, Adam (and the whole human race) entered into a state of unrighteousness. He condemned himself, and pronounced himself unrighteous "even before God formally rejected him from his state of justification."[38] Adam, however, could not escape this state of unrighteousness. He has remained in this state ever since, "knowing the Law, but not doing it; admiring not loving; assenting, not following; not utterly without the Law, yet not with it; with the Law not within him, but before him."[39] The Law for Adam became a source of confrontation. "What had been a law of innocence, became a law of conscience; what was freedom, became a bondage; what was peace, became dread and misery."[40] Although not explicitly stated, the implication is that what happened to Adam happened to the whole human race.

The righteousness that was lost through Adam, and could not be regained through the Jewish dispensation, was restored through the salvific event of Jesus Christ. Newman teaches that Christ saves us from the state of unrighteousness by bringing us back again to righteousness. Jesus effects what the Law "contemplates and enjoins, but cannot accomplish, our righteousness."[41] Christ accomplishes this "by that great gift of His passion, the abiding influence of the Holy Ghost, which enables us to offer to God an acceptable obedience, such as by nature we cannot offer."[42] The righteousness that comes in Jesus Christ is real and not merely imputed. It is real because it comes from the Holy Spirit who pours God's gift into our hearts, and thus makes us acceptable to God. Again, Newman's listeners were reminded that it is the Spirit who makes us acceptable. It is grace that makes us acceptable and the Divine Presence in us that makes us pleasing to God.[43]

---

34. *PPS*, 5:1051.
35. *PPS*, 5:1052.
36. *PPS*, 5:1052.
37. *PPS*, 5:1052. Here Newman stated: "After the Fall, Adam forfeited the presence of the Holy Spirit; he no longer fulfilled the law; he lost his righteousness and he knew he had lost it."
38. *PPS*, 5:1052.
39. *PPS*, 5:1052.
40. *PPS*, 5:1052.
41. *PPS*, 5:1053.
42. *PPS*, 5:1053.
43. *PPS*, 5:1058–59.

Although the Mosaic Law could not bring regeneration, it did represent God's revelation. Newman holds that the Law of Moses "represented the Law of God in its place and age; was the fullest revelation of it, and the nearest approximation to it, then vouchsafed; and was that Law, as far as it went."[44] During its time, the Jewish law had a divine character. "It was the light of God shining in a gross medium."[45] It did not teach the Jewish people everything, but it taught them a lot, and it was the only means available at the time.[46]

In his sermon, "Judaism of the Present Day," preached on 28 February 1841, Newman pointed out that while the Jews under the old law received God's grace, they did not receive regeneration. The source of God's grace for the Jews under the old law was their faith.[47] Aided by God's grace, the Jews "did good actions" and had "holy desires and tempers."[48] Because of their faith, the Jews did have some graces, but not all. They did not receive the promise, that is, regeneration in Jesus Christ.[49] Consequently, Newman concluded that the Jews, under the old law, did not receive the "great gift of the Spirit."[50] They did not receive the grace of the indwelling of the Holy Spirit that comes through regeneration in Jesus Christ.[51] Newman makes a distinction between grace and regeneration. The clear implication of this distinction is that Newman holds that the people of Israel in the Old Testament did receive some type of grace, but not the grace of regeneration, and therefore, presumably, they did not receive the indwelling of the Holy Spirit.

The Holy Spirit outside the Church

From the discussion above, it appears that the only way to receive regeneration and the indwelling of the Holy Spirit is through baptism within the Christian Church. However, for Newman, other ways are possible. In his sermon, "Faith the Title for Justification" (24 January 1841), Newman offers an explanation of how those who are not baptized Christians can be justified and receive

44. *PPS*, 5:1051.
45. *PPS*, 5:1051.
46. *PPS*, 5:1051.
47. *PPS*, 6:1298.
48. *PPS*, 6:1298.
49. *PPS*, 6:1298. Newman further stated that "in modern language, their faith *apprehended* the promise, yet they had it not" (*PPS*, 6:1295). He added: "It is equally clear *what* the promise is which is spoken of—regeneration" (*PPS*, 6:1295).
50. *PPS*, 6:1295.
51. *PPS*, 6:1298. Newman writes that "they [the Jews] did not have that regenerate life within them which Christians are promised . . . they had not the indwelling Spirit" (*PPS*, 6:1298).

salvation.⁵² Reflecting upon the relationship between faith and justification, Newman analyzes the statements in the New Testament that seem to teach that faith alone is the only means to justification. For Newman, faith does not automatically confer justification. It is, rather, the title to justification. To say that faith is a title means that one cannot say that everyone who has faith is justified. Faith can exist as the title for justification whether one is actually justified or not. The possession of the title is distinct from the possession of justification. Some who have the title are justified; some are not.⁵³

Though Newman states that faith is a title to justification, faith "cannot serve in the place of baptism."⁵⁴ "None are justified but those who are grafted into the justified body; and faith is not an instrument of grafting, but a title to be grafted."⁵⁵ Since baptism grafts a person into the Church, the privileges of justification are only available to those who have entered the Church.⁵⁶ Newman then reflects upon the consequences of this view. If the Christian way is the only way, then there are great numbers, vast multitudes, who through their own fault or the fault of their fathers, cannot receive the privileges of regeneration. The vast majority of the human race cannot participate in either the power of the Holy Spirit or the fullness of justification—"at least according to the provisions of the Gospel covenant."⁵⁷

Reluctant to accept the harsh consequences of this reflection, Newman introduces an exception to this general rule: "But in spite of this, we may humbly yet confidently say, that where there is true faith, there justification shall be; there it is promised, it is due, it is coming, somehow, somewhile."⁵⁸ So it seems that, in some cases, those who have true faith but are not baptized can be justified, and, as a result, can receive the Holy Spirit and be regenerated and saved. Those who have faith are entitled: "[I]f they call, they shall be answered,—if they knock, it shall be opened to them."⁵⁹ However, we do not know who really has this true faith or when God bestows it upon a person.⁶⁰ Newman then adds that it is a great comfort to know that God's power is not

---

52. *PPS*, 6:1282–94.
53. *PPS*, 6:1284–87.
54. *PPS*, 6:1292.
55. *PPS*, 6:1292.
56. *PPS*, 6:1292. This privilege is suspended for those who have seceded from the Church, or those who have sinned grievously, or those born in a schismatical or heretical sect.
57. *PPS*, 6:1292.
58. *PPS*, 6:1292.
59. *PPS*, 6:1293.
60. *PPS*, 6:1293. Here Newman stated that we do not know what "power of influence" God gives to those who do not have the particular "gifts and endowments of the Covenant of the Gospel."

limited to "the bounds of His heritage," but that everyone, within the Church and out of the Church, who calls on the "Name of the Lord with a pure and perfect heart shall be saved."[61]

Although we do not know how this grace of justification is bestowed, some speculations emerge in this sermon. Perhaps some, like the Jews, are retroactively justified through the salvific actions of Jesus Christ and will be received into the glory and grace of the Church at the second coming. Some might be justified at the moment of death.[62] Or, some might receive justification in this life through some "extraordinary dispensation unknown to us and to themselves."[63] Others will perhaps have their eyes opened in this world and eventually be received into the Church.[64] Even though the precise means through which the Holy Spirit communicates grace outside the Church remain obscure, Newman clearly affirms that it is possible to be justified without being explicitly baptized and received into the Church.[65]

Avery Dulles agrees that Newman admits the possibility, in exceptional cases, of justification without baptism; however, Dulles observes that Newman does not, as a general rule, maintain that faith can serve in the place of baptism.[66] In his sermon, "Judaism of the Present Day," Newman states that this view should not be seen as a slight to baptism; he also suggests that those who are justified through baptism might have a "higher acceptance" than those who are justified without baptism.[67] Newman evidently believed that some, who have the true faith, can receive the indwelling of the Holy Spirit and be regenerated, without being baptized.

Evaluation: The Nature of the Indwelling and Original Sin

In his *Parochial and Plain Sermons*, Newman did not fully and sufficiently explain the nature of the change that occurs in believers through the indwelling of the Holy Spirit. This limitation is partially the result of another inadequacy in these sermons, namely, Newman's vagueness about the doctrine of original

---

61. *PPS*, 6:1293.

62. *PPS*, 6:1292. In his sermon, "Judaism of the Present Day," Newman mentioned that martyrs who are not baptized can be justified "in their streaming blood" at the moment of death (*PPS*, 6:1296).

63. *PPS*, 6:1292. In his sermon, "Judaism of the Present Day," Newman also said that some who are not baptized could be justified in God's own secret way (*PPS*, 6:1296).

64. *PPS*, 6:1292.

65. This view is confirmed in his sermon, "Judaism of the Present Day," where Newman states "that if a man has faith, he has or will be justified" (*PPS*, 6:1297).

66. Avery Dulles, *Newman* (London: Continuum, 2002), 26–27.

67. *PPS*, 6:1296–97.

sin. Clearly, Newman intended to teach that the indwelling of the Holy Spirit effects a real change in the being of a person. As a result of the indwelling, a believer enters into a new state, becomes a new creation, is exalted in the scale of beings, is given a new place and office, is said to be a partaker in the divine nature.[68] Yet, the precise nature of this change is obscured by the vagueness of Newman's description of original sin in the *Parochial and Plain Sermons*.

Vincent Blehl maintains that in these sermons Newman did not clearly distinguish between original sin and the tendency to sin, which is an effect of original sin.[69] Newman focuses more on the effects of original sin and the human proneness to sin without the gift of the indwelling of the Holy Spirit. In these sermons, he concentrates on showing how, in the concrete, people sin in spite of their best efforts; and how they are prone to sin and do commit great sins, unless prevented by the grace of God.[70] However, he does not present a clear position on the nature of the corruption involved in original sin—whether it is total or partial.[71]

In the *Parochial and Plain Sermons*, Newman discusses the change more existentially. The most obvious observation that can be made about the nature of the change is that, before the indwelling of the Holy Spirit, a person is in sin, both original and actual, and that, after receiving the Spirit, a person is free from all sin. Newman often contrasts the "natural" human person and the person after the indwelling of the Holy Spirit. The natural person cannot do anything good, only evil. According to nature, the human person is evil, not good. Yet, when Newman speaks about the natural human person, he is not describing the essential nature of the human person, but the concrete situation

---

68. *PPS*, 2:367–68.
69. Blehl, *White Stone*, 49.
70. Blehl, *White Stone*, 49.
71. Blehl, *White Stone*, 49. Blehl pointed out that "[i]n an early sermon, 'On the Corruption of Human Nature,' he [Newman] declines to discuss the extent of man's corruption, whether total or partial, but concentrates on showing how men in the concrete despite their best efforts actually sin and how great sins man is prone to and will commit unless prevented by the grace of God." Newman first preached "On the Corruption of Human Nature" at Saint Clement's on 19 September 1824, and repeated it (with revisions) on a half-dozen other occasions—the final time at St. Mary the Virgin on 12 December 1841. As a Catholic, Newman did not allow this sermon to be published in Copeland's edition of the *Parochial and Plain Sermons* because of its harshness (Blehl, *White Stone*, 58, note 1). Blehl also found it difficult to define the precise nature of Newman's understanding of original sin in the *Parochial and Plain Sermons*, because of their ambiguity about the nature of the corruption (*White Stone*, 58, note 1). As a Catholic, Newman made a distinction between what he calls the Protestant and Catholic views on original sin: the Protestant view sees original sin as a corruption of human nature, while the Catholic view considers it as the privation of sanctifying grace.

of the human person under sin, and with a proneness to sin, after the Fall. This is the situation that Newman describes when he says that, without grace, the nature of the person is evil, and not good.[72] Consequently, on the existential level, the nature of the change is clear. Before the indwelling of the Holy Spirit, the natural person is in sin, prone to sin, and can do no good. After the infusion of the Holy Spirit, a person receives the grace of regeneration and, as a result, all sins—original and actual—are removed. However, in these sermons, Newman never speaks about the ontological nature of the change, and, as a result, his position on the ontological nature of the change remains unclear and undeveloped.

REGENERATION AND GRACE

When Newman distinguishes between the grace of regeneration that comes through baptism and the grace that the Jews had before Christ, he did not fully explain the form of grace that does not regenerate and does not result in the indwelling of the Holy Spirit. With this distinction, Newman seems to admit that there can be more than one form of grace. Yet, at this point in his theological development, he does not possess a formal theology of grace that distinguishes between different types of graces. Peter Sheehan points out that, as an Anglican, Newman understands grace in its general scriptural meaning in which grace refers to a number of God's gifts.[73] As an Anglican, Newman was not aware of the Catholic theology that distinguished between different forms of grace.[74] Actually, it is the context of his sermon, "Judaism in the Present Day," that explains Newman's radical distinction between Christian regenerating grace and the grace of the Jews. He was arguing against those evangelical Christians who maintained that faith alone is needed for justification and that baptism is simply a formality similar to circumcision. Christians who say that faith without baptism is sufficient for regeneration are in the same state as the Jews under the old law.[75] They have faith and grace, but they lack regeneration through the indwelling Spirit. In stressing the role of baptism, Newman also is arguing in favor of the Church, its sacraments, its teachings, and against those evangelicals who taught that faith alone is necessary. In

---

72. *PPS*, 5:1042–45.

73. Peter F. Sheehan, *The Realization of the Divine Presence Through the Indwelling of the Trinity, According to John Henry Cardinal Newman* (Dissertation, Pontificium Athenaeum Angelicum, Rome: 1956), 123–24.

74. Perhaps the distinction in Catholic theology between habitual sanctifying grace and actual grace might offer some possibilities for understanding Newman's distinction.

75. *PPS*, 6:1297–1300.

making his point, Newman tends to stress the role of baptism and the Church in regeneration.

This obscurity in Newman's notion of the grace that does not regenerate and result in the indwelling of the Holy Spirit raises a question for contemporary theology. If grace is understood in a personal and relational sense—as is the tendency in contemporary Catholic theology—then are not the three persons of the Trinity, including the indwelling Spirit, present in every moment of grace, including actual grace? So, the question arises, can there be grace without the indwelling of the Holy Spirit? And, if this relationship with the Trinity is accepted in a personal and loving faith, does not the Holy Spirit dwell in those persons and bring about regeneration?

It is clear that Newman was moving in this direction. Even in a sermon where the point insists on the necessity of baptism and the Christian Church, Newman accepts a retroactive regeneration for the Jews. Jews who died without regeneration are regenerated, after the fact, through the saving grace that comes in and through Jesus Christ.[76] Newman points to David as an example. Although while on earth David did not receive God's generating grace, he is now with Christ in the Spirit and is justified.[77] As was seen in the sermon, "Faith as the Title for Justification," Newman goes even further and teaches that, by exception, Jews, and perhaps others, can be regenerated and receive the indwelling of the Holy Spirit through their faith and without baptism and the Church.

The Indwelling of the Holy Spirit: The Foundation of Newman's Spirituality

As the central doctrine in Newman's theology, the indwelling of the Holy Spirit is the foundation of his notion of Christian spirituality. Supporting this view, William Lamm maintains that Newman "took as the central doctrine of his preaching the great truth of the 'Divine Indwelling.'"[78] Newman views the indwelling of the Holy Spirit as the most fundamental doctrine of Christian faith and makes it "the basis of a true Christian life."[79] Later in the same work, Lamm adds that the indwelling of the Holy Spirit "is the central doctrine of Newman's whole teaching on the way to holiness, to a true Christian life."[80]

---

76. *PPS*, 6:1298–99.

77. *PPS*, 6:1299.

78. Lamm, *Spiritual Legacy*, 17. On the same page Lamm adds, "It [the Divine Indwelling] is this which gives unity to his [Newman's] teaching,"

79. Lamm, *Spiritual Legacy*, 17–18.

80. Lamm, *Spiritual Legacy*, 41.

In the sermon, "Mental Prayer," Newman says that the indwelling of the Holy Spirit "implants here and at once a new principle within us, a new spiritual life."[81] Actually, it gives us a spiritual life.[82] In his *Meditations and Devotions*, a later Catholic work, Newman meditates on the central role that the indwelling of the Holy Spirit has played in his own spiritual development.[83] In his sermons he speaks about the Holy Spirit initiating the believer into a state of holiness.[84] Lamm says that, for Newman, being a Christian meant living and walking in the presence of the Holy Spirit.[85]

The spiritual life for the Christian is a lifelong process of realizing the presence of the indwelling of the Holy Spirit in the heart and mind of the believer. Realizing the Spirit's presence is not solely an intellectual act. It is not merely a notional assent to the theoretical doctrine of the indwelling of the Holy Spirit. It is not merely freedom from mortal sin. Nor is it mere imagining. It is not mere enthusiasm or excitement.[86] For Newman, when believers realize a truth of faith, "it becomes an influential principle within them, and leads to a number of consequences both in opinion and in conduct."[87] Realizing means bringing a truth into consciousness, dwelling upon it, and contemplating it vividly.[88] To realize a truth means to grasp it and bring it home to oneself. When a Christian realizes the presence of the Spirit, this presence becomes a principle of action; "realizing" is practical and fruitful knowledge.[89] The believer feeds upon the presence of the Holy Spirit and, little by little, grows into the transformations brought through this presence.[90] Realizing the presence of the Spirit brings us a new self-consciousness that makes us real and shows us who we really are.[91] The Spirit effects a transformation of the whole

---

81. *PPS*, 7:1538.

82. *PPS*, 7:1539. Newman tells his congregation, "... the new birth of the Holy Spirit ... gives us a spiritual life; it opens the eyes of our mind, so that we begin to see God in all things by faith, and hold continual intercourse with Him by prayers; and if we cherish these gracious influences, we shall become holier and wiser and more heavenly, year by year ..."

83. *MD*, XIV, 396–404. In this work, Newman speaks about the Holy Spirit as the source of life in all things, as the light and life of his own soul, as the font of love, the source of all grace, and as the life of the Church.

84. *PPS*, 5:1074.

85. Lamm, *Spiritual Legacy*, 17.

86. Lamm, *Spiritual Legacy*, 210–11.

87. *PPS*, 6:1350.

88. *PPS*, 6:1348. See Lamm, *Spiritual Legacy*, 210–11.

89. Lamm, *Spiritual Legacy*, 211–14.

90. *PPS*, 3:566. See Lamm, *Spiritual Legacy*, 214.

91. Lamm, *Spiritual Legacy*, 210.

consciousness of the person at the deepest level of one's being. To realize the presence of the Holy Spirit means to make a real assent to the indwelling of the Holy Spirit.[92]

Implications for Contemporary Spirituality

There are a number of implications for Newman's understanding of spirituality for contemporary Christians. One of the most significant is that Newman emphasizes that Christian spirituality is rooted in a personal relationship with God, and not in a notional assent to the external expressions of the truths of revelation. In his sermon, "The Indwelling Spirit," Newman teaches that the Holy Spirit comes in the same manner as Christ—"by a real and personal visitation."[93] As a result of the indwelling of the Holy Spirit, a believer enters into a personal relationship with the Father and the Son.[94] As Charles Dessain points out, Newman's teaching on the indwelling of the Holy Spirit demonstrates that he saw that the essence of Christianity [true Christianity] is the "presence of persons."[95] Dessain elsewhere notes that Newman retrieves the New Testament notion of faith, which emphasizes that faith is a personal relationship of intimacy and friendship with the Father and the Son.[96] Newman describes this relationship as the culminating point in Christian revelation.[97] Dessain also shows that Newman, in developing his understanding of the indwelling of the Holy Spirit, was struggling to overcome an impersonal view of grace. Rather than viewing grace as a habit or disposition within a person, Newman stresses that grace is the personal indwelling of the Holy Spirit.[98] Grace is not a thing, but a personal relationship.

Newman's analysis of the gifts of the Holy Spirit also offers some concrete spiritual direction for Christians today. Through the indwelling of the Holy

---

92. Lamm, *Spiritual Legacy*, 215–16. Lamm maintains that, when Newman speaks about realizing the presence of the Spirit, he is speaking about an experience that comes through the response of faith. Newman is not speaking about a mystical experience. Dr. Zeno supports this interpretation and maintains that Newman never had a mystical experience; see Dr. Zeno, Capuchin, *John Henry Newman: His Inner Life* (San Francisco: Ignatius, 1987), 276.

93. *PPS*, 2:367.

94. *PPS*, 2:368–71.

95. Charles Stephen Dessain, *John Henry Newman* (Stanford: Stanford University Press, 1971), 20.

96. Charles Stephen Dessain, "The Biblical Basis of Newman's Ecumenical Theology," in *The Rediscovery of Newman: An Oxford Symposium*, ed. John Coulson and A. M. Allchin (London: Sheed & Ward, 1967), 102.

97. Dessain, "Biblical Basis," 102.

98. Dessain, "Biblical Basis," 112–16.

Spirit, Christians receive the gifts of the Holy Spirit—which are love, truth, peace, joy, and unity. One of the main effects of the indwelling of the Holy Spirit on the lives of Christians is love. The Holy Spirit "lives in the Christian's heart, as the never-failing fount of charity."[99] In his sermon, "Faith and Love," Newman says that we love because the Holy Spirit has made it our nature to love. To this, he adds that "[l]ove is the immediate fruit and evidence of regeneration."[100] Love is described as the motion of the new spirit within believers that is given to them through the indwelling of the Holy Spirit.[101] Vincent Blehl characterizes this aspect of Newman's thought by stating that the Holy Spirit creates a loving disposition in the heart of the Christian, "after the pattern of Christ whose incarnation and whole life was one of condescending assiduous love."[102] Newman summarizes his understanding of the relationship between the indwelling of the Holy Spirit and love as follows: "Charity is another name for the Comforter."[103]

The second gift conferred through the indwelling of the Holy Spirit is truth. In his sermon, "The Indwelling Spirit," Newman states that the Holy Spirit conveys the Christian system of truth into "the hearts of each individual Christian in whom He dwells."[104] Peace is the third gift bestowed upon the believer through the indwelling of the Holy Spirit. This peace springs from trust and innocence and places one at leisure. Without this peace, one is "anxious, thinks of oneself, speaks hurriedly, and has no time for the interests of others."[105] The fourth gift conferred by the Spirit is joy. Newman preaches that doubt, gloom, and impatience are expelled through the indwelling of the Holy Spirit. These are replaced by joy in the gospel, hope of heaven, the harmony of a pure heart, the triumph of self-mastery, sober thoughts, and a contented mind.[106]

The fifth gift bestowed on believers through the indwelling of the Spirit is unity. In the sermon, "The Communion of Saints" (14 May 1837), Newman speaks about the indwelling of the Holy Spirit as a source of unity.[107] He states that the Holy Spirit comes into the souls of all who believe, takes possession of

---

99. *PPS*, 2:373.
100. *PPS*, 4:931.
101. *PPS*, 4:933.
102. Blehl, *White Stone*, 97.
103. *PPS*, 4:937.
104. *PPS*, 2:372.
105. *PPS*, 2:372.
106. *PPS*, 2:373.
107. *PPS*, 4:839–49.

them, and "knits them all together into one."[108] The Holy Spirit is the source of unity in the Church. What makes the Church one is the fact that it is alive. If it were dead, it would consist of as many parts as it has members. Yet, the Church is one; it is the Holy Spirit who makes the Church one by giving it life at Pentecost.[109] From this sermon, clearly, the unity of the Church includes not only those living on earth but the communion of saints in heaven.[110]

Newman's understanding of the universal presence of the Holy Spirit provides contemporary Christians with a theological basis for being open to the presence of the Holy Spirit outside the church. Although holding that the primary locus for conferring the indwelling of the Holy Spirit is in the Church through baptism, Newman believes that the Holy Spirit can be present in people who are outside the Church. This teaching is consistent with Newman's notion of a universal revelation, which is found in various writings: his Second University Sermon, "The Influence of Natural and Revealed Religion Respectively,"[111] *The Arians of the Fourth Century*,[112] and the *Grammar of Assent*.[113] His point is a reminder to Christians today that the presence of the Holy Spirit is much more pervasive than most people realize. The Holy Spirit pervades the Church at all levels: pope, bishop, priest, laity, women and men. The Holy Spirit is present in all Christian religions, in all of the religions of the world, in the workings of nature, and all forms of human thought, as well as in other places. Newman reminds us that no one controls the Holy Spirit. We must be constantly open to the presence of the Spirit wherever the Spirit is found.

In the *Parochial and Plain Sermons*, Newman provides Christians today with guidelines for an understanding of holiness that stresses the importance of personal growth. Although the indwelling of the Holy Spirit brings freedom from all forms of sin, it does not free a person totally from the effects of original sin. Even after baptism and regeneration, Christians are prone to sin—even grievously at times. It is the continual presence of the Holy Spirit that enables

---

108. *PPS*, 4:840.
109. *PPS*, 4:841.
110. *PPS*, 4:840–42.
111. Sermon II (13 April 1830), "The Influence of Natural and Revealed Religion Respectively," John Henry Newman, *Fifteen Sermons Preached Before the University of Oxford Between A.D. 1826 and 1843* (Notre Dame: University of Notre Dame Press, 1997), 16–36.
112. John Henry Newman, *The Arians of the Fourth Century* (Westminster, MD: Christian Classics, 1968), 80–89, available at http://www.newmanreader.org/works/arians/index.html.
113. John Henry Newman, *An Essay in Aid of a Grammar of Assent*, ed. I. T. Ker (Oxford: Clarendon, 1985), 431.

believers to overcome sins committed after baptism, to perform good acts, and to continue to be open to God. For Newman, the indwelling of the Holy Spirit is the source of holiness.[114] The Spirit plants the seeds of holiness within the believer.[115] As he states in his sermon on "Mental Prayer" (13 December 1829), "[T]he new birth of the Holy Spirit sets the soul in motion in a heavenly way; it gives us good thoughts and desires, enlightens and purifies us, and prompts us to seek God."[116]

Although the indwelling of the Holy Spirit is the source of holiness, the Spirit does not make us perfect all at once. We are not "unreprovable, and unblemished in holiness yet."[117] Since the indwelling of the Holy Spirit does not eliminate the tendency to sin or sin's attraction, we are not immediately made into perfect human persons. As Newman stated in his sermon, "Love of Religion a New Nature" (3 May 1840), "A holy man is by nature subject to sin equally with others."[118] As a result, the quest for holiness is a process. Only gradually will a believer be able to overcome sin and all the other obstacles to holiness.[119]

The Holy Spirit patiently guides and directs us. In his sermon on "Christian Repentance" (20 November 1831), Newman puts it this way: "We may not so limit the mysterious work of the Holy Spirit. He condescends to plead with us continually, and what He cannot gain from us at one time, He gains at another. Repentance is a work carried on at diverse times, and but gradually and with many reverses perfected."[120] Newman described this growth in holiness in his sermon, "Mental Prayer": "[W]e shall become holier and wiser and more heavenly, year by year, our hearts being ever in a course of change from darkness to light, from the ways and works of Satan to the perfection of Divine obedience."[121] However, a perfect holiness will never be achieved in this life.

As Newman asserted in his sermon, "The Law of the Spirit": "They who persevere to the end, will be perfect in soul and body, when they stand before God in heaven."[122] What can be seen in Newman's description of holiness is the

---

114. Blehl, *White Stone*, 96.
115. Blehl, *White Stone*, 38.
116. *PPS*, 7:1539.
117. *PPS*, 5:1059, "The Law of the Spirit" (12 January 1840).
118. *PPS*, 7:1526.
119. Blehl, *White Stone*, 51.
120. *PPS*, 3:542.
121. *PPS*, 7:1539.
122. *PPS*, 5:1059.

merging of the two points he learned from Thomas Scott at the time of his 1816 conversion, "*Holiness rather than peace*," and "*Growth the only evidence of life.*"[123]

---

123. John Henry Newman, *Apologia Pro Vita Sua*, ed. and intro. A. Dwight Culler (Boston: Houghton Mifflin, 1956), 26, available at http://www.newmanreader.org/works/apologia65/chapter1.html.

3

Coming to Terms with the Past
The Role of History in the Spirituality of John Henry Newman

Kenneth L. Parker

In 1968, Professor Joseph Ratzinger stated in the opening pages of his *Introduction to Christianity* that Giovanni Battista Vico's argument against the static scholastic concept of truth, *verum est ens* (being is truth), and Vico's assertion that *verum quia factum* (truth is what is made), ended the apologetical power of the "old metaphysics" and required Christians to think *historically* about their faith.[1] He went further in his 1969 commentary on the Second Vatican Council's constitution, *Dei Verbum*. After reviewing the conciliar debate over Vincent of Lérins's well-known dictum, *quod semper, quod ubique, quod ab omnibus* (what [has been held] always, everywhere, by all)—which Trent and Vatican I had enshrined in conciliar documents—Ratzinger explained why *Dei Verbum* had excluded it. He noted that Vincent's canon is no longer "an authentic representative of the Catholic idea of tradition," for his static *semper* (always) is not "the right way of expressing this problem." Ratzinger stated that our "new orientation simply expresses our deeper knowledge of the problem of historical understanding . . ."[2]

Yet this need to come to terms with historical consciousness was already evident in authoritative voices of the nineteenth century and has been expressed

---

1. Joseph Ratzinger, *Einführung in das Christentum* (München: Kösel, 1968), 34–38; *Introduction to Christianity* (New York: Seabury, 1969), 31–34.

2. Herbert Vorgrimler, ed., *Commentary on the Documents of Vatican II*, 4 vols. (New York: Herder & Herder, 1969), 3:187–88.

in various ways ever since. When Leo XIII opened the Vatican Archives in 1879, the paleographical school attached to it adopted a motto endorsed by him: *Nihil est quod ecclesiae ab inquisitione veri metuatur* (The church has nothing to fear from the quest for truth).[3] In 1950, the Dominican theologian, Marie-Dominique Chenu, put it this way: "Truth is no less true for being inscribed in time."[4] Pope John Paul II reaffirmed this in 1999. During his noteworthy apology for the execution of Jan Hus in 1415, the pope stated: "Faith has nothing to fear from historical research."[5]

During the nineteenth century, static understandings of Christian truth began to give way to visions of Christian faith claims that reflected growth and development. While the quest for the origins of this historical consciousness is elusive, John Henry Newman's *Essay on the Development of Christian Doctrine* (1845) may be credited with crystallizing awareness of the need for a historical understanding of Christian truth claims.[6] Newman's *Essay* was written during his last years as an Anglican theologian, and was birthed out of his spiritual struggle over whether to become a Roman Catholic, after decades of hostility toward the Catholic Church. Though this work has exercised enormous influence in the history of modern Christianity, it remains—at its source—an artifact of one man's search for a new path in his journey of faith. In the opening pages Newman stated that Vincent of Lérins's canon was a hypothesis no longer sufficient to address the rise of critical historical scholarship over the previous three centuries.[7] He rejected static understandings of truth and argued for a living tradition, ever growing, flowering, and bearing fruit.[8]

The influence of Newman's theory of development is not conjecture. In August 1855, a correspondent reported to Newman the pope's view that "though it ought not to be publically talked of," Newman's theory of development was "the private opinion of the Holy Father himself."[9] A year later, on 17 March 1856, *Singulari Quidem* presented the pope's own application

---

3. Owen Chadwick, *Catholicism and History: The Opening of the Vatican Archives* (Cambridge: Cambridge University Press, 1978), 143.

4. Fergus Kerr, *Twentieth-Century Catholic Theologians: From Neoscholasticism to Nuptial Mysticism* (Oxford: Wiley-Blackwell, 2007), 28.

5. John Paul II, "Address of the Holy Father to a Symposium on John Hus, 17 December 1999," accessed 27 June 2013, http://www.vatican.va/holy_father/john_paul_ii/speeches/1999/december/documents/hf_jp-ii_spe_17121999_jan-hus_en.html.

6. See Kenneth L. Parker and Erick Moser, eds., *The Rise of Historical Consciousness among the Christian Churches* (Lanham, MD: University Press of America, 2012).

7. John Henry Newman, *An Essay on the Development of Christian Doctrine* (London: James Toovey, 1845), 28 (hereafter, *Dev*).

8. *Dev*, 37.

of Newman's theory of doctrinal development: "We should not conclude that religion does not progress in the Church of Christ. There is great progress! But it truly is the progress of faith, which does not change. The intelligence, wisdom, and knowledge of everybody should grow and progress, like that of the whole Church of the ages. In this way we might understand what we used to believe obscurely; in this way posterity might have the joy of understanding what used to be revered without understanding."[10] Explicit appeals to Newman's theory of development have become commonplace since Vatican II. In his 1986 article on the ecclesiology of Vatican II, Cardinal Ratzinger praised Newman's concept of development, and described it as one of the "decisive and fundamental concepts of Catholicism." He noted that Vatican II "had the merit of having formulated it for the first time in a solemn magisterial document." He criticized those who cling to a literal test of Scripture or patristic teaching for banishing Christ to the past and characterized their practice as "an entirely sterile faith that has nothing to say to the present . . ."[11] In 2005, during his first Christmas address to the Curia, Pope Benedict XVI extolled what he called the "hermeneutic of reform," and appealed to development in continuity with tradition—rather than rupture—as the guiding principle of Vatican II. He explained that where this hermeneutic had been applied, it had borne new life and new fruit, and achieved "renewal in the continuity of the . . . Church which the Lord has given to us."[12]

This chapter will sketch out a monumental landscape on a small canvas. I will argue the following thesis: John Henry Newman's theory of doctrinal development enabled the Roman Catholic tradition to rearticulate the faith in an intellectual ethos permeated by the rise of historical consciousness, because his own struggle toward conversion to Roman Catholicism became a prism through which the principles of a new apologetical hermeneutic—which incorporated critical historical scholarship into its argumentation—could be perceived and applied. This was an integral part of Newman's spirituality that has had an enduring significance. As Sandra Schneiders has observed, "only a theology that is rooted in the spiritual commitment of the theologian and

---

9. Birmingham Oratory Archives, Various Collections, Essay on Development: Fr. James Stanton to John Henry Newman, 17 August 1855. I am grateful to C. Michael Shea for this reference.

10. Pius IX, *Singulari Quidem*, in *The Papal Encyclicals 1740-1878*, ed. C. Carlen (Raleigh, NC: McGrath, 1981), 341. Many thanks to C. Michael Shea for directing me to this encyclical.

11. Joseph Ratzinger, "The Ecclesiology of the Second Vatican Council," *Communio* 13 (1986): 241–42.

12. Benedict XVI, "Address of His Holiness Benedict XVI to the Roman Curia," 22 December 2005, accessed 27 June 2013, http://www.vatican.va/holy_father/benedict_xvi/speeches/2005/december/documents/hf_ben_xvi_spe_20051222_roman-curia_en.html.

oriented toward praxis will be meaningful in the Church of the future."[13] There can be no meaningful distinction between theology and spirituality, for they are inextricably connected. How Newman came to terms with the Christian past is critical to understanding his spiritual journey, as well as his vocation as a theologian. Benjamin King has aptly observed, Newman "can be described as writing history in the first person."[14] The "metanarrative" of development became an outgrowth of Newman's personal struggle.[15]

The argument will be made in three parts. First, Newman's early Anglican understandings of the Christian past and their uses in doctrinal disputes will be examined, and his disillusionment with his earlier presuppositions will be considered. Second, Newman's cultivation of the theory of development will be explored in the context of his conversion. Finally, the role his theory played in the decades following his 1845 conversion to Roman Catholicism will be briefly analyzed. In this way, we can better understand why the twentieth century's first non-neoscholastic prefect of the Congregation for the Doctrine of the Faith came to describe Newman's theory as one of the "decisive and fundamental concepts of Catholicism."[16] Through Newman's theory we will also appreciate why his conception of doctrinal development remains an essential path to understanding Benedict XVI's appeal for a "hermeneutic of reform" that can bear new life and new fruit in our time.

Newman's Early Understanding of the Christian Past

Newman's earliest understandings of the Christian past were cultivated in the wake of his evangelical conversion in 1816. During this intense adolescent quest for an interiorized faith, two visions of Christian history shaped his life of faith. In the *Apologia Pro Vita Sua* he recalled two works, "each contradictory to each," that planted seeds of "intellectual inconsistency which disabled me for a long course of years."[17] These works were Joseph Milner's *History of the Church of Christ* and Bishop Thomas Newton's *Dissertations on the Prophecies.* From Milner, he learned to love the Church Fathers as exponents of primitive

---

13. Sandra Schneiders, "Spirituality in the Academy," *Theological Studies* 50 (1989): 677.

14. Benjamin King, "Newman and the Church Fathers: Writing Church History in the First Person," *Irish Theological Quarterly* 78, no. 2 (2013): 150.

15. For more on metanarratives of the Christian past, see Kenneth L. Parker, "Re-visioning the Past and Re-sourcing the Future: The Unresolved Historiographical Struggle in Roman Catholic Scholarship and Authoritative Teaching," in *Studies in Church History*, 49 vols. (Woodbridge, UK: Ecclesiastical History Society and Boydell, 2013), 49:384–411.

16. Ratzinger, "Ecclesiology," 241–42.

17. John Henry Newman, *Apologia Pro Vita Sua* (London: Longman, 1864), 62 (hereafter, *Apo*).

Christianity; and from Newton, he came to fear the pope as Antichrist. While Milner sought to trace out the pure thread of faith that had been preserved unalloyed through the centuries, Newton's vision of the Christian past highlighted a corrupted dark age that ended when the power of the papacy had been effectively challenged in the sixteenth century.

These works instilled in Newman two historiographical traditions: one that emphasized continuity and stasis—a legacy of the patristic era—and the other that defined a past marked by primitive purity, corrupted by the rise of papal authority, and restored by champions of the Reformation. Though Newman read Edward Gibbon three years later and expressed enthusiasm for his historical methodology and literary style, he regretted Gibbon's eighteenth-century skepticism.[18] While he recognized the importance of history in defense of the faith, he remained unaffected by the historical-critical scholarship flourishing in Germany during this period.[19] Indeed, he took pride in this intellectual deficit. What he did know was filtered through the judgment of trusted friends like Edward Pusey, who had studied there and rejected the rationalism of German Protestantism.[20]

The young Newman yearned for responsible historical scholarship in defense of the faith. Newman's sensibilities as a zealous young Christian, attuned to the rising historical consciousness of his era, should not be underestimated. The significance of the historiographical traditions that Milner and Newton represented shaped the struggles of his early adult years and contributed to the crisis of his late twenties (when he embraced high church Anglicanism), and then again in his late thirties (when new doubts, intellectual ferment, and spiritual crisis led to his conversion to Roman Catholicism). These two metanarratives of the Christian past must be briefly considered before looking more closely at Newman's life as a scholar and leader of the Oxford Movement.[21]

Through Joseph Milner's *History of the Church of Christ*, Newman received a vision of history promoted by such ancient authorities as Eusebius of Caesarea

---

18. John Henry Newman, *Autobiographical Writings* (New York: Sheed & Ward, 1957), 41, 44 (hereafter, *AW*).

19. I am currently preparing a critically annotated bibliography of the books Newman used during his time as a fellow of Oriel College. It is clear from Newman's letters and diaries, and my own research on his reading habits in the Oriel College library during the 1820s and 1830s, that Newman's scholarship was more dependent on seventeenth- and earlier eighteenth-century scholarship, than the more recent historical-critical methods of the late eighteenth and early nineteenth centuries.

20. Benjamin O'Connor, "The Oxford Movement," in *Authority, Dogma, and History*, ed. Kenneth L. Parker and Michael Pahls (Bethesda, MD: Academica, 2008), 20.

21. Parker, "Re-visioning the Past and Re-sourcing the Future," 384–411.

and Augustine of Hippo. In his introduction, Milner explained that his history rested on two premises: first, that he would supply his reader with "real facts"; and second, that he would not doubt the credibility of ancient historians. He lamented the historiographical trends of the eighteenth century, observing that "we condemn the ancients by wholesale, without giving them a hearing: we suspect their historical accounts, without discrimination."[22]

Newman's scholarship reflected Milner's concern that the ancients be heard and their wisdom communicated to the current age. Through reading long extracts from Augustine and other Church Fathers in Milner's *History*, he came to prize their writings as the great repository of Christian truth. In this manner, Newman received, in the first months of his evangelical conversion, a model of history grounded in the historiographical assumptions of ancient Christian writers. These presuppositions influenced his studies for over twenty-five years.

Eusebius, Augustine, and other ancient Christians declared that Christian truth had been given to the apostles, and preserved through each generation. Eusebius of Caesarea (260–340 CE), often referred to as the father of church history, composed the first synthetic historical account of Christianity, from its origins to the early fourth century. His *Ecclesiastical History* became the foundation on which subsequent histories were written. Eusebius's historiography dominated Milner's account of early Christianity. He was by far the most often-quoted ancient historian. Eusebius opened his history by stating, "I have purposed to record in writing the successions of the sacred apostles, covering the period stretching from our Saviour to ourselves."[23] By successions, Eusebius meant more than the succession of bishops. He referred to the whole intellectual, spiritual, and institutional life of the Church. As Kirsopp Lake, a translator of this work observed, "It cannot be too strongly emphasized, that Eusebius, like all early church historians, can be understood only if it be recognized that whereas modern writers try to trace the development, growth, and change of doctrines and institutions, their predecessors were trying to prove that nothing of the kind ever happened."[24] Eusebius labored to expose "the names, the numbers and the age of those who, driven by the desire of innovation to the extremity of error, have heralded themselves as the introducers of Knowledge, falsely so-called, ravaging the flock of Christ unsparingly, like grim wolves."[25] While Eusebius's *History* chronicled events

---

22. Joseph Milner, *History of the Church of Christ*, 5 vols. (London: T. Cadell & W. Davies, 1810), 1:xi.

23. Eusebius of Caesarea, *Eusebius: Ecclesiastical History*, trans. Kirsopp Lake, 2 vols., Loeb Classical Library (London: Heinemann, 1926), 1:7.

24. Eusebius, *Ecclesiastical History*, 1:xxxiv–xxxv.

25. Eusebius, *Ecclesiastical History*, 1:6–7.

and the acts of Christians in the first three centuries, it denied the mutable or innovative nature of time. For Eusebius, the goal of the believer was to be unswervingly faithful to the tradition of the apostles.

Augustine of Hippo (354–430 CE) used prophetical texts to ground his theology of time, and identified seven periods of abrupt change, or dispensations, in God's interaction with humanity; each of them was approximately a millennium in length. These dispensations paralleled the days of creation. Augustine claimed to live in the sixth dispensation, or the last millennium before Christ's return and the beginning of an eternal Sabbath rest. During the sixth dispensation, also called the Age of the Church, nothing new would be revealed until Christ's second coming, because Satan was bound by the Church's presence. Augustine's historiography created a sense of stasis in the sixth dispensation.[26]

This patristic vision of the Christian past, which was both linear and static—in which Christian truth was communicated inter-generationally without qualitative alteration or change—proved a powerful force in shaping Newman's understanding of the faith, and his connection to it. Newman's early awareness of this way of engaging Christians of the earliest generations shaped his imagination, and during his twenties drew him into a study of their writings. Even as Newman imbibed from Milner this patristic metanarrative of Christian history, he engaged another vision of the past found in Bishop Thomas Newton's *Dissertations on the Prophecies* (1803), a vision that had emerged in the late medieval and early modern period. This understanding of the Christian past identified the institution of the papacy with the Antichrist.

The controversial Avignon period of the papacy and the Great Western Schism that followed raised doubts about the monarchical model of authority the papacy had come to assume by the fourteenth century. For some, these doubts were spiritualized. John Wyclif (1330–1384) was the first author to gain a wide audience for identification of the papacy with the Antichrist. Wyclif, like his medieval counterparts, rejected innovation and accepted Augustine's seven dispensations. Yet Wyclif's teaching on the papacy struck at the heart of Western Christianity's historiography. Augustine's sixth millennium, the age of the Church, resolved the problem of time in the fourth and early fifth centuries—but by the fourteenth century it was strained to the breaking point. Wyclif found in Revelation 20 an explanation for the challenge faced by the Western Church of his era. While Augustine focused on the first six verses, in

26. Anthony Kemp, *The Estrangement of the Past: A Study in the Origins of Modern Historical Consciousness* (Oxford: Oxford University Press, 1991), 18–32; Ernst Breisach, *Historiography: Ancient, Medieval, and Modern* (Chicago: University of Chicago Press, 1983), 84–88.

which Satan is bound and the saints reign for a thousand years, Wyclif focused on Rev. 20:7-9, in which Satan is loosed "to deceive the nations." During this second millennium, errors and false doctrine would abound, even at the heart of the Church. Wyclif identified the deceiver in that prophecy with the bishop of Rome.[27]

Wyclif's counterpart in classical studies was Petrarch (1304–1374). Using images of light and darkness, he identified the period after Titus as an epoch of darkness, when Rome's Golden Age ended, and Europe slipped into a period of barbarity. Petrarch divided history into three distinct periods: the classical, the middle (or dark) ages, and the modern. In the modern period, Europe, and particularly the Italian region, would reject the dark barbarous middle age, and restore and revitalize its golden classical past.[28]

In the sixteenth century, Luther and those who followed him used these two themes as they developed an alternative understanding of the Christian past. Petrarch's model was adopted to divide Christian history into three ages: first a period of primitive purity, followed by an age of corruption and decline that was ultimately overcome by the sixteenth-century Reformation—which reappropriated and reapplied ancient, primitive ideals. The pope was the source of this corruption, and identified as the Antichrist foretold by the prophets.[29]

When Newman read Thomas Newton's *Dissertations on the Prophesies* in 1816, it was this vision of history that he also absorbed. Newton observed, "That night of ignorance was so thick and dark, that there was hardly here and there a single star to be seen in the entire hemisphere. But no sooner was there any glimmering or dawning of a reformation, than the true notion of anti-Christ, which had been so long suppressed, broke out again."[30] Explaining that Wyclif had introduced this teaching while at Oxford University, Newton took comfort in the events of the sixteenth century, observing, "The power of the pope is nothing near so great now as it was some ages ago: It received its death-wound at the Reformation of which it may languish for a time, but will never entirely recover."[31]

Enough has been presented to illustrate the intellectual inconsistency—created in part by these conflicting historiographical

27. Kemp, *Estrangement*, 66–75.
28. Breisach, *Historiography*, 181; Kemp, *Estrangement*, 98–104.
29. Kemp, *Estrangement*, 75–83.
30. Thomas Newton, *Dissertations on the Prophecies*, 2 vols. (London: F. C. and J. Rivington, 1803), 2:118. For a more extensive examination of his treatment of the pope as Antichrist, see 2:117–21, 241–44, 387–99.
31. Newton, *Dissertations on the Prophecies*, 2:399.

metanarratives—that Newman struggled with during his early years of evangelical fervor. On the one side, he embraced a vision of Christian history that asserted timeless, changeless truth, dating from the period of the apostles; and on the other side, he perceived a Christian past marked by periods of purity, corruption, and reformation, which had as its chief protagonist the pope as Antichrist. The impact of these two metanarratives of Christian history deeply marked Newman's theological studies and interior spiritual life from the late 1810s to the early 1840s. While the Reformation model of history dominated his thinking during the evangelical phase of Newman's life, during the latter half of his twenties, Newman radically reoriented his Anglican loyalties, and the ancient patristic model of the Christian past came to the fore. Yet, it must be stated that both had been so deeply impressed on his religious imagination that Newman tended to employ them as subject and circumstance required. These were not abstract scholarly speculations for Newman, but crucial to his personal experience of faith and his perception of England's spiritual dilemma. Christian truth was at stake, and his passion to defend it led to an intense study of early Christianity as a lens through which to understand the faith in his times.

ARIANS OF THE FOURTH CENTURY (1833)

With his migration from evangelical to high church Anglicanism during the 1820s, Newman developed a deep appreciation for ancient Christianity, and its relevance in Britain's social and political crises of the late 1820s and early 1830s. His studies of the ancient Christian past became a prism through which he critiqued Anglicanism's contemporary dilemma.[32] His purpose was to defend the doctrinal continuity of the English Church with primitive Christian teaching. Early in 1831, Newman corresponded with Hugh James Rose, a leading member of the high church party and an editor of the *Theological Library*, a collection of works intended for Anglican ordinands. He proposed an apologetical defense of the historical continuity between the ancient creeds and the Thirty-nine Articles. Rose convinced him to write a history of the ecumenical councils instead.[33]

When Newman's first book was completed in late 1832, it had changed form again, and was titled *Arians of the Fourth Century*. This work wove

---

32. For historical context, see Peter Nockles, *The Oxford Movement in Context: Anglican Highchurchmanship, 1760-1857* (Cambridge: Cambridge University Press, 1994). For a close examination of Newman's work on *Arians*, see King, *Newman and the Alexandrian Fathers*, 70–126.

33. John Henry Newman, *The Letters and Diaries of John Henry Newman* (Oxford: Clarendon, 1979), 2:321–22 (hereafter, *LD*).

together an engaging, scholarly study of Christianity's first great doctrinal controversy, with a running commentary on his own times. To account for anomalies in early patristic teaching that complicated his use of the ancient metanarrative of the Christian past, Newman argued for a *disciplina arcani* (secret tradition), which he claimed the Church had received from the apostles, but only revealed as time and circumstance required.[34]

During his research on Arianism in the summer of 1831, Newman came under the influence of the Baroque-era Jesuit, Dionysius Petavius (Denis *Pétau*, 1583–1651), whose historiographical argument for a stable apostolic deposit of faith depended on a *disciplina arcani* to account for apparent alterations in Christian teaching during antiquity. According to Petavius, this hidden tradition had been handed down through the succession of bishops and only became part of the Church's public teaching as controversy and need required.[35] In Newman's study of the Arian controversy, he treated change in doctrinal matters as a test and mark of heresy. Under the influence of George Bull's *Defence of the Nicene Creed* (1685), Newman became convinced that a stable (static) tradition was the hallmark of orthodoxy and that ancient Christianity provided the benchmark for any assessment of Christian truth claims.[36]

In the first sections of his book, Newman described an early church reluctant to reduce its central teachings to texts and formulas. He claimed primitive Christianity enjoyed the peculiar privilege of freedom from creeds and articles of faith, because it distinguished between exoteric teaching, intended for the general public, and esoteric teaching, reserved for the fully initiated Christian. This esoteric teaching, the *disciplina arcani*, came to the Church from the apostles. The doctrines it taught were not found in Scripture, but were confirmed in biblical texts, and acknowledged as apostolic in origin.[37]

By the fourth century, problems of novel and heretical ideas forced Church leaders to respond with clear definitions in creeds and articles of faith, issued by ecumenical councils. Over time, the *disciplina arcani* ceased to exist, even in theory. What survived from this tradition had been passed on through the creeds of the councils, as new heresies required its publication. Newman stated that these creeds were "in some sense of apostolical authority still; and at least [serve] the chief office of the early traditions, viz. that of interpreting

---

34. John Henry Newman, *Arians of the Fourth Century* (London: J. G. and F. Rivington, 1833), 55–72 (hereafter, *Ari*).

35. *Ari*, 78ff.

36. Stephen Thomas, *Newman and Heresy: The Anglican Years* (Cambridge: Cambridge University Press, 1991), 180.

37. *Ari*, 59–61.

and harmonizing the statements of Scripture."[38] Newman, echoing Milner, emphasized that the creeds should be received as facts, not opinions, for "these doctrines were the subject of an Apostolic Tradition; they were the very truths which had been lately revealed to mankind."[39] Through this line of argument, Newman sought to establish the normativity of primitive Christian teaching, and assert an Anglican claim to be faithful followers and defenders of that apostolic heritage.

To deepen the connection he identified between his age and the ancient church, Newman associated those who threatened his understanding of orthodoxy with the taint of ancient heresy. By analogy, Newman associated "liberals" of his age with the ancient Eclectics, suggesting that their reforming efforts in the church and society threatened traditions received from the apostles and preserved through the ages in the English Church. He observed, "Who does not recognise in this old philosophy the chief features of that recent school of liberalism and false illumination, political and moral, which is now Satan's instrument in deluding the nations?"[40]

After finishing *Arians*, Newman spent the winter of 1833 traveling in Greece and Italy with Hurrell Froude and Froude's father. He parted with them in Rome to travel through Sicily. While there he suffered a serious illness that brought with it a deep sense of spiritual crisis. He emerged from that illness with an ambiguous, but profound sense of purpose.[41] At the end of May 1833, his Sicilian servant found him weeping by his bed and asked what troubled him. Newman reported that he could only say, "I have a work to do in England."[42] As he journeyed back to England, he penned his famous hymn, "Lead Kindly Light," which expressed a powerful need to follow a providential light "amid the encircling gloom." In Newman's narrative of his life, clarity came with John Keble's Assize sermon, "National Apostasy," preached in Oxford shortly after his return.[43] What followed was a more strident application of Newman's tendency to write history in the first person, as he and his colleagues in the Oxford Movement used the resources of the past to defend priorities they valued and that they perceived to be under threat.

---

38. *Ari*, 62.
39. *Ari*, 148.
40. *Ari*, 117.
41. Frank Turner, *John Henry Newman: The Challenge to Evangelical Religion* (New Haven: Yale University Press, 2002), 146–53.
42. *Apo*, 99.
43. *Apo*, 100; Turner, *Newman*, 153–54.

The Oxford Movement

In the summer of 1833, Newman joined others in a campaign to defend the Church of England from parliamentary acts and elements within the Church itself that they perceived as threats to Anglican orthodoxy. The movement declared the Church of England to be the one true church in England, and asserted that their church must preserve and transmit the Catholic tradition, received from the apostles through primitive Christianity and defended by the Caroline divines. They attacked the innovations of Protestantism from within, and raised the alarm against politically active Catholics and Dissenters in Parliament.[44]

To justify this polemical position, Newman promoted three historiographical assumptions that creatively altered the received Reformation model of history. First, instead of one period of primitive purity and Catholic orthodoxy, there were two: the early centuries of Christianity and the period of the Caroline divines. Second, instead of one source of decadence and corruption, there were two: the papacy and the sixteenth-century Protestant Reformers. Third, the true source of reform was not the sixteenth-century Reformation, but a "second Reformation," inaugurated by Newman and his colleagues. This adaptation reflected the crises of the times, for the target of this polemic was not (at least initially) Roman Catholicism, but the Protestantism of those who wielded power in England.

Yet even as Newman creatively adapted the metanarrative he had internalized from the writings of Bishop Newton and others, he retained and employed—as circumstance and polemic required—the ancient metanarrative of unaltered truth received from the apostles and preserved by the best of the Anglican tradition through the centuries. This model supported Newman's claim that the Oxford Movement reflected the true expression of Anglicanism. He used the early Church Fathers, not only in the *Tracts for the Times*, but also in essays published by the *British Magazine* between 1833 and 1836 to reinforce this claim.

In a *British Magazine* article Newman later titled, "What says Vincent of Lerins?" he urged his readers to think of the Fathers primarily as witnesses to unchanging truth: "[T]heir treatises are, as it were, *histories*,—teaching us, in the first instance, matters of fact, not of opinion."[45] In another *British Magazine*

---

44. For context, see Nockles, *Oxford Movement*, *passim*; Benjamin O'Connor, "An Introduction to the Oxford Movement," in *Authority, Dogma, and History: The Role of Oxford Movement Converts in the Papal Infallibility Debates*, ed. Kenneth L. Parker and Michael J. G. Pahls (Bethesda, MD: Academica, 2009), 9–43; Thomas, *Newman and Heresy*, 50–62.

article, Newman directly challenged the historiography of Protestantism. Noting that some asserted that the Catholic system was "foreign to the pure gospel," he stated that one must look to the data of history for proof. After reviewing the beliefs and practices of the early Fathers, Newman observed that "witnesses of the faith of Rome, Africa, Gaul, Asia Minor, Syria, and Egypt, certainly do not represent the opinions of Luther and Calvin. They stretch over the whole of Christendom . . . they coalesce in one religion; but it is not the religion of the Reformation."[46] The series of articles ended in 1836 with this strongly worded conclusion: "If Protestantism is another name for Christianity, then the Martyrs and the Bishops of the early Church, the men who taught the nations, the men who converted the Roman Empire, had themselves to be taught, themselves to be converted. Shall we side with the first age of Christianity or with the last?"[47] Newman rejected Protestantism because its principles clashed with those he found in early Christianity. It was a novelty that had arisen in the previous three centuries, and therefore did not merit the assent of the English people. Though tainted by Protestant heresy, the English Church had been preserved from apostasy by those faithful to the Caroline divines.

Newman argued instead for an Anglican tradition that had found a middle way between the corruptions of Roman Catholicism and the innovations of Protestantism. He promoted an Anglican *via media*, which existed in continuity with the ancient church, and formed the foundation for what he styled England's second, true Reformation. This call for a "return" to the Anglican *via media* creatively wedded the two models of history Newman had received in his earliest years of adolescent fervor. During this time, these two models of history worked well for Newman and complemented one another. They shaped his understanding of truth and anchored his commitment to Anglican spirituality, as he understood it.

If Protestantism was one extreme to be avoided by this middle way, Roman Catholicism was the other extreme. The rising political fortunes of Roman Catholics heightened the anti-Roman fears of many Anglicans, including high churchmen. While the Tractarians acknowledged many similarities between their position and Romanism, crucial differences divided them. For Newman, the most compelling difference was their understanding and use of history.

---

45. John Henry Newman, "Letters on the Church of the Fathers, no. IX," *British Magazine* 6 (1834): 288–89. This essay was included in: John Henry Newman, *Historical Sketches*, 3 vols. (London: Longmans, Green & Co., 1897), 1:385–86. Subsequent essays from the *British Magazine* will be quoted from the 1897 edition of *Historical Sketches* (hereafter, *HS*).

46. *HS*, 1:403.

47. *HS*, 1:442.

In the *Lectures on the Prophetical Office of the Church*, published in 1837, he stated that Anglicans differed with Romanists "in our view of historical facts."[48] The difference between the two traditions rested in their appeals to antiquity; for when controversy grew animated, Roman Catholics "supersede the appeal to Scripture and Antiquity by the pretence [sic.] of the infallibility of the Church."[49] In contrast, Anglicans tested their doctrines against Scripture and apostolic teaching preserved by the Church Fathers. Applying the metanarrative of changeless continuity of apostolic teaching, he observed, "Ancient Consent is, practically, the only, or main kind of Tradition which now remains to us."[50] Newman argued that the Roman system was "a Tradition of men, that is, not continuous, that it stops short of the Apostles, that the history of its introduction is known." The Roman system rested upon "what is historically an upstart Tradition." He insisted that arguments against Romanism based on patristic literature were the surest ground for controversy because they rested on historical facts.[51]

Changeless continuity became the basis for his assertion that the Oxford Movement represented a restored and purified primitive Christian practice—against the innovations of Protestantism on the one hand and the corruptions of Roman Catholicism on the other.[52] As he explained to Samuel Rickards in July 1834, "We are a 'Reformed' Church, not a 'Protestant [Church].'" Denouncing the sixteenth-century Reformation and the "Puritanic spirit" of the Elizabethan and Jacobean reigns, he asserted that the Catholic character of the English Church endured: "We, the while, children of Holy Church, whencesoever brought into it, whether by early training, or after thought, have had one voice, that one voice which the Church has had from the beginning. As far as I can make out, the great and holy men of every age have not much differed from each other—Hooker and Taylor from St Bernard, St Bernard from St Chrysostom."[53] As the evidence from this period illustrates, Newman skillfully wedded the ancient model of history to a modified version of the Reformation model of history; and in so doing, he identified primitive Christianity and the Caroline divines with continuity of Christian truth, Roman

---

48. John Henry Newman, *The Via Media of the Anglican Church*, 2 vols. (London: J.G. and Rivington, 1837), vol 1, *Lectures on the Prophetical Office of the Church* , 59 (hereafter, *VM*). Vol 2 has a different title, *Occasional Letters and Tracts*. It is not quoted in this chapter.

49. *VM*, 1:60.

50. *VM*, 1:63.

51. *VM*, 1:48–49.

52. *VM*, 1:1–32.

53. *LD*, 4:314–15.

Catholicism and Protestantism with innovation or corruption of that truth, and the Anglicanism of the Oxford Movement as the engine of true Reformation.

While Newman's Anglican spirituality in this period rested on this complex appropriation of the Christian past, at least one of his disciples, Samuel Francis Wood, challenged him to look at the Christian past through a different lens. In 1835 and 1836, Wood pressed Newman to consider the possibility of development as a historiographical model on which to base his understanding of Christian history. While Wood did not succeed in the short term, by the early 1840s, Newman was forced by life circumstances to revisit this theory.

Developmentalism

On 19 November 1835, Samuel Wood, a former student and devoted disciple of John Henry Newman, wrote to his Oxford contemporary and close friend, Henry Edward Manning, full of news from a country holiday with mutual friends. Wood noted that he looked forward to receiving from Manning reflections on the nature of "tradition," based on Vincent of Lérins's *Commonitorium*, from which the Vincentian canon had been culled. Manning's project eventually became Tract 78 (published 2 February 1837).[54]

In anticipation of that exchange, Wood offered Manning "a few dogmas of my own on the same subject." Before setting out six points in a document he titled "Scripture and Tradition," Wood expressed the hope that Manning would not think him "very *Popish*."[55] Wood had reason for concern. The theory he set forth resonated with "Romish" caricatures attacked in tracts Newman had published. Wood's key point touched on the issue of "development." He stated, "In common with other societies the Church has the inherent power of expanding or modifying her organization, of bringing her ideas of the Truth into more distinct consciousness, or of developing the Truth itself more fully." He went on to observe, "It follows then that doctrines may be true, though not traceable* to the Apostles: *i.e. we may not have need to trace them, etc."[56]

In another letter to Manning dated 18 December 1835, Wood conceded that the apostles were divinely illuminated and conscious of the "whole range of Christian doctrine." Yet he doubted the early church had been capable of apprehending the entirety of Christian truth in its fullness. Comparing the growth of the church to human development, Wood considered it more natural

---

54. James Pereiro, *Ethos and the Oxford Movement: At the Heart of Tractarianism* (Oxford: Oxford University Press, 2008), 239.

55. Pereiro, *Ethos*, 240.

56. Pereiro, *Ethos*, 241.

that, like a human person in the midst of struggle, using the divine word as its guide, the church might "evolve, comment on, and exhibit the whole counsel of God" over time. This did not cast "a shadow of disparagement on the Primitive church, because it shows the moral necessity of the progress I contend for." He argued that one could discern development of doctrines between the Gospels and the Epistles. Wood went on at length to demonstrate how doctrinal truths had developed from their nascent character in Scripture to settled doctrines centuries later. In a postscript, he emphasized that the Rule of Faith—the "*summa Fidei*"—had concluded with the apostles and that no additions should be made to the Scriptures. Yet he framed a crucial question in human developmental terms: "[W]as their Faith *fully exhibited* in the teaching of the infant Church?"[57]

Two weeks later, on 1 January 1836, Wood wrote to Newman on the same topic. Returning a draft of what became Newman's third letter to Abbé Jager, Wood expressed satisfaction that while they used the term "Rule of Faith" somewhat differently, their differing views were reconcilable. He pressed against his mentor's critique of his theory of development, observing: "I do not see how my notion can disparage the early Church, even as an historical fact." Quoting Vincent of Lérins's *Commonitorium*, Wood assumed that God intended "*profectus religionis*" (progress of religion) in the church. While he considered early Christian teaching the foundation of the church's doctrinal system, "It surely will not be said that Her authority was exhausted by its first exercise." Indeed Wood insisted that "the full body and perfection of Divine truth could not be ecclesiastically exhibited, at once, in a moment," without violating the ordinary way God deals with humans or acknowledging the limited capacity of the human mind to understand. In a striking passage that resonates with Newman's 1845 description of historical developments, Wood stated: "The course of events, corruptions, and schisms, might interrupt its [a doctrine's] subsequent application, and this is our grievous loss, but no invalidation of the authority itself, or disproof that a 'profectus' [progress] was designed." It does not depreciate the early church's role in the "*profectus*," "to show that it was humanly impossible she could do more."[58]

Four weeks later, on 29 January 1836, Samuel Wood sent Henry Manning a detailed letter on Newman's weeklong visit to London. The bulk of the text explored the intense resistance Newman had to Wood's theory of development. Newman staked out a firm Reformation vision of history that seemed impenetrable, despite Wood's best efforts.[59]

---

57. Pereiro, *Ethos*, 244–46.
58. Pereiro, *Ethos*, 246–47.

Far from dissuading Wood, Newman's line of argument had convinced him that his theory of development was not mere "idle speculation," but "involves practical consequences of very great weight in our present condition." Wood observed that Newman's "violent repugnance" toward sixteenth-century reformers and their doctrines was justified by principles so extreme "they opened one's eyes to their unsoundness."[60]

To make his case, Newman had asserted that after the church ceased to be one, the right of any part of the church to "propound" articles of faith had been suspended. Newman condemned the reformers for attempting to deduce doctrines from Scripture—like justification by faith—and considered their appeals to the early fathers perverse. Wood observed that the effect of Newman's approach was "not merely to *refer* us to antiquity but to *shut us up* in it, and to deprive, not only individuals but the Church, of all those doctrines of Scripture not fully commented on by the Fathers." In this way, Newman condemned England's "Reformed Church" in the same manner that he condemned the Tridentine Roman Catholic Church.[61] Indeed, Newman had already staked out a firm commitment to this vision of history in Tracts 31, 39, and 41. Just that month he had employed it in Tract 71 against "Romanists." It was the central historiographical point of his argument in his *Lectures on the Prophetical Office of the Church*, published the following year. Yet Wood remained firm in his convictions and pressed his former Oriel mentor.

Wood concluded that Newman's position required Anglicans to suspend judgment and not fully accept their church's teaching on justification and other doctrines, because they were not rooted explicitly in ancient teaching. It removed from serious consideration large portions of the Church of England's heritage, "under the pretense of respect for primitive antiquity." Wood found this unduly dismissive of doctrines expounded by "many holy men" and the good fruit that had come of their teaching. His unease over Newman's heavy-handed application of the Reformation vision of history caused Wood to ask: "How then am I to prevent them from being wrested from me . . . on *what theory* are they to be defended?"[62]

Wood's resolution of this dilemma was his theory of development. Taking up again the human developmental analogy, he stated that in the individual Christian and in the life of the church, "there is a natural course of the mind,"

---

59. Pereiro, *Ethos*, 248.
60. Pereiro, *Ethos*, 248.
61. Pereiro, *Ethos*, 248–49.
62. Pereiro, *Ethos*, 249.

that starts with the "external Objects of faith" and moves on to examine "their inward operations on the soul, and its condition as affected by them." He went on to identify different classes of subjects, and the order in which they attract consideration. While regretting that corruption and schisms had disrupted the unity of the church, Wood rejected Newman's modified Reformation vision of history, and insisted that each church—and even parties within churches—must play their part "in building the temple of the Lord." In his view, it was "no disparagement of the early Church" to look to later Christian history for things that would have been impossible for early Christians to discern.[63] Wood's assessment of the power of his theory is worth quoting at length: "Surely in thoughts like these one may see glimpses of a beautiful and comprehensive system which holding fast primitive antiquity on the one hand, does not reject the later teaching of the Church on the other, but bringing out of its stores things new and old, is eminently calculated to break up existing parties in the Church, and unite the children of light against those of darkness."[64] Wood's developmental vision of history left Newman unmoved in January 1836. Wood explained to Manning, "I have endeavoured in vain to gain entrance into Ns. [Newman's] mind on this subject, and have tried each joint of his intellectual panoply, but its hard and polished temper glances off all my arrows."[65] Wood closed by professing ongoing devotion to the "positive parts" of Newman's system, and expressed a willingness to "wait calmly in the sure trust that . . . God will reveal this also unto us."[66] He stated this in full knowledge that Newman would not seek to move forward with Wood's developmental vision of history.

Evidence from Newman's *Lectures on the Prophetical Office of the Church*, published in 1837, demonstrates that Wood was accurate in his reading of Newman's disposition at that time. Yet by 1839 and 1840, life circumstances had softened Newman's resistance. His studies of the Monophysite controversy during the summer of 1839 created an interior crisis that caused him to confide in others that he had glimpsed a "vista" that led to a destination he could not yet perceive. In 1840, Newman's *Tract 90* attempted to defend his vision of Oxford Movement Anglicanism—as the preservation of primitive Christian truth claims—against the Oxford Movement's critics. Bishops and the popular press denounced his vision of Anglicanism. This and several other factors forced Newman to face a hard reality: that his understanding of Anglicanism was not shared by the Church of England's leadership and the vast majority of

63. Pereiro, *Ethos*, 248–50.
64. Pereiro, *Ethos*, 250.
65. Pereiro, *Ethos*, 250.
66. Pereiro, *Ethos*, 250.

Anglican laity.[67] By 1841, Newman began a process of de-conversion from the Anglican Church, though he only came to realize it by degrees. Analyzing the reasons, Newman came to appreciate that his understanding of "antiquity" and "catholicity" did not argue in favor of his *via media* Anglicanism. While Anglicans took refuge in antiquity, the Roman appeal to catholicity seemed to favor the historical "corruptions" that he had denounced during the preceding decade.[68] Newman spent the next five years struggling toward an alternative understanding of the Christian past, one that ultimately enabled him to become a Roman Catholic.

Newman's Theory of Doctrinal Development

Newman's understanding of the history of Christian doctrine underwent a metamorphosis during this period.[69] In place of appeals to primitive Christianity, he argued for a theory of doctrinal development that might span centuries, but would come to a true conclusion under the providential guidance of the Holy Spirit. In a significant turn, Vincent of Lérins's dictum was no longer deemed sufficient given the rise of critical historical scholarship over the previous three centuries.[70] He rejected the static vision of truth and argued for a living tradition, ever growing, flowering, and bearing fruit.[71] He asserted that development and growth in the Christian doctrinal tradition occurred despite periods of controversy and disorder. Owen Chadwick concluded that Newman pursued this development "according to the strict canons of historical scholarship."[72]

This vision of the Christian past departed radically from his Oxford Movement rhetoric, but opened a way forward toward a Christian communion that he could recognize as Catholic.[73] While much has been written about

---

67. Kenneth L. Parker, "The Role of Estrangement in Conversion: The Case of John Henry Newman," in *Christianity and the Stranger: Historical Essays*, ed. Francis Nichols (Atlanta: Scholars, 1995), 193–99.

68. *Apo*, 259–61.

69. Kenneth L. Parker and C. Michael Shea, "Johann Adam Möhler's Influence on John Henry Newman's Theory of Doctrinal Development: The Case for a Reappraisal," *Ephemerides Theologicae Lovanienses* 89, no. 1 (2013): 73–95.

70. *Dev*, 28.

71. *Dev*, 37.

72. Owen Chadwick, *From Bossuet to Newman* (Cambridge: Cambridge University Press, 1987), 147. Benjamin King, following Newman's contemporary and friend, James Mozley, disagrees with Chadwick. King, *Newman and the Alexandrian Fathers*, 216.

73. Jay Hammond's analysis of this turbulent period is perhaps the clearest dissection of the issues at stake as Newman struggled for a justification for his conversion to Roman Catholicism. Jay Hammond,

Newman's theory of development and its impact, we must never forget the brilliant but bewildered man in his Littlemore retreat, searching for convincing reasons to become Roman Catholic. He found it through a historicized understanding of tradition—a theory of development. Newman was received into the Catholic Church in October 1845, just before finishing his essay on development.[74] Though other scholars had tentatively explored earlier concepts of development and organic growth of doctrine (he mentioned Möhler and de Maistre in his opening pages), it was Newman's essay that crystallized the concept. No doubt the notoriety of his conversion played a role, but his struggle to find a way to appropriate a historicized vision of tradition resonated with some in his newfound spiritual home. Though appropriation of this theory was slow and the scholastic vision of the Christian past continued to dominate Roman Catholic discourse for more than a century, its impact was felt within the first decade, and gained strength and influence over time.

Reception of Newman's Theory of Development

Newman began his life as a Catholic under a cloud of suspicion. His essay on development received a chilly reception, from Protestants and Roman Catholics alike. Even former friends, like Edward Manning (still an Anglican), found it incompatible with Roman Catholic thought. He observed, "[T]he Tridentine Doctors would have severely censured the modern theories of development, or gradual rise as false, and dangerous."[75] Philip Schaff concluded that "Romanism cannot give up the principle of stability, without unsettling its own foundations."[76]

However, Manning and Schaff underestimated the flexibility of the Roman Catholic tradition to adapt in the face of changing circumstances. When Newman arrived for studies in Rome in 1846, he found suspicion among Roman theologians about the orthodoxy of his theory and engaged in a dialogue with Giovanni Perrone, the *doyen* of the Roman School. Though

---

"The Interplay of Hermeneutics and Heresy in the Process of Newman's Conversion from 1830-1845," in *Authority Dogma and History*, 45–76.

74. Thomas, *Newman and Heresy*, 228.

75. Bodleian Library, Oxford, MS Eng. Lett.c. 662, fol. 68r. Manning to unknown correspondent, 10 March 1846. To William Gladstone he expressed doubts about the viability of Newman's theory of development, and asserted that whatever its influence, the impact would not be seen soon, "Certainly not for a long time." Pitts Library, Emory University, Manning Papers, Box 1, Folder 22, Manning to Gladstone, 6 March 1846.

76. Philip Schaff, *What Is Church History?: A Vindication of the Idea of Historical Development* (Philadelphia: J. B. Lippincott & Co., 1846), 47n.

Perrone did not warm to his theory based on any compulsion to historicize the Catholic concept of tradition, his prior reading of Möhler had opened a way toward dialogue. Perrone found common ground with Newman through the Suarezian distinction between *explicit* revelation and implicit elements of the deposit of faith that only become defined in the midst of controversy.[77]

Only eight years later, at the episcopal assembly preceding the promulgation of *Ineffabilis Deus* (the definition of the Immaculate Conception), an American archbishop, Francis Kenrick, forced a delay in the publication of the final text by harshly critiquing assertions in the proposed draft that the Church had always taught this dogma. Kenrick observed, "It is not true that tradition has always been clear in the Church on the Conception. For some centuries it was not mentioned."[78] He also noted that Pius V had rebuked those who had spoken as though their opinion on the Immaculate Conception was dogma.[79] Five years after the promulgation of the bull, Kenrick published a review article of the events of the assembly and closely followed Newman's theory in his argument. He outlined the incorporation of this devotion into the life of the church in the early modern and modern period, and the cautious but increasingly supportive role played by popes in these developments.[80] Francis Kenrick's use of Newman's theory in an episcopal assembly is a crucial landmark in the incorporation of Newman's theory into the magisterial teaching of the Catholic Church.[81] It would not be the last.

77. C. Michael Shea, "The Role of Newman's Theory of the Development of Christian Doctrine in the Events Leading to the Definition of Papal Infallibility at the First Vatican Council," in *Authority, Dogma, and History*, 80–85. Also see Walter Kasper, *Die Lehre von der Tradition in der Römischen Schule* (Freiburg im Breisgau: Herder, 1962), 119–30. I am grateful to Michael Shea for his insights on this subject.

78. "Non esser vero che sempre sia stata *chiara* la tradizione nella Chiesa sul Concepimento: per diversi secoli non se ne parlò." Vincenzo Sardi, *La Solenne Definizione del Dogma dell'Immacolato Concepimento di Maria Santissima*, 2 vols. (Rome: Tipografia Vaticana, 1905), 2:208. There was an explicit discussion about Newman's theory of development in the episcopal convocation in November 1854. Francis Kenrick's recommendation that the phrase "vult sileri de Scriptura, traditione, et perpetuo Ecclesiae sensu" be excised sparked a sharp reaction from Schrader and others, for they suspected Newman's theory was implied. For the full exchange, see Sardi, 2:210–11.

79. For matters summarized in this paragraph, see Sardi, 2:180–81, 198–214, 231–32, 307, 309.

80. Francis P. Kenrick, "Article I—1. De Immaculato Deipare conceptu Caroli Passaglia commentarius. Romae, 1854, 1855, 3 Tomi, 4to.—2. *The Immaculate Conception of the Most Blessed Virgin Mary a Dogma of the Catholic Church*. By J. D. Bryant, M.D. Boston, 1855.—3. *L'Immaculée Conception de la Bienheureuse Vierge Marie considerée comme dogme de Foi*. Par Mgr. J. B. Malou, Évêque de Bruges. Bruxelles, 1856, 2 Tomes, 6 vols." in *Brownson's Quarterly Review*, New York Series, 4:417–37 (October 1859): 429.

81. For a more complete account of Francis Kenrick's role at the episcopal convocation in November 1854, see Kenneth L. Parker, "Francis Kenrick and Papal Infallibility: How Pastoral Experience in the American Missions Transformed a Roman Ultramontanist," in *Pluralism and Tradition: Essays in Honor of*

During the First Vatican Council in 1870, Newman opposed the defining of papal infallibility because of historical evidence, and applied his theory of development in letters written to minority bishops. In a letter to Bishop Ullathorne, he asked, "What have we done to be treated, as the faithful never were treated before? When has definition of doctrine de fide been a luxury of devotion, and not a stern painful necessity? Why should an aggressive insolent faction be allowed to 'make the heart of the just to mourn, whom the Lord hath not made sorrowful?'"[82] In a letter to Bishop David Moriarty, he drew distinctions between right and wrong developments.[83] Yet his *Essay on Development* was on the minds of minority bishops as they struggled with the likely outcome. Moriarty wrote, "Strange to say, if ever this definition comes you will have contributed much towards it. Your treatise on development has given the key. A Cardinal said the other day—'We must give up the first ten centuries, but the infallibility is an obvious development of the supremacy.' Of course development was ever at work in the Church, but you brought it out and placed it on a pedestal."[84] In response to the bishop's letter, Newman observed that his understanding of development had been "attacked by various persons and praised by none—till at last it is used against me. However, I cannot be sorry for it, for without it I never should have been a Catholic."[85] Yet in the wake of the council, as he and others struggled with the implications of the new dogma, Newman consoled a disciple with an appeal to the historical development of doctrines: "Looking at early history, it would seem as if the Church moved on to perfect truth by various successive declarations, alternately in contrary directions, and thus perfecting, completing, supplying each other. Let us have a little faith in her, I say. Pius is not the last of the Popes. . . . Let us be patient, let us have faith, and a new Pope, and a re-assembled Council may trim the boat."[86] Newman's words of advice seemed to presage the events of the mid-twentieth century, when many Catholic scholars and church leaders became convinced that neoscholasticism could no longer address the pressing questions of their era.

William Shea, ed. Kenneth Parker, Peter Huff, and Michael Pahls (Lanham, MD: University Press of America, 2008), 189–90. For Newman's early influence on the Roman School, see C. Michael Shea, "Newman's Early Legacy: Giovanni Perrone and Roman Readings of the *Essay on the Development of Christian Doctrine* 1845-1854" (unpublished Ph.D. dissertation, Saint Louis University, forthcoming 2014).

82. *LD*, 25:18–19; also see 17.
83. *LD*, 25:58.
84. *LD*, 25:58 n. 2.
85. *LD*, 25:58.
86. *LD*, 25:310.

As Professor Ratzinger stated in his *Introduction to Christianity*, the apologetical power of the "old metaphysics" had ended. Christians need to think *historically* about their faith.[87] Newman's *Essay on Development* had provided the key.

Conclusion

Nicholas Lash observed, "Newman was one of the first catholic theologians seriously to attempt to hold in tension the demands of historical consciousness and the christian conviction that the gospel of Jesus Christ is irreplaceable and unchangeable."[88] When Yves Congar published his *True and False Reform in the Church* in 1950,[89] the papal nuncio to Paris, Archbishop Angelo Roncalli—the future Pope John XXIII—wrote in his copy of the book, "A reform of the Church—is it possible?"[90] Fifty-five years later, Pope John XXIII's successor not only answered in the affirmative, but extolled the "hermeneutic of reform"—and by extension the concept of development—as the truest way to understand the impact of Vatican II. While we affirm that truth is whole and complete—in God—we can no longer escape the reality that our understanding of that truth comes through incarnated experience. Christian faith does not simply affirm that God became flesh and dwelt among us in the person of Jesus Christ, but that the "embodiment" of God's truth continues to struggle toward full maturity in the Body of Christ, of which we are all a part. Newman's effort to appropriate historical consciousness and incorporate it into his life of faith, like a gestalt image, changed his perspective and opened a vista full of possibilities. It also shook apodictic certainties he had constructed on ephemeral foundations. Like Newman, our appreciation of doctrinal development and the implications of a historicized understanding of tradition continues to unfold. However, it is crucial that we remember that this insight came into the life of the Church through the prism of John Henry Newman's spiritual crisis, his struggle to rethink Christian history "in first person," and thus discover a way to become a Roman Catholic. His insight is not a static truth or one birthed in an era that transcends our twenty-first-century experience. To follow Newman's example means that we take seriously the "hermeneutic of reform,"

---

87. Ratzinger, *Einführung*, 34–38; *Introduction to Christianity*, 31–34.

88. Nicholas Lash, *Newman and Development: The Search for an Explanation in History* (New York: Sheed & Ward, 1975), 2.

89. Yves Congar, *Vrai et fausse réforme dans l'Église* (Paris: Cerf, 1950).

90. Elizabeth Teresa Groppe, *Yves Congar's Theology of the Holy Spirit* (Oxford: Oxford University Press, 2004), 22.

rethink Christian history "in first person," and thus discover insights that God's providence intends to impart in our age.

4

Sympathy in the Spiritual Theology of John Henry Newman

Donald G. Graham

Introduction

In July 1865, after his friends Frederic Rogers (Lord Blachford) and Dean Church had made him a gift of a violin, Newman told Church: "I never wrote more than when I played the fiddle. I always sleep better after music. There must be some electric currents passing from the strings through the fingers into the brain and down the spinal marrow. Perhaps thought is music." Some twenty-two years earlier, in his sermon, "The Theory of Development in Religious Doctrine," while reflecting upon those representations under which the mind considers reality, he suggests that if "the slender outfit" of the notes of the scale can precipitate so "vast an enterprise" as the melodic universe of harmony then surely music can suitably signify both creation and that "divinity in the theology of the Church, which those who feel cannot communicate . . ."[1] In his efforts to communicate the incommunicable, including the mystical sympathy shared by members of the Holy Family, Newman sometimes had recourse to musical metaphor.

> When, for our sakes, the Son came on earth and took our flesh, yet He would not live without the sympathy of others. For thirty

---

1. As related by Edward Short, *Newman and His Contemporaries* (New York: T. & T. Clark, 2011), 383–84. See John Henry Newman to R. W. Church, 11 July 1865, *The Letters and Diaries of John Henry Newman* (London: Nelson; Oxford: Clarendon, 1961), 22:9 (hereafter, *LD*), and *Fifteen Sermons Preached before the University of Oxford*, new edition (London: Longmans, Green, 1892), 346 (hereafter, *US*). I am grateful to my friend, Dr. H. Daniel Monsour, former associate editor of the *Collected Works of Bernard Lonergan* (Lonergan Institute, Regis College, University of Toronto, 1988) for his close reading of and comments upon this chapter.

years He lived with Mary and Joseph and thus formed a shadow of the Heavenly Trinity on earth. O the perfection of that sympathy which existed between the three! Not a look of one, but the other two understood, as expressed, better than if expressed in a thousand words—nay more than understood, accepted, echoed, corroborated. It was like three instruments absolutely in tune which all vibrate when one vibrates, and vibrate either one and the same note, or in perfect harmony.[2]

My goal in this chapter is to spotlight Newman's sense of sympathy within the scope of his spiritual theology in order to suggest its power to animate contemporary Christian spirituality and theology. Meanings of sympathy from the nineteenth century to our own range from feelings of pity and sorrow for someone else's misfortunes, to a common understanding between people, to agreement with, or approval of an opinion or aim, to relating harmoniously to something else.[3] In Newman's theological lexicon, this range of meanings is often condensed so that sympathy comes to denote that graced strengthening of character, ennobling of spirit, and expanding of heart that enable one to: (1) identify with another's circumstances and to confirm him or her in dignity; (2) rejoice together in that which is true, good, and beautiful; (3) commiserate with the fragile, vulnerable, and wounded, without necessarily affirming either the reasons for, or nature of, their afflictions, (4) apply the salve of healing compassion to the sin-scalded. To this end, I trace how Newman situates sympathy within the trajectory of the mystery of salvation regarding the life of the Trinity, the office of the Divine Son, the mission of the God-man, and the sanctification of the saints. In each case, I analyze how Newman's understanding of sympathy operates in the specified context and briefly state its relevance for contemporary Christian spirituality and theology. First, however, I want briefly to clarify two questions: What do I mean by spiritual theology, and why should we attend to Newman's spiritual theology?

---

2. John Henry Newman, "Our Lord Refuses Sympathy" (10 March 1855), in *Prayers, Verses, and Devotions* (San Francisco: Ignatius, 1989), 345–46. This is a compilation of three reprints the first translated and adapted by Newman, the other two being his own works: *The Devotions of Bishop Andrewes* (Oxford and London: John Henry Parker, 1843), *Meditations and Devotions* (London: Longmans, Green, 1903), and *Verses on Various Occasions* (London: Longmans, Green, 1903) (hereafter, *VV*).

3. A paraphrase of "sympathy," accessed 5 June 2012, at http://oxforddictionaries.com/definition/sympathy.

Jordan Aumann describes spiritual theology as the "part of theology that, proceeding from the truths of divine revelation and the religious experience of individual persons, defines the nature of the supernatural life, formulates directives for its growth and development, and explains the process by which souls advance from the beginning of the spiritual life to its full perfection."[4] In a searching essay, "Theology and Sanctity," Hans Urs von Balthasar depicts the deficiencies of a theology that is inappropriately dogmatic or spiritual.

> The impoverishment brought about by the divorce between the two spheres is all too plain; it has sapped the vital force of the Church of today and the credibility of her preaching of eternal truth. This impoverishment is felt considerably more strongly by those who have to preach to modern pagans than by professors in their seminary lecture rooms. It is the former who look round for some example of the conjunction of wisdom and holiness. They long to discover the living organism of the Church's doctrine, rather than a strange anatomical dissection: on the one hand, the bones without the flesh, 'traditional theology'; on the other, flesh without bones, that very pious literature that serves up a compound of asceticism, mysticism and spirituality and rhetoric, a porridge that, in the end, becomes indigestible through lack of substance. Only the two together (corresponding to the prototype of revelation in scripture) constitute the unique 'form' capable of being 'seen' in the light of the faith by the believer, a unique testimony, invisible to the world, and a 'scandal' to it.[5]

Although almost fifty years have elapsed since Balthasar wrote these words, they retain their bite. Regrettably, encounters with "dry-bones" theologies and "thin indigestible" flavor-of-the-day spiritualities are still not uncommon. How unusual it is to find someone whose theological writing is shot through with spiritual insight, and whose spiritual insight is watermarked with creedal profession. In part, the abiding attractiveness of Blessed John Henry Newman resides in the fact that he regularly provides theological substance and spiritual nourishment.[6] Indeed his grasp of revelatory truths and artful application of

---

4. Jordan Aumann, *Spiritual Theology* (New York: Continuum, 2006), 22.

5. Hans Urs von Balthasar, "Theology and Sanctity," in *Explorations in Theology I: The Word Made Flesh*, trans. A. V. Littledale with Alexander Dru (San Francisco: Ignatius, 1989), 192–93.

6. See C. S. Dessain, *Newman's Spiritual Themes* (Dublin: Veritas, 1977); Vincent Blehl, SJ, *The White Stone: The Spiritual Theology of John Henry Newman* (Petersham, MA: St. Bede's, 1993); and Ian Ker,

their principles to everyday living, which emerges from an authentically lived Christian life within the ambit of the Great Tradition, have led some to say that he is a modern Father of the Church[7] who will surely be numbered among her Doctors.[8]

Trinitarian Sympathy

Though Newman rarely speaks of sympathy relative to the Trinity in se, there is a notable exception. In his reflection, "Our Lord Refuses Sympathy," which forms the second of his series of thoughts upon "Hope in God—Redeemer" in his Meditations on Christian Doctrine, we discover this rich fare.

> SYMPATHY may be called an eternal law, for it is signified or rather transcendentally and archetypically fulfilled in the ineffable mutual love of the Divine Trinity. God, though infinitely One, has ever been Three. He ever has rejoiced in His Son and His Spirit, and they in Him—and thus through all eternity He has existed, not solitary, though alone, having in this incomprehensible multiplication of Himself and reiteration of His Person, such infinitely perfect bliss, that nothing He has created can add aught to it. The devil only is barren and lonely, shut up in himself—and his servants also.[9]

Five theological considerations come to the fore in Newman's pithy account of triune sympathy. First, his speech about the mystery of the tri-personal God's sympathy observes traditional conventions. Inasmuch as he acknowledges the ineffability of divine love, it is apophatic. Inasmuch as he recognizes that our universal human experience of sympathy can participate, and be fulfilled in, "the mutual love of the Divine Trinity," it is analogical.[10] Indeed, my opening

Healing the Wound of Humanity: The Spirituality of John Henry Newman (London: Darton, Longman & Todd, 1993).

7. See Lawrence Cross, "John Henry Newman: A Father of the Church?" *Newman Studies Journal* 3, no. 1 (Spring 2006): 5–11 (hereafter, *NSJ*).

8. Drew Morgan argues that Newman is an authentic spiritual master and Christian witness whose widely diffused, relevant, and durable writings represent a mature sapiential synthesis that draws deeply from ecclesial sources and, consequently, meets the six *Procedural Norms and Doctrinal Criteria for Judgment Concerning the Eminence of Saints Proposed as Doctors of the Church* by the Congregation for the Doctrine of the Faith. See Drew Morgan, CO, "John Henry Newman—Doctor of Conscience: Doctor of the Church?," *NSJ* 4, no. 1 (Spring 2007): 5–23.

9. *VV*, 345.

10. Here it is good to recall Lateran IV (1215), which says: "For between creator and creature there can be noted no similarity so great that a greater dissimilarity cannot be seen between them." *Fourth Lateran*

description of the range of meanings of sympathy in Newman's theological lexicon of sympathy suggests the scope of his analogical understanding. And, inasmuch as he typifies this fulfillment as being transcendently and archetypically fulfilled in the Trinity, he speaks in an eminent way about how triune love always transcends this analogical understanding.

Second, speech of triune sympathy is coincidentally speech of the mystery of the oneness of Divine Nature and threeness of the divine persons who eternally live and dance "in" each other. In his words, it is about the "mutual love of the Trinity." As Newman says in another place regarding the doctrine of circumincessio, "This doctrine is not the deepest part of the whole, but it is the whole, other statements being in fact this in other shapes. Each of the Three who speak to us from heaven is simply, and in the full sense of the word, God, yet there is but one God; this truth, as a statement, is enunciated most intelligibly when we say the Father, Son, and Holy Ghost, being one and the same Spirit and Being, are in each other . . ."[11] Third, this means that the Trinitarian foundation for understanding sanctified human sympathy is perichoretic Divine Life, that is, communio. However, in divine communio, literally entering into the other's situation is only metaphorical, for the perfect, dynamic, superabundant, eternal union of the divine persons is without beginning or end, growth, interruption, impediment, or impairment. In the language of St. Thomas, divine persons do not have relationships per se, but are subsistent relations, that is, pure relations in and toward each other.[12] Sympathy, in the inner life of the Trinity, then, is not a "movement" to supply a lack, to heal, to restore, to build up, to clarify, to reorient, or to cleanse; rather it is divine love considered from the perspective of that exultant, overflowing delight which each divine person eternally expresses because of their shared life of love. As Newman says above, "[The Father] ever has rejoiced in His Son and His Spirit, and they in Him—and thus through all eternity He has existed, not solitary, though alone, having in this incomprehensible multiplication of Himself and reiteration of His Person, such infinitely perfect bliss, that nothing

---

Council in *Decrees of the Ecumenical Councils*, 2 vols., ed. Norman P. Tanner, SJ (Washington, DC: Georgetown University Press, 1990), 1:232.

11. John Henry Newman, *Select Treatises of St. Athanasisus in Controversy with the Arians*, 2 vols., 5th ed. (London: Longmans, 1895), 2:72.

12. See St. Thomas Aquinas, *Summa Theologica*, translated by the Fathers of the English Dominican Province, 5 vols. (Allen, TX: Christian Classics, 1981), *ST* 1, qq. 27–43, and in particular, q.40 a.2. See also Giles Emery, OP, *The Trinitarian Theology of St. Thomas Aquinas*, trans. Francesca Aran Murphy (Oxford: Oxford University Press, 2010), 114–20, and William J. Hill, *The Three-Personed God: The Trinity as a Mystery of Salvation* (Washington, DC: Catholic University of America Press, 1982), 69–78.

He has created can add aught to it." Here Newman characterizes sympathy as an eternal aspect of the exultant, overflowing delight of the tri-personal God. Elsewhere he affirms that this self-same God is mercifully generous in the acts of condescension in creation, Incarnation, redemption, and deification.[13] Hence he indirectly indicates that while divine sympathy *ad intra* is typified by joyous delight, divine sympathy *ad extra* is typified by merciful and generous life-giving acts. Sanctified sympathy resembles Trinitarian sympathy insofar as human relationships of heart, mind, and soul manifest joyous delight, and insofar as we lovingly transcend self-interest to enter into the lives of others often at the universal fault-lines of our experience of contingency and sin-brokenness.

Fourth, according to Newman's embrace of the logic of *circumincessio*, divine persons necessarily are "sympathetic" in a manner that corresponds to them as distinct persons, as Father, Son, and Holy Spirit. Though he does not overtly pursue this matter as regards the Father and the Holy Spirit, he does, at various points, explicitly unfold the meaning of the sympathy of the Son. Hence it is worthwhile here to cite his characteristic teaching on the distinctiveness of the Son prior to pursuing below what this distinctiveness means in the key of sympathetic love. In Newman's judgment, "[T]his is what makes the doctrine of our Lord's Eternal Sonship of such supreme importance, namely, that He is God because he is begotten of God; and they who give up the latter truth, are in the way to give up, or will be found to already have given up, the former. The great safeguard to the doctrine of our Lord's Divinity is the doctrine of His Sonship; we realize He is God only when we acknowledge Him to be by nature and from eternity Son."[14]

Fifth, Newman tells us that divine sympathy and, analogously, sanctified human sympathy, are recognizable by way of contrast: they are not demonically barren, but supernaturally fruitful; not lonely, but heart-warmingly engaged; not self-enclosed, but self-communicating. Divine sympathy signifies the deepest possible interpersonal sharing of the Divine Life. Analogously, then, sanctified sympathy, far from residing in the superficial warmth of platitudes

---

13. On Newman's doctrine of Divine Condescension, see Rino La Delfa, "Christ and the Face of the One and Triune God in John Henry Newman," *Louvain Studies* 35 (2011): 266–78. For Newman's attentiveness to theological "rules" and "cautions" in his consideration of the condescension of the Son, see his 27 July 1874 editorial comments upon Aubrey de Vere's poem, "Condescensio," *LD*, 27:97. The poem appears, incorporating Newman's suggestions, in Aubrey de Vere, *May Carols*, 3rd edition, enlarged (London: 1881), 217–18.

14. John Henry Newman, 26 April 1836, "Christ, the Son of God Made Man," *Parochial and Plain Sermons*, 8 vols. (Westminster, MD: Christian Classics, 1966–68), 6:57–58 (hereafter, *PPS*).

uttered at a distance,[15] represents the penetration of the other's situation in a life-giving manner that is simultaneously communion-establishing, difference-respecting, and joy-fulfilling. In a few words, Blessed Newman affirms much.

Relevance

In view of these positions, I want to suggest one way in which Newman's view of divine sympathy might orient contemporary Christian theology and spirituality in the task of the New Evangelization, that is, the mission of the baptized to re-propose the gospel in a winsome and accessible manner to those in secularized societies experiencing a crisis of faith.[16] Recent reports indicate that a growing number of North Americans, especially the young, no longer self-identify with a religion. As well, religiously nonaffilitated "Nones" are increasingly gravitating toward atheism.[17]

We can benefit here from attending to aspects of Michael Buckley's analysis of the origins of modern Western atheism. In part, Buckley argues that atheism "depends upon theism for its vocabulary, for its meaning, and for the hypotheses it rejects." Consequently he contends that contemporary atheism is attributable to the historical movement away from an impoverished Enlightenment idea of the Christian God toward the denial of the divine.[18] To the extent that Buckley is correct, proclamation of the Living God of Divine sympathy comprehended from within the relational logic of circumincessio and typified by joy, fecundity, friendship, and self-communication would exert a curative influence upon the "self-alienation of religion itself" and contribute to

---

15. "If a brother or sister is poorly clothed and in lack of daily food, and one of you says to them, 'Go in peace, be warmed and filled,' without giving them the things needed for the body, what does it profit?" (James 2:15-16).

16. See *The New Evangelization for the Transmission of the Christian Faith*, Synodus Episcoporum Bulletin, XIII Ordinary General Assembly of the Synod of Bishops, 7–28 October 2012, accessed 20 July 2013 at http://www.vatican.va/news_services/press/sinodo/documents/bollettino_25_xiii-ordinaria-2012/02_inglese/b33_02.html.

17. See *"Nones" on the Rise: One-in-Five Adults Have No Religious Affiliation*, The Pew Forum on Religion & Public Life in the United States, released 9 October 2012, accessed 17 April 2013 at http://www.pewforum.org/uploadedFiles/Topics/Religious_Affiliation/Unaffiliated/NonesOnTheRise-full.pdf. The short-form *2011 Canadian Census* excludes reference to religion. The *2001 Canadian Census* is the most recent official record. It notes that Canadians who have "no religion" grew from 1 percent in 1971 to 16 percent in 2001. Among those aged 25–44, the 2001 figure is 40 percent. See "Religions in Canada," *2001 Census: analysis series*, accessed 30 April 2013 at http://www12.statcan.gc.ca/english/census01/products/analytic/companion/rel/pdf/96F0030XIE2001015.pdf, 10, 19.

18. Michael J. Buckley, SJ, *At the Origins of Modern Atheism* (New Haven: Yale University Press, 1987), 15, 363.

a renewal of evangelization. Proclamation of Trinitarian sympathy would also form a piece with Newman's personalist approach. This approach is rightfully associated with his emphasis upon the commanding Divine voice in conscience as a foundation of his own belief in God[19] and his Christian apologetic. This apologetic leans heavily upon the manner in which the image of Christ historically has lit up the hearts of believers, and the way in which the credibility of their lives convinces and calls others to travel the Way.[20] For Newman, then, the testimony of conscience and the historical witness of the saintly evince the God of Jesus Christ and Jesus Christ who is God.

While the Newmanian emphasis upon the preeminent place of personalism in the proclamation of the gospel conditions his rejection of William Paley's (1743–1805) mechanistic watchmaker argument from design,[21] it does not constitute a rejection of natural theology[22] or the dogmatic teaching of Vatican I on the natural knowability of God.[23] Newman opposed the practice of natural theology as represented by Paley primarily because he thought it detached the apologetic effort from the graced, personal encounter with the Trinitarian God

---

19. John Henry Newman, *Apologia Pro Vita Sua: Being a History of His Religious Opinions*, ed. Martin J. Svaglic (Oxford: Clarendon, 1967), 216–17 (hereafter, *Apo*); and, *Callista: A Tale of the Third Century* (London: Longmans, Green, 1922), 314–15. See also Gerard Hughes, "Conscience," in *The Cambridge Companion to John Henry Newman*, ed. Ian Ker and Terrence Merrigan (Cambridge: Cambridge University Press, 2009), 189–220, esp. 207–17.

20. See John Henry Newman, 22 January 1832, "Personal Influence, the Means of Propagating the Truth," *US*, 75–98, and his *An Essay in Aid of a Grammar of Assent*, ed. I. T. Ker (Oxford: Clarendon, 1985), 297–312 (hereafter, *GA*). See also Avery Cardinal Dulles, SJ, *John Henry Newman* (New York: Continuum, 2002), 58–61.

21. On Newman's "suspicion of scientific considerations" in arguments for the existence of God, see John R. Connolly, *John Henry Newman: A View of Catholic Faith for the New Millennium* (Lanham, MD: Rowman & Littlefield, 2005), 98, and on Paley, see Kevin Mongrain, "The Eyes of Faith: Newman's Critique of Arguments from Design," *NSJ* 6 no. 1 (Spring 2009): 68–86. William Paley drew upon contemporary science, especially, biology and astronomy in *Natural Theology* (1802) to argue that the complexity, perfection, and design of the universe lead the mind to embrace a divine designer. His famous analogy of the purposeful design of a watch with the mechanistic makeup of the universe has been an occasion for unrelenting attack by Darwinian thinkers like Richard Dawkins; see, e.g., *The Blind Watchmaker* (Harlow, UK: Longman & Scientific Technical, 1987). On the analogy itself, see William Paley, *Natural Theology* (New York: Oxford University Press, 2006), 7. These details on Paley are drawn from Patrick J. Fletcher, "Newman and Natural Theology," *NSJ* 5, no. 2 (Fall 2008): 26–42 at 27.

22. See Newman, *GA*, 53 and Charles R. Amico, "William Paley's Argument from Design and Newman's Critique," *The Natural Knowability of God according to John Henry Newman with Special Reference to the Argument from Design in the Universe* (Rome: Urbaniana, 1986), 38–56.

23. "Dogmatic Constitution on the Catholic Faith," *First Vatican Council* in *Decrees of the Ecumenical Councils*, 2:806.

of sympathy in four ways. First, the divinity yielded by this natural theology is largely a product of, and shaped by, the Newtonian system and often leads to pantheism or deism. Second, while natural theology might indirectly say something of God's power or intelligence, it is practically mute about what lives at the heart of religion. As Newman writes, "Half the world know nothing of the argument from design—and, when you have got it, you do not prove by it the moral attributes of God—except very faintly. Design teaches me power, skill and goodness—not sanctity, not mercy, not a future judgment, which three are of the essence of religion."[24] Third, in such a scheme, natural theology deprives theology of its proper place in mediating and interpreting the revelation of God, along with its seat at the round table of learning and knowledge itself. Fourth, by restricting the method of inquiry to the natural realm, this sort of theological inquiry adopts the materialistic viewpoint of the physical sciences.[25]

I think Newman would be very supportive of contemporary efforts to reflect philosophically upon the data of science in the light of revelation.[26] However, I also believe that he would be ill-disposed to trod the failed apologetic path detailed by Buckley, of which Paley seems a step on the way: a path in which belief in God ultimately rests upon impersonal deductions like those once derived from Cartesian principles, Newtonian mechanics, and Enlightenment reason. In our scientific-technological culture, as we ponder theological-spiritual-pastoral strategies and resources to harness in service of the New Evangelization, we must respect the natural light of reason and appropriately draw upon, and integrate the data of science into, our philosophizing and theologizing. However, in our exercise of this responsibility, let us weigh Newman's preference for the apologetic power of proclaiming the triune God whom we know, love, and serve in faith, over and against his reluctance to invest in renovated natural theology arguments severed from the light of the Christ event.[27]

---

24. John Henry Newman to William Robert Brownlow, 13 April 1870, *LD*, 25:97.

25. In this paragraph, I am indebted to Fletcher, "Newman and Natural Theology," 41–42.

26. See John Henry Newman, "Christianity and Physical Science," and "Christianity and Scientific Investigation," in *The Idea of a University*, ed. I. T. Ker (Oxford: Clarendon, 1976), 346–67 and 368–86. For a reflection upon these Dublin lectures see John T. Ford, CSC, "John Henry Newman: The Relationship Between Theology and Science," *NSJ* 4, no. 2 (Fall 2007): 54–63.

27. See Edward Jeremy Miller, "Newman on the Tension between Religion and Science: Creationism, Evolution and Intelligent Design," *NSJ* 7 no. 1 (Spring 2010): 5–19. In "Theories of Evolution," Stratford Caldecott associates the ID movement with "the tradition of William Paley," accessed 22 April 2013 at http://www.secondspring.co.uk/articles/Evolution.pdf,1–12; 3.

Sympathy of the Son

While reflecting upon St. Athanasius' use of the term "condescension" in his extended 1872 essay, "Causes of the Rise of Arianism and Successes of Arianism," Newman speaks of how the Son and the Holy Spirit exercise "ministrative offices" in creating, preserving, governing, and correcting "this vast, minutely complex universe" not merely "from the era of redemption" but "from the beginning of all things."[28] Though he acknowledges a ministrative office of the Holy Spirit, Newman's attention here is Christologically concentrated. He neatly sidesteps pitfalls inherent in the fourth-century theologies of Arius, Asterius, and Eusebius, which protected the Father's transcendence at the cost of the Son's divinity, by exploiting the congruity of the eternal Son with creation. In this regard, Newman's reading of Athanasius aligns with the recent findings of patristic scholar Khaled Anatolios. In *Retrieving Nicaea*, Anatolios argues that St. Athanasius construes divine transcendence and immanence as "attributes that belong to divine being as such and are harmonized through the category of *philanthrōpia*, God's love for humanity," which love finds particular, filial expression in the acts of creation and incarnation.[29] Accordingly, Anatolios argues that Athanasius understands God to bridge the gap between divine ontological perfection and the contingency of creation by his merciful *philanthrōpia* expressed in the Son's creating and becoming incarnate.[30]

In similar fashion, Newman refers creation and incarnation to "the special Office which it was congruous to His Person to undertake, and which He did voluntarily undertake as being the Son and the Word of the Father . . . the Second Divine Person, in order to create, submitted to descent, such as was befitting in a Son, and as was compatible, rigorously so, with His co-equality and indivisible unity with the Father."[31] By characterizing the eternal Son as

---

28. For a consideration of the doctrinal nexus of creation, incarnation, and sacramentality, see John Thiel, "Creation, Contingency, and Sacramentality," *CTSA Proceedings* 67 (2012): 46–58.

29. Khaled Anatolios, *Retrieving Nicaea: The Development and Meaning of Trinitarian Doctrine*, foreword by Brian E. Daley, SJ (Grand Rapids: Baker, 2011), 104.

30. Anatolios, *Retrieving Nicaea*, 104. Compare Newman's citation of Athanasius (*Orations* 2:64) on this point: "'The Word,' says Athanasius, 'when in the beginning He framed creatures, condescended ([*sunkatabebēke*]) to them, that it might be possible for them to come into being. For they could not have endured His absolute, untempered nature, and His splendour from the Father, unless, condescending with the Father's love for man, He had supported them, and taken hold of them, and brought them into substance.'" See *Tracts Theological and Ecclesiastical* (London: Longmans, Green, 1902), 202 (hereafter, *TT*).

31. *TT*, 194–95.

archetype and fashioner of the cosmos into which he enters and, subsequently, redeems as son of Mary, Newman speaks about the fittingness of contemplating creation relative to the eternal *genesis* of the Son.[32] For the "Son interprets and fulfils the designs of the Eternal Mind, not as copying them, when He forms the world, but as being Himself their very Original and Delineation within the Father. Such was the doctrine of the great Alexandrian School, before Athanasius as well as after."[33] Hence Newman understands the possibility of creation, incarnation, and in fact, all of salvation history, mysteriously to reside in the divine act by which the Father eternally begets the Son.[34] Happily, this theological reading neither diminishes divinity nor eternalizes the world. It bridges heaven and earth in the person of the eternal Son who originates, fashions, and impresses himself upon the created order. In so doing, he forges the possibility of a sacramental language by which we can converse intelligibly concerning how the transcendent, triune God makes himself immanently present through creation in the Son. Such a reading ushers in an understanding of how the foregoing is motivated by the merciful condescension of the ontologically perfect eternal Son. Divine filial sympathy is another way of speaking about the love of the eternal Son expressed in the cosmic dimension of his salvific work: that is, by his entering into, embracing, and assuming unto himself the contingency of the created order. Indeed, in a sermon that focuses almost exclusively on St. Paul's exemplary exercise of the gift of sympathy, Newman's opening line and paragraph remind his hearers that the redemptive mission of the Incarnate Son is conjoined to his prior office of originating the cosmos. "There is no one who has loved the world so well, as He who made it. . . . He loved them before He redeemed them, and He redeemed them because he loved them. This is the 'philanthropy' or 'humanity' of God our Saviour of which the inspired writers speak."[35]

Relevance

In the past few decades, Christian theology and spirituality have awakened to the reality of pressing environmental threats to our planet and its inhabitants.[36]

---

32. See *TT*, 218–19, 199–207, 230–31.

33. *TT*, 218.

34. *TT*, 230–32.

35. "St. Paul's Gift of Sympathy," in *Sermons Preached on Various Occasions* (London: Longmans, Green, 1900), 106 (hereafter, *OS*).

36. *The Catechism of the Catholic Church* (San Francisco: Ignatius, 1994) asserts a moral imperative to respect the integrity of creation as part of the common good and the universal destination of goods in paragraphs 2401–2. Pope emeritus, Benedict XVI, frequently addressed this topic as evidenced in

Though reasonable people debate degrees of danger and best courses of action, they recognize that deforestation, desertification, water depletion, pollution, problematic resource extraction, warming, overfishing, and alike require remedy. At the intersection of these environmental concerns, many scientific, economic, political, educational, psychological, sociological, health, cultural, and religious issues are interlaced. In this context, I want to suggest one modest yet seminal way in which Newman's view of divine-filial sympathy serves an environmentally engaged Christian theology and spirituality.

It is a commonplace that Enlightenment rationalism has bequeathed to us the reductive tendency to dissolve nature into discrete manipulables. Sadly, this dissolution and manipulation desensitizes us to the sacramentality of nature, intensifies our propensity to dominate and, at length, leads us to privilege autonomy, individuality, and immanence over relatedness, community, and transcendence.[37] Widespread dissatisfaction with this dissolution has supported upsurges in divers phenomena like holistic medicine, organic farming, back to the land movements, homeschooling, the greening of just about everything, and interest in Buddhist, Hindu, aboriginal, and environmental spiritualities, all of which are guided by something other than that mythical creature: detached, neutral, all-knowing Enlightenment rationality.[38]

By contrast to Enlightenment rationalism, Newman's neopatristic accenting of divine-filial sympathy honors the trinitarian, cosmic ordering of salvation. For him, as for the Fathers, there is no point in the redemptive drama at which human actors should handle the created order as a stage prop, that is, merely as a series of discrete objects open to endless reshaping and subject only to the limits of the manipulator's power.[39] Rather the Divine Son's sympathetic originating, entering into, embracing, and assuming unto himself

---

Jacqueline Lindsey's edited collection of his writings, *Environment* (Huntington, IN: Our Sunday Visitor, 2012). During his "Homily for Inaugural Mass of Petrine Ministry," Pope Francis spoke of environmental care relative to the patronal protection of St. Joseph for the Universal Church; see accessed 27 April 2013 at http://www.news.va/en/news/pope-homily-for-inaugural-mass-of-petrine-ministry.

37. Gerard Manley Hopkins poem evocatively expresses this self-alienation. "And all is seared with trade; bleared, smeared with toil;/ And wears man's smudge and shares man's smell: the soil/Is bare now, nor can foot feel, being shod." "God's Grandeur," *Hopkins: Poems and Prose* (New York: Knopf, 1995), 14.

38. For agricultural, historical-philosophical, pedagogical, and architectural reactions to and interpretations of this complex matter, see Wendell Berry, *The Art of the Commonplace: The Agrarian Essays of Wendell Berry*, ed. Norman Wirzba (Berkeley, CA: Counterpoint, 2003); Charles Taylor, *A Secular Age* (Cambridge, MA: Belknap, 2007); Stratford Caledecott, *Beauty for Truth's Sake: On the Re-Enchantment of Education* (Grand Rapids: Brazos, 2009); and Christopher Alexander et al., *A Pattern Language: Towns, Buildings, Construction* (New York: Oxford University Press, 1977).

that which is created not only vitalizes the entirety of the economy of salvation, but also bestows upon the created order a Trinitarian-filial dignity deserving of sacral stewardship. It also supplies a thoroughgoing theological rationale for Catholic environmentalism without "capitulating to the excesses of modern Romanticism."[40]

Sympathy of the God-Man

Commentators silently pass over the extent to which Newman's Pauline, New Adam Christology underwrites his spirituality of sympathy. Yet his description of the manner in which grace makes possible St. Paul's sympathetic identification with "the whole race of Adam"[41] clearly emerges from his New Adam Christology, a Christology that has a privileged place in his articulation of the mystery of the Incarnate Word.[42] As Newman's interpretation of Pauline spirituality rests upon the Apostle's understanding of New Adam Christology, I briefly examine this Christological understanding prior to examining the spirituality that is expressive of it.

In this regard, Roderick Strange and Benjamin King observe that Newman's Christology bears the impress of St. Cyril of Alexandria's thought.[43] King notes that Newman favors speaking of Christ as "Man" using an uppercase "M" without the indefinite article since he studiously desires to avoid speaking of the Son as "a man" in order to emphasize that "Jesus Christ is a person only

---

39. See Kilian McDonnell, *The Baptism of Jesus in the Jordan: The Trinitarian and Cosmic Order of Salvation* (Collegeville, MN: Liturgical 1996), and Alexander Schmemann, *For the Life of the World*, 2nd ed. (Crestwood, NY: St. Vladimir's Seminary Press, 1973), 72–75.

40. Stratford Caldecott, "Creation as a Call to Holiness," 1–7; 1, accessed 27 April 2013 at www.secondspring.co.uk/articles/scaldecott18.htm. On these excesses, see *Jesus Christ, The Bearer of the Water of Life: A Christian Reflection on "The New Age,"* Pontifical Council for Culture and Pontifical Council for Interreligious Dialogue (2003), accessed 27 April 2013 at http://www.vatican.va/roman_curia/pontifical_councils/interelg/documents/rc_pc_interelg_doc_20030203_new-age_en.html#top.

41. "St. Paul's Characteristic Gift," 25 Jan. 1857, *OS*, 96.

42. On references to Christ as the New Adam, see John Henry Newman, *Lectures on the Doctrine of Justification* (London: Longmans, Green, 1900), 89, 93, 105, 157–62, 192–94, 202, 211; *Essays Critical and Historical*, 2 vols. (London: Longmans, Green, 1897), 1:250–52; *Discourses Addressed to Mixed Congregations* (London: Longmans, Green, 1902), 64, 298–99, 305; *Certain Difficulties Felt by Anglicans in Catholic Teaching Considered*, 2 vols. (London: Longmans, Green, 1897), 1:277; *TT*, 214, 224, 378; *Ath*, 2:61, 120, 132, 187, 206, 274, and *LD*, 13:342, 19:36.

43. Roderick Strange, *Newman and the Gospel of Christ* (Oxford: Oxford University Press, 1981), 56–62, and Benjamin John King, *Newman and the Alexandrian Fathers: Shaping Doctrine in Nineteenth-Century England* (Oxford: Oxford University Press, 2009).

by virtue of the divine Word—he is the second hypostasis of the Trinity rather than '*a* man'—and this hypostasis is Son of God, not son of Joseph."[44]

The same Christological form of address surfaces in his 1834 sermon, "The Incarnation," in which Newman shifts from speaking about "our Lord and Christ . . . taking our flesh, not sullied thereby, but raising human nature with Him" to saying that "Man has redeemed us, Man is set above all creatures as one with the Creator, Man shall judge man at the last day."[45] The significance of this Christological form of address for Newman's spirituality of sympathy lies in its orthodoxy, clarity, and intensity. First, the Cyrilline formulation is one indication of the falsity of the charge leveled by some critics[46] that Newman failed to ensure in his writings the orthodox position that the *enhypostasized* human soul of the God-man functioned fully as a human soul.[47] For such critics, the formulation "taking our flesh . . . raising human nature" would be susceptible of an Apollinarian reading that does not do sufficient justice to the rational-affective dimension of the human being. However, the second formulation—"Man has redeemed us . . . Man shall judge man at the last day"—unambiguously includes all that the human being "is."

Second, the clarity of Newman's formulation—"Man redeems man"—underscores that divine redemption occurs in, and through, the humanity of the eternal Son who was conceived, born, lived, died, rose, ascended, and sent his Spirit. The formulation intensifies, in a twofold manner, the dogmatic truth that the Word assumed our humanity in every respect, save that of sin. Use of the same word of both subjects—"Man" and "man"—signifies that a full humanity is possessed both by the Lord who redeems, and by human beings who are redeemed. Use of the uppercase "M" and lowercase "m" signifies the sense in which the fullness of this common humanity is possessed differently: by the Divine Word in virtue of the hypostatic union, and by human persons in virtue of their natural conception. Each point is important. If the humanity possessed by the Lord is not full, then humankind is not saved; again, if the one

---

44. King, *Newman and the Alexandrian Fathers*, 157.

45. *PPS*, 2:39, "The Incarnation," 25 December 1834.

46. Newman's critics include Gabriel Daly, review of *Newman and the Gospel of Christ*, by R. Strange, *Journal of Ecclesiastical History* 35 (1984): 289–90; Hilda Graef, *God and Myself: The Spirituality of John Henry Newman* (London: Peter Davies, 1967), 51–53; and Stephen Thomas, *Newman and Heresy: The Anglican Years* (Cambridge: Cambridge University Press, 1991), 65.

47. For a defense of Newman against this charge, see Donald G. Graham, *From Eastertide to Ecclesia: John Henry Newman, the Holy Spirit, & the Church* (Milwaukee: Marquette University Press, 2011), 89–121.

possessing the full humanity does not possess it in virtue of the hypostatic union, then humankind is not saved, for only God is capable of effecting salvation.

Third, Newman's New Adam, Cyrilline formulation makes intelligible the intensification of the genuinely human experience undergone by the God-man. This point about the intensification of the genuinely human experience of the God-man is paramount for Newman's spirituality of sympathy. Since he understands the Spirit-filled enhypostasized humanity of the eternal Son to amplify his experience of the human condition, in precise proportion to the immeasurable depth of his divine person, the God-man's thoroughly human sympathy is spectacularly intensified by his soul's intimate union with his divine person. Dramatic expression of this insight occurs in Newman's meditation on the "Familiarity of Jesus": "Thou art more fully man than . . . Thy own sweet Mother. As in Divine knowledge of me Thou art beyond them all, so also in experience and personal knowledge of my nature. Thou art my elder brother. How can I fear, how should I not repose my whole heart on one so gentle, so tender, so familiar, so unpretending, so modest, so natural, so humble? Thou art now, though in heaven, just the same as Thou wast on earth: the mighty God, yet the little child—the all-holy, yet the all-sensitive, all-human."[48] In his post-1855 meditation upon this "overwhelming" mystery, Newman avoids hyperbole.[49] My unfolding of Newman's understanding of sympathy in his spiritual theology finds its most complete Christological justification in this passage's avowal of the all-embracing manner in which our race's "elder brother" enters into the human circumstance without dilution of divinity or negation of humanity. Framed in the language of the intercommunion of hearts,[50] Newman suggests that because the Lord is "elder brother," like the beloved disciple (John 13:22-25), each of us should "repose" his or her "whole heart" upon him.[51] Consequently, the Gospel injunction to "be not afraid" (Matt. 14:26-27; Mark 5:22; Luke 2:11; John 14:27) emerges from the human heart of the God-man and extends to every corner of human living. Even death has no dominion over this personal field of divine-human sympathy.

---

48. *VV*, 386.

49. Newman held that understanding the Incarnation was, in one sense, more "overwhelming" than understanding the Trinity. Until we encounter the former mystery we think ourselves experts about the experience of being human, while of the latter mystery, we claim no direct knowledge prior to revelation. See 8 March 1835, "The Humiliation of the Eternal Son," *PPS*, 3:156.

50. See Donald G. Graham, "Blessed Newman's Sacred Heart Theology and the 'intercommunion of hearts,'" *Downside Review* 129, no. 457 (2011): 14–37.

51. On the "Johannine origin" of devotion to the Lord under the symbol of his human heart, see Timothy Terrence O'Donnell, *Heart of the Redeemer: An Apologia for the Contemporary and Perennial Value of the Devotion to the Sacred Heart of Jesus* (San Francisco: Ignatius, 1989), 37–53.

The definitiveness of God's covenantal love radicalized in the incarnation of the eternal Son is now eternalized in his ascension and sitting down at the right hand of the Father. Far from being confined to his earthly sojourn, the God-man's affectivity is eternalized as an aspect of his enhypostasized divine personhood. Filial sympathy is understood by Newman, then, both as integral to the God-man's redemptive mission, and as revelatory of the Father's *philanthrōpia*.

Relevance

Obviously the question of "what happens when I die?" is always relevant. Juan Vélez states that Newman rebuts "the 19th century denial of possible eternal damnation" in his *Plain and Parochial Sermons* whereas, in *The Dream of Gerontius*, he focuses upon "God's merciful dispensation that broadens the narrow fundamentalist perspective of heaven or hell" and intertwines eschatology "with Christology and Christian anthropology."[52] Christian theological conversation about our final end historically oscillates between the Origenist pole of *apocatastasis*, which affirms the universal salvation of all souls, and the Calvinist pole of the positive reprobation of the damned, which affirms that some are condemned from all eternity without reference to their freely willed actions.[53] Of late, though differing on many matters, and qualifying this particular matter differently, many Catholics and Protestants have boldly underscored God's universal salvific will.[54] Fundamentalist Christians have

---

52. Juan R. Vélez, "Newman's Theology in the Dream of Gerontius," *New Blackfriars* 82, no. 967 (2001): 387, and "The Dream of Gerontius," *PVD*, 691–726. On the sympathy of mind and heart shared by Newman and the composer who popularized his work, see Mary Katherine Tillman, "An Introduction to 'The Dream of Gerontius' by Cardinal John Henry Newman and Sir Edward Elgar," *NSJ* 1 no.1 (Spring 2004): 42–48.

53. Figures such as Friedrich Schleiermacher (1768–1834) have tacked closer to the former position, while those like St. Augustine of Hippo (354–430) have moved nearer to the latter position. See "Apocatastasis," "Origen," "Origenism," and "Predestination," *The Oxford Dictionary of the Christian Church*, ed. F. L. Cross and E. A. Livingstone, 2nd rev. ed. (Oxford: Oxford University Press, 1983), 69–70, 1008–9, 1010, and 1117–18. See also Louis Bouyer of the Oratory, "Predestination," *Dictionary of Theology*, trans. Rev. Charles Underhill Quinn (Tournai, Belgium: Desclée, 1965), 359–62; and Henri Rondet and Karl Rahner, "Predestination," *Encyclopedia of Theology: The Concise Sacramentum Mundi* (Tunbridge Wells, UK: Burns & Oates, 1975), 1277–81.

54. See Hans Urs von Balthasar, "*Praedestinatio Gemina*," *The Theology of Karl Barth: Exposition and Interpretation*, trans. Edward T. Oakes, SJ (San Francisco: Ignatius, 1992), 174–88; Rob Bell, *Love Wins: A Book About Heaven, Hell and the Fate of Every Person Who Ever Lived* (New York: HarperOne, 2012); Karl Rahner, "Christianity and the Non-Christian Religions," *Theological Investigations*, vol. V, *Later Writings*, trans. Karl-H. Kruger (Baltimore: Helicon, 1966), 115–34; Ralph Martin, *Will Many Be Saved?: What*

continued to preach fire and brimstone, leaving little room inside the tent of salvation for those not explicitly professing Christ. Obviously, I do not intend to engage and address seriously this wide-ranging discussion of things eschatological, and the attendant issue of the salvation of non-Christians.[55] However, I do think that Blessed Newman's spiritual theology of sympathy has pastoral and theological wisdom as it pertains to facing our own approaching particular judgment.

We often reify God by conceiving of the Divine Mystery, to put it crudely, as the biggest and strongest of realities in the universe.[56] Then, at the moment of our maximum vulnerability, we cower as if the Grim Reaper were coming for us. Admittedly, this image recalls pagan festivals of the dead at the end of harvest time more than the Christian vigil of All Saints. The image does not represent the feelings of many Christians. Yet the recounting itself points to an awkward fact: many of us marked with the sign of the crucified sometimes imagine God more as a stern competitor than as our Savior. For most of us, including the theologically literate, the grasp of doctrines concerning predestination, heaven, hell, and purgatory remains existentially secondary to, and rests upon, our yearnings for life, love, justice, goodness, beauty, and wholeness. Newman's spiritual theology of the sympathy of the God-man stands at the service of these truths by showing the heart "where" to find true satisfaction.[57]

In the climactic passage of his 1834 Christmas sermon, "The Incarnation," Newman treats of judgment on the Last Day. At the outset, he underscores the Son's eternal origin as "Only-begotten." At the end, his radical solidarity with his brothers and sisters occupies center stage. The core of this commonality is the fact that the judge by way of his assumption of our humanity has entered fully into our "imperfections" and "infirmities": "no stranger shall judge us, but He who is our fellow, who will sustain our interests." The task of judgment is placed within the ambit of his appointment to "assign the final measurement and price upon His own work" of redemption. Judgment, then, is never separated from the Son's desire to "plead his sacred wounds in token

Vatican II Actually Teaches and Its Implications for the New Evangelization (Grand Rapids: Eerdmans, 2012).

55. For reflections on Newman's thought on these issues, see Terrence Merrigan, "Newman and Religions," *Louvain Studies* 35 (2011): 336–49, and Francis McGrath, F.M.S., *John Henry Newman: Universal Revelation* (Tunbridge Wells, UK: Burns & Oates, 1997).

56. See Robert Barron, "The Noncompetitively Transcendent and Coinherent God," *The Priority of Christ: Toward a Postliberal Catholicism* (Grand Rapids: Brazos, 2007), 190–255.

57. "The life of Christ brings together and concentrates truth concerning the chief good and the laws of our being, which wander idle and forlorn over the surface of the mortal world, and often appear to diverge from each other." John Henry Newman, 13 April 1830, "The Influence of Natural and Revealed Religion Respectively," *US*, 27.

of our forgiveness . . . and from his pierced side to pour forth his choicest blessings upon them." In fact, judgment emerges out of the elder brother's sympathetic identification with his accused siblings in order to winnow the wheat from the chaff so "that not a grain shall fall to the ground." Newman predicates "full sympathy in all our imperfections" to the eternal Son and makes it clear that our "fellow" and "brother" will judge us. At the moment of our maximum vulnerability, rather than cower because the Grim Reaper has come for us, he proposes that we walk through the door of judgment to face our eternal brother's sympathetic scrutiny and embrace. Here, as elsewhere, Newman shows that such truths live only in the Person of Christ who is Truth enfleshed, crucified, risen, and ascended.[58]

SANCTIFIED SYMPATHY

Critical to understanding the place of sanctified sympathy in Newman's spiritual theology are two sermons that he preached in the University Church in Dublin during 1857: "St. Paul's Characteristic Gift," and "St. Paul's Gift of Sympathy."[59] "In St. Paul's Characteristic Gift," Newman enumerates features common to saints "from the beginning to the end of history": they excel in their human formation and responsibilities due to grace, perform heroic deeds, pattern theological virtues, reach "a rare and special union with their Maker and Lord," perform penance, and attain heaven without the intervention of Purgatory.[60] Then he distinguishes between two classes of these saints: those "who are so absorbed in the divine life, that they seem, even while they are in the flesh, to have no part in the earth or in human nature" and those "in whom the supernatural combines with nature, instead of superseding it,—invigorating it, elevating it, ennobling it; and who are not the less men, because they are saints."[61] Of the former, he mentions St. John, St. Mary Magdalen, hermits, holy Virgins, and others "whose lives belong to the science of mystical theology."[62] Of the latter, he mentions "many of the early Fathers, St. Chrysostom, St. Gregory Nazianzen, St. Athanasius, and above all, the Great Saint of this day, St. Paul the Apostle,"[63] to which list he later appends his own patron, St. Philip Neri.[64] Though he refuses to calibrate degrees of holiness, Newman

---

58. *PPS* 2:39–40.
59. "St. Paul's Characteristic Gift," *OS*, 91–105; 12 Feb. 1857, "St. Paul's Gift of Sympathy," *OS*, 106–20.
60. *OS*, 91.
61. *OS*, 91–92.
62. *OS*, 92.
63. *OS*, 93.

distinguishes this second grouping of saints precisely by their capacity to enter into and identify with the situations of others and, in so doing, to glorify God.[65] As he states,

> They do not put away their natural endowments, but use them to the glory of the Giver; they do not act beside them, but through them; they do not eclipse them by the brightness of divine grace, but only transfigure them. They are versed in human knowledge; they can throw themselves into the minds of other men; and all this in consequence of natural gifts and secular education. While they themselves stand secure in the blessedness of purity and peace, they can follow in the imagination the ten thousand aberrations of pride and passion, and remorse. . . . Thus they have the thoughts, feelings, frames of mind, attractions, sympathies, antipathies of other men, so far as these are not sinful, only they have these properties of human nature purified, sanctified, and exalted; and they are only made more eloquent, more poetical, more profound, more intellectual, by reason of their being made more holy.[66]

Shorn of its lyricism, Newman's view of holiness corresponds to a conventional Christian humanism that, regardless of its permutations, rests upon the Thomistic principle that grace perfects, and does not destroy nature.[67] Newman finds this view presaged in the prominent epigram of former African slave and Roman playwright, Terence (c. 190–158 BCE), whom he cites from his play, *The Self-Tormentor*: "I am a man; nothing human is without interest to me."[68] Though Terencian and Christian humanism have a resemblance, Newman distinguishes them by reference to the gracious process of purification, sanctification, and elevation that equips saints, especially the tentmaker from Tarsus, to glorify God precisely in and through their humanizing task of evangelization and cultural engagement. As he says, "The world is to them a book, to which they are drawn for its own sake, which they read fluently, which interests them naturally,—though, by the reason of grace which dwells

---

64. *OS*, 96.
65. *OS*, 92–94.
66. *OS*, 92–93.
67. See *ST* I 1.8ad2. As Newman says, "There are Saints in whom grace supersedes nature; so was it not with this great Apostle; in him grace did but sanctify and elevate nature." *OS*, 113–14.
68. "'Homo sum, humani nihil a me alienum puto'" *OS*, 95. See Terence, *Andria, Et Heauton Timorumenos*, ed. Andrew F. West (Charleston, SC: Nabu, 2011), I.i.25.

within them, they study it and hold converse with it for the glory of God and the salvation of souls."[69] He contends that St. Paul's characteristic gift of sympathy transcends Terence's embrace of everyman embedded in the universal dignity of human nature. Grounding his view in Pauline New Adam Christology, Newman explains, "Now this, in a fulness of meaning which a heathen [like Terence] could not understand, is, I conceive, the characteristic of this great Apostle . . . human nature, the common nature of the whole race of Adam, spoke in him, acted in him, with an energetical presence, with a sort of bodily fulness, always under the sovereign command of divine grace, but losing none of its real freedom and power because of its subordination . . . St. Paul felt all his neighbours, all the whole race of Adam, to be existing in himself."[70] Significantly, the Pauline gift of sympathy transcends the Terencian embrace of everyman in terms of its "fulness of meaning" which, in the passage immediately above, Newman classifies according to sympathy's penetration, scope, power, freedom, and ordering of human nature to its proper ends under the tutelage of grace.[71] Though Newman does not develop this taxonomy of graced nature according to which we consider sanctified sympathy precisely in terms of its depth, power, freedom, and ends, he is specific about its outcome: "And the consequence is, that, having the nature of man so strong within him, he is able to enter into human nature, and to sympathise with it, with a gift peculiarly his own."[72]

Relevance

In the course of examining St. Paul's life, gifts, and apostolic ministry, the relevance of Newman's view of sanctified sympathy comes to the fore. He appreciates the manner in which St. Paul, "spiritual father of the Gentiles," values Greek literature both in itself and as "preparatory to the Gospel."[73] He discerns value in St. Paul's positive assessment of a desire for the living God in the misdirected Lycaonian impulse to worship him (Acts 14:11).[74] He praises the Apostle's missionary strategy of drawing souls by "the cords of Adam."[75] Although St. Paul's graced capacity to identify with the "whole race

---

69. *OS*, 93.

70. *OS*, 95–96.

71. Penetration is indicated by the phrase, "a sort of bodily fulness," scope by the phrase, "the common nature of the whole race of Adam," freedom, power, and ordering to proper ends by the phrase, "losing none of its real freedom and power because of its subordination" (*OS*, 95–6).

72. *OS*, 96.

73. "St. Paul's Conversion Viewed in Reference to His Office," 25 January 1831, *PPS*, 2:99 and *OS*, 98.

74. *OS*, 98.

of Adam" is understood by Newman relative to his exercise of the apostolic office, the graced capacity itself is not characterized as a charism peculiar to that office. Rather, in these embryonic examples, Newman identifies the Pauline exercise of sanctified sympathy with a broad, richly textured Christian humanism respectfully and confidently operative in a modality that is, at once, educational, cultural, and evangelical. This view of sanctified sympathy fits well with the universal call to holiness issued by the fathers of Vatican II, inviting the entire people of God to share in the corporate mission of bringing Christ to the world in and through the daily, priestly offering of the totality of their efforts, expertise and experience, family life and friendships, worship and work.[76]

Finally, I think that Newman's view of sanctified sympathy is opportune because it privileges and promotes medicinal attitudes and actions of mind and heart. We live at a time when factionalism rents not only those societies that the Church inhabits, but, sometimes, the body of Christ itself. While factions often are formed and fueled by moral failures to embrace truth, their ongoing existence is largely due to the demonizing of the "other" rather than recognizing what Christ sees: his own image, bruised and battered. Newman's sanctified sympathy impels and endows those who "stand secure in the blessedness of purity and peace" to understand "the ten thousand aberrations of pride and passion, and remorse" that afflict the sin-scalded in order to enter into their "thoughts, feelings, frames of mind, attractions, sympathies, [and] antipathies," to preserve their dignity and to cauterize their sins. In turn, this holy capacity to sympathize with the sin-scalded, out of the love of Christ crucified, equips saints to overcome factionalism by binding up, and anointing broken persons and communities with the salve of grace. In this fashion, saints image the One who, in Newman's words, "fulfills the one great need of human nature," the One who is "the Healer of its wounds, the Physician of the soul."[77] Our Church and the world stand in need of such holy healing.

---

75. *OS*, 120.

76. Second Vatican Council, "Dogmatic Constitution on the Church (De Ecclesia)," 39–42 in Tanner, *Decrees of the Ecumenical Councils*, 2:880–84.

77. *GA*, 299; see also "Prayer, Novena of St. Philip," *PVD*, 211. Though this Christological title was not uncommon among the Fathers, Newman seems to have derived it from St. Ignatius of Antioch (35–107 CE): "'There is one physician,' says S. Ignatius, 'fleshly and spiritual, generate and ingenerate, God come in the flesh, in death true life, both from Mary and from God, first passible, then impassible, Jesus Christ our Lord'" (*Ep.ad Eph*.7); *Ath*, 2:215.

Conclusion

I hope this glance at Newman's view of sympathy has shown how it has a legitimate place in his spiritual theology as it concerns the Trinity, Divine Son, God-man, and the gifts of creation and sanctity. Along the way, I have suggested that Newman's neopatristic thought is a wellspring of Christian spirituality and theology from which contemporary seekers can draw water on topics as diverse as the New Evangelization, environmental concerns, eschatology, and cultural engagement. In closing, conscious of the limitations of this chapter and the greatness of the Mystery approached, I am put in mind of Newman's response to Spencer Northcote upon being pressed to document publicly the reasons for his conversion: "Catholicism is a deep matter—you cannot take it up in a teacup."[78]

---

78. As cited in Wilfrid Ward, *The Life of John Henry Cardinal Newman: Based on His Private Journals and Correspondence in Two Volumes* (New York: Longmans, Green, 1913), 1:121.

5

Trinity, Imagination, and Belief in the Spirituality of John Henry Newman

Theodore J. Whapham

INTRODUCTION

The doctrine of the Trinity is a significant theme in the writings of John Henry Newman. In addition to the lengthy historical treatment of the Arian Controversy in the fourth century, reference to the Trinity appears frequently in works like the *Grammar of Assent* and *An Essay on the Development Doctrine*. Despite this fact, Newman's references to the Trinity have not frequently been the subject of study. Perhaps it is because these contributions have tended to be seen as among his least original.[1] However, some recent scholarship has recognized a seminal contribution to his approach to the Trinity, particularly in the *Grammar of Assent*.[2]

This chapter, accordingly, will present John Henry Newman's treatment of the doctrine of the Trinity as it is presented in *A Grammar of Assent* with an eye to its seminal quality in relationship to contemporary Trinitarian theology, as exemplified by Wolfhart Pannenberg, and contemporary spirituality. The chapter will begin with a discussion of the purpose of the *Grammar* and a brief summary of Newman's terminology. This will be followed by an in-depth examination of Newman's notion of the Trinity in the *Grammar*. In the final section, the chapter will discuss the significance of Newman's notion of the Trinity for his understanding of spirituality and the implications of his notion of spirituality for contemporary theology.

---

1. Roderick Strange, "Newman and the Mystery of Christ," in *Newman After a Hundred Years*, ed. Ian Ker and Alan G. Hill (Oxford: Clarendon, 1985), ix–x.

2. Terrance Merrigan, "Newman on Faith in the Trinity," in *Newman and Faith*, ed. Ian Ker and Terrence Merrigan (Louvain: Peeters, 2004), 93.

The *Grammar* and Its Terminology

In chapter five of *An Essay in Aid of a Grammar of Assent*, Newman seeks to argue how it is possible for the Christian of ordinary intellect to make a real assent to the doctrine of the Trinity. However, before analyzing Newman's argument it will be necessary first to explain his larger goals in the *Grammar* and his technical use of some key terms.

Newman's *Grammar of Assent* was one of his later works and the product of an extended reflection on the rationality of the faith of ordinary Christians. Newman was concerned to show how it was possible for the ordinary person of faith to be certain of the key statements of the Christian faith despite the fact that they surpass rational comprehension. Further, he wanted to demonstrate that this was possible through the "ordinary" processes of reflection and not simply the province of theologians, philosophers, and other specialists.[3] Such an effort is understandable as a reaction to many developments in the philosophy of religion and the theology of the early nineteenth century that sought to place theological knowledge on more solid ground. For example, Henry Mansel in his 1858 Bampton Lectures, titled *The Limits of Religious Knowledge*, argued that knowledge of the personal God was directly related to the individual's experience of dependence and the sense of moral obligation.[4] This knowledge, however, was understood in direct relation to the degree that the individual reflected upon this experience and sense. In other words, knowledge of God is immediately connected to scholarly reflection upon these experiences. Mansel's own argument echoes the work of Friedrich Schleiermacher who similarly argued that theological knowledge was based upon reflection of the experience of absolute dependence and as a result relegated reflection on the Trinity to the appendix of his Christian Faith as a second-order proposition.[5]

Newman begins his argument by distinguishing two types of assent: notional and real. Assent refers to the mind's manner of asserting the truth of

---

3. In 1860 Newman wrote to Charles Meynell and mentioned a book that he intended to write, the object of which "would be to show that a given individual, high or low, has as much right (has as real rational grounds) to be certain, as a learned theologian who knows the scientific evidence." John Henry Newman, *Letters and Diaries of John Henry Newman*, vol. 25 (Oxford: Clarendon, 1973), 29.

4. Henry Longueville Mansel, *The Limits of Religious Thought* (London: John Murray, 1867), vii–xix, accessed June 1, 2013, *American Theological Library Association (ATLA) Historical Monographs Collection: Series 1*, EBSCO*host*.

5. Friedrich Schleiermacher, *On Religion: Speeches to Its Cultured Despisers*, ed. Richard Crouter, *Cambridge Texts in the History of Philosophy* (Cambridge: Cambridge University Press, 1996); Friedrich Schleiermacher, *The Christian Faith*, 2nd ed., trans. H. R. Mackintosh and J. S. Stewart (Philadelphia: Fortress Press, 1928), 738–39.

an idea.⁶ Notional assent is holding to the truth of a proposition that is the result of rational reflection and abstraction from experience. Newman connects this form of assent to professing an idea, having an opinion, and engaging in speculation. While this form of assent is very important for the development of general principles and reflection on a wide variety of general phenomena, Newman asserts that it is necessarily a weaker and less vivid form of assent because it deals with generalities and abstractions.

Real assent is the strongest and most powerful form of assent because it is drawn from concrete experience and enjoys an affective component. Newman explains that real assent is also called belief or certitude and that this way of holding the truth of a thing is the rarest and most powerful form of assent.⁷ The power of real assent or belief is rooted in the fact that it leads to action. He holds that the detailed images that the mind produces from its experiences of the concrete world can incite the imagination, the affections, and appetites; these in turn drive the will to act. Notional assent does not have the same power to affect the will.⁸

For example, the notion that motherhood is a noble vocation is a relatively simple idea to which most would be willing to assent. However, Newman points out that the capacity of the nobility of motherhood to excite action to defend motherhood or to become a mother stems not from this abstract proverb about motherhood (regardless of its truth or the aptness of its expression). Rather, it is from the individual's concrete experience with one's own mother, or other mothers, or indeed of being a mother, that has the power to excite the will and move a person to take action. Newman puts the matter plainly: "Persons influence us, voices melt us, looks subdue us, deeds inflame us. Many a man will live and die upon a dogma: no man will be a martyr for a conclusion."⁹

The imagination is the faculty of the mind that draws concrete experience to mind and creates a mental image.¹⁰ These mental images need not be visual or of something tangible, nor is Newman unaware that the imagination may be mistaken. Nonetheless, for Newman the imagination is the source of the concepts that are the object of real assent, and it is the imagination that

---

6. John Henry Newman, *An Essay in Aid of a Grammar of Assent* (Notre Dame: University of Notre Dame Press, 1979), 29–31 (hereafter *GA*).

7. *GA*, 86–87.

8. *GA*, 87.

9. *GA*, 89.

10. For a more extensive treatment of Newman's understanding of imagination see Terrence Merrigan, *Clear Heads and Holy Hearts: The Religious and Theological Ideal of John Henry Newman* (Louvain: Peeters, 1991), 48–81.

provides the vividness that drives the will. In developing his understanding of the imagination, Newman is interested primarily in describing a faculty of the mind that while rational is "more delicate, versatile, and elastic than verbal argumentation."[11] It is this capacity of the imagination to draw concrete experiences to mind and drive the will that connects the assent of faith with real assent. Here Newman is making it clear that the assent of faith is not primarily a notional or purely rational activity, but something that is more intimate and personal. However, because the imagination is itself a mental faculty it has a semi-rational quality and therefore is not fundamentally opposed to reason.

After establishing his key terms and providing an analysis of the structure of assent, Newman turns to the relationship between assent and religion.[12] His goal in this section is to demonstrate that it is possible to rationally assent to the key doctrines of Christianity. First, he argues that most children make a real assent to the oneness of God through the development of their conscience.[13] Christopher Pramuk observes that Newman's argument from conscience speaks of a pre-reflective, pre-verbal apprehension of God that is universal, as opposed to only an innate moral sense of right and wrong.[14] This pre-reflective understanding of the divine excites the emotions and awakens the image of the living God in the soul: "[I]f on doing right, we enjoy the same sunny serenity of mind, the same soothing, satisfactory delight which follows on our receiving praise from a father, we certainly have within us the image of some person, to whom our love and veneration, look, in whose smile we find our happiness, for whom we yearn, towards whom we direct our pleadings, in whose anger we are troubled and waste away."[15]

THE TRINITY IN THE *GRAMMAR OF ASSENT*

However, Newman's most important example and test for his claims about the possibility of real assent to Christian faith is the Trinity. He begins by underscoring the importance of belief in a personal God for the Catholic faith. In this context, he is anxious to distinguish himself from the deists and pantheists of his own age.[16] Again, Newman sets out to describe whether it

---

11. *GA*, 217.
12. *GA*, 93–135.
13. *GA*, 95–109.
14. Christopher Pramuk, "'They Know Him by His Voice': Newman on the Imagination, Christology, and Theology of Religions," *Heythrop Journal* 48, no. 1 (2007): 66.
15. *GA*, 101.
16. This emphasis can be seen throughout chapter five of the *Grammar*. For example, in his conclusions about the personal God revealed in the conscience, Newman emphasizes that these emotions require an

is possible to have a real apprehension (or understanding) of this doctrine that would allow for a real assent. In other words, Newman sets out to establish whether the doctrine of the Trinity can provide the sort of vivid experience within an individual that might permit real assent. Moreover, he wants to establish that this real assent is not only possible for experts who have studied the history, theory, and development of the doctrine, but that it is the ordinary way of understanding the faith among "average" Christians.[17] In particular, Newman has in mind the doctrine of the Trinity as it is expressed in the Athanasian Creed,[18] which he deems to be "the most simple and sublime, the most devotional formulary to which Christianity has given birth."

One should not underestimate the audacity of Newman's attempt to establish the possibility of real assent to the doctrine of the Trinity, either in the nineteenth century or today. During the nineteenth century, there was a decline of interest in Trinitarian theology. Stanley Grenz argues that, in part due to the influence of Schleiermacher, the Trinity was increasingly seen as the most speculative and impractical of Christian doctrines.[19] This assertion is further confirmed by the rival notions of monotheism and an increase of insistence on the Trinity as a mystery of faith that surpasses human understanding.[20] As a result, even more traditional Christians shied away from

---

intelligent being and not simply an inanimate object (GA, 100–101). Later, in his discussion in the same chapter he emphasizes the connection between belief in the Trinity and belief in a Personal God (GA, 111). Today it might be more relevant to point out that it is the doctrine of the Trinity (as articulated at Nicaea and in the Athanasian Creed) that distinguishes most of Christianity from each of the other major world religions. Pramuk echoes this sentiment in his work, which draws upon Newman to develop a Christocentric inclusivism that recognizes God's saving work through Christ in all of creation, including the diversity of religions. Pramuk, "'They Know Him by His Voice,'" 76–81.

17. The term "average Christian" is used in this context advisedly; the author is aware of many complications involved with such a term. However, what is intended is the average Christian who attends services and naturally (although largely unreflectively) holds the church's traditional teaching regarding the Trinity. It is intended to contrast with the assent and reflection that is characteristic of a theological professional for example.

18. Although the Athanasian Creed is less familiar to most contemporary Catholics in the United States, it is the ancient creed of the church that most directly discusses the doctrine of the Trinity. It, along with the Apostles' Creed and the Niceno-Constantinopolitan Creed, is one of the key ecumenical creeds that doctrinally unites mainline Protestant, Catholic, and Orthodox Christians.

19. Stanley Grenz, *Rediscovering the Triune God* (Minneapolis: Augsburg Fortress Press, 2004), 6–32.

20. With regard to rival versions of monotheism, one need only think of deism and the pantheism of Spinoza and Hegel. Further, in the same year the *Grammar of Assent* was published, the First Vatican Council in the constitution *Dei Filius* reasserted the Church's teaching that the existence of God could be established through the use of reason alone, but that other mysteries of the faith could not be established by reason. Rather these mysteries "so far surpass the created understanding that, even when a revelation

the doctrine of the Trinity. Despite the theological environment of the day, however, Newman argues how the Trinity might be apprehended by all the faithful through a rational process that leads to real assent. Indeed, Newman suggests that this process is not only possible, but that the Trinity is the source and *telos* of all Christian worship. As a result, this real assent to the Trinity is not only possible for Christians; it is the ordinary faith of the believer.[21]

Newman first expounds on the challenge that the doctrine of the Trinity presents because it is known only through revelation and because of the doctrine's relative complexity. He asserts that the doctrine of the Trinity is comprised of nine propositions that are to be held simultaneously by the believer. He presents these statements as follows:

> 1. There are Three who give testimony in heaven, the Father, the Word or Son, and the Holy Spirit. 2. From the Father is, and ever has been, the Son. 3. From the Father and the Son is, and ever has been, the Spirit. 4. The Father is the One Eternal Personal God. 5. The Son is the One Eternal Personal God. 6. The Spirit is the One Eternal Personal God. 7. The Father is not the Son. 8. The Son is not the Holy Ghost. 9. The Holy Ghost is not the Father.[22]

Newman argues that each of these propositions, when considered separately, presents itself vividly to the mind and the experience of the faithful. After laying out each of these elements of the doctrine of the Trinity, he explains how each is found in common experience: that sons come from fathers and that an eternal, personal God exists. Newman is claiming that the concrete contents of each of these statements are the objects of ordinary experience and not technical terms. This differs from a number of theologians writing on the doctrine of the Trinity in the middle of the twentieth century. Karl Barth and Karl Rahner each famously argued that the terms connected with the doctrine of the Trinity were highly technical and could not be understood in their modern sense. In particular, these theologians were concerned that the term "person" needed to be replaced in theological discourse with terms such as *Subsistenzweisen* (modes

---

has been given and accepted by faith, they remain covered by the veil of that same faith and wrapped, as it were, in a certain obscurity, as long as in this mortal life we are away from the Lord" (*Dei Filius*, Denzinger, 1796). Clearly, the council fathers have in mind in this passage the mystery of the Trinity (among others).

21. Ono Ekeh, in his excellent study of Newman's understanding of the Trinity, emphasizes this doxological context of the Trinitarian faith of the believer. Ono Ekeh, "John Henry Newman on the Mystery of the Trinity," *Irish Theological Quarterly* 74 (2009): 202–23; 205–6.

22. *GA*, 119.

of subsisting) or *Seinweisen* (modes of being) that they felt would do better to avoid confusion.[23]

However, Newman argues that the real force of each of these claims can be found in Scripture and in the church's liturgical life. He argues that the New Testament is filled with references to the Trinity that are directly related to the aforementioned nine theses. From the Prologue of John's Gospel to Paul's doctrine of justification, the New Testament speaks in rich detail of the experience of the apostolic community that gives rise to Trinitarian faith. In fact, Newman as a young man solidified his faith in Christianity by collecting a series of biblical texts in support of the doctrine of the Trinity and a commentary on the Athanasian Creed that included a verse-by-verse scriptural support for its propositions.[24] Newman was still in possession of these documents, written at the age of sixteen, when he wrote his *Apologia*, and apparently, it is the image from these pages that he drew upon in this context.

Further, Newman appeals to the liturgical services for Christmas, Epiphany, Ascension, and Corpus Christi in particular as grounding for the Trinitarian faith of the community. "What are these great festivals but comments on the words, 'The Son is God'? Yet, who will say that they have the subtlety, the aridity, the coldness of mere scholastic science?"[25] Ono Ekeh describes this liturgical context for the Trinity as "the source and end of faith."[26] From the sign of the cross to the baptismal formula, Newman helps his readers understand that the liturgical life of the Church is irrevocably Trinitarian. In this way, it is clear that for Newman the entire spiritual life of the Christian is grounded in the Trinity.

Newman suggests that the doctrine of the Trinity is only considered a mystery from the position of notional apprehension or theological reflection.[27] In the creeds and in the liturgy of the Church, the Trinity is always described as a subject of devotion rather than of speculation. Thus the creeds and liturgical life of the Church are fundamentally an act of prayer, an act of devotion, and in this sense an experience that leads to action.

---

23. Karl Barth, *Church Dogmatics* I/1, trans. G. W. Bromiley, 2nd ed. (Edinburgh: T. &T. Clark, 1975), 295–384; Karl Rahner, *The Trinity*, trans. Joseph Donceel, with an introduction by Catherine Mowry LaCugna (New York: Crossroad, 1997), 110.

24. John Henry Newman, *Apologia Pro Vita Sua*, ed. David J. DeLaura (New York: W. W. Norton, 1968), 17.

25. *GA*, 122.

26. Ekeh, "Newman on the Trinity," 203.

27. *GA*, 118–19. Since the Trinity is a mystery, Newman maintains that you can only make a notional assent, and not a real assent, to the Trinity as a whole. See also *GA*, 114–15.

Therefore, Newman asserts that considered separately the nine claims that underpin the doctrine of the Trinity are each the object of the real assent of the faithful. They are not the result of ivory-tower speculation, but grounded in the faith life of the community. In this sense, the doctrine of the Trinity can be the object of belief or a real assent, because the doctrine of the Trinity is no more than the hold of each of these propositions on the believer's imagination. However, when attempting to hold all of these propositions in the imagination at the same time, the mind inevitably turns to one image or another.[28]

IMPLICATIONS FOR NEWMAN'S SPIRITUALITY AND CONTEMPORARY THEOLOGY

This section of the chapter addresses the great value that Newman's presentation of the doctrine of the Trinity has for contemporary theology and spirituality. Three key implications of Newman's work will be discussed and analyzed. Of fundamental importance to these implications is the significance of Newman's grounding of real assent in the imagination. The role of the imagination in assenting to the Trinity secures its value for the spirituality of ordinary Christians, underscores the practical import of the doctrine of the Trinity, and emphasizes the need for believers to draw upon multiple images of the divine.

The first implication of Newman's notion of the Trinity for contemporary theology and spirituality is that his treatment of the Trinity demonstrates his concern for the spiritual life of the ordinary believer. Connected to this is the idea that traditional doctrines matter (or should matter) for the ordinary lives of the faithful. It is clear from this presentation of Newman's treatment of the doctrine of the Trinity that his major concern is to demonstrate the possibility of real assent to the content of Christianity among the faithful. To this extent, assent to Christian faith can be a rational act, even in its most complex concepts among the ordinary faithful. Moreover, Newman holds that Christian faith, in ordinary practice, is fundamentally Trinitarian. This central reality can be seen throughout the testimony of Scripture and the public and private prayer life of Christians.

While Newman is certainly familiar and comfortable with the lives of academics, clerics, and monastics, his treatment of the Trinity in chapter five of the *Grammar* is a discussion of the ground and end of faith for the spiritual lives of all Christians. This Trinitarian faith engages the whole life of the believer—one's affective, rational, and volitional dimensions. In fact, this faith is

---

28. *GA*, 116.

most powerful and practical because of its capacity to enliven the emotions and motivate people to take actions in their everyday lives.

This emphasis on the spiritual lives of ordinary Christians sets Newman's Trinitarian spirituality apart from much of the history of Christian spirituality. Sandra Schneiders notes that while the biblical history of the term "spirituality" points to life lived in the Spirit, over the centuries "this life tended to be understood less as the common pursuit of all Christians and more as the special enterprise of souls seeking perfection. The seeking of perfection was understood as ever more individualized and interiorized and centered more exclusively in the practice of specialized spiritual exercises thus requiring more intensive spiritual guidance by trained directors."[29] This tendency can be seen in many classics of Christian spirituality such as *The Rule of Saint Benedict*, *The Interior Castle*, and *Spiritual Exercises*, each of which acts as a guide toward the path to perfection intended for religious communities. Newman's own goals in discussing the Trinity in the *Grammar of Assent*, however, are focused on defending the life in the Spirit for all Christians and precisely not as the avenue of specialists. Moreover, as the previous discussion has demonstrated, Newman's understanding of real assent to the Trinity requires no special practice other than participation in the personal and public prayer life of the church. No special guides or spiritual directors are necessary; and because this spiritual life is rooted in the imagination (a faculty of the mind that is both rational and affective) it drives the individual to action and thus inherently drives the individual believer into relationship with the broader community.

This approach to life in the indwelling Spirit of the Trinitarian God corresponds nicely to Schneider's definition of spirituality as "the experience of consciously striving to integrate one's life in terms not of isolation and self-absorption but of self-transcendence toward the ultimate value that one perceives."[30] Newman's treatment of the Trinity is thus inherently spiritual, but corresponds much more closely to Schneider's influential, contemporary definition than to definitions of spirituality dominant in his own time. This point underscores the lasting significance of Newman's Trinitarian spirituality

---

29. Sandra M. Schneiders, "Theology and Spirituality: Strangers, Rivals, or Partners?," *Horizons: Journal of the College Theology Society* 13 (1986): 260.

30. Schneiders, "Theology and Spirituality," 266. Schneiders narrows this definition to specify Christian spirituality as referring to Christian religious experience that is "affective as well as cognitive, social as well as personal, God-centered and other directed all at the same time" (267). For more on the connection between Newman's spirituality and the indwelling Spirit, see John Connolly, chapter two of this volume, "The Indwelling of the Holy Spirit: The Foundation of Newman's Spirituality," 43–45.

especially for contemporary efforts to develop a lay spirituality that is grounded in the sacramentality of daily life and mundane activities.

It is also important to point out that while embracing a holistic approach to the Trinity that is deeply aware of the importance of the imagination as the source for faith, Newman does not reject the cognitive or notional aspect of faith. On the contrary, his reflection on the possibility of real assent to the Trinity takes place in the context of a meditation on the doctrine of the Trinity, particularly as it is expressed in the Athanasian Creed. Notional apprehension thus helps to deepen and enliven real apprehension. This insight suggests that theological reflection on traditional doctrines can help to intensify the lived experience of the faithful—even doctrines that may appear on the surface to be deeply speculative and impractical. Rather, as both Newman's and Schneiders's work suggests, the spiritual and the theological necessarily go hand in hand and enjoy a dialectical relationship. Theology must always remain grounded in the spirituality of lived experience and spirituality; spirituality, if it is to grow, must be aided by theological reflection on the teachings of the Christian community. This connection does not necessitate that all of the faithful undertake advanced studies in theology. Instead, the relationship between faith and theology points to the value and importance of adult faith formation and to the value of what might be called the ordinary theology of the faithful.

The second implication of Newman's notion of the Trinity for contemporary theology and spirituality is that Newman, like Wolfhart Pannenberg, grounds his treatment of the Trinity in the concrete spiritual experience of the earliest Christians and in the lives of Christians today. Thus the doctrine of the Trinity is practical because it is grounded in experience, it enlivens our spiritual imaginations, and it drives us to action.

As noted earlier, Newman's argument for the possibility of real assent to the doctrine of the Trinity is grounded in the believer's experience of each of the component claims that make up the doctrine, and the imagination that brings the images of these experiences to the mind. This is a significant departure from the work of many others during the nineteenth century who viewed the doctrine of the Trinity as an afterthought and as the most impractical of theological doctrines.[31] However, in the second half of the twentieth century there was a resurgence of interest in Trinitarian theology.

---

31. Such an approach differs markedly from Schleiermacher's famous treatment of the doctrine of the Trinity as an appendix to *The Christian Faith*. There, famously, Schleiermacher radically shifted the locus of the treatment of the doctrine of the Trinity to an afterthought since he argued that it was at best an impractical, speculative second-order proposition related to the human experience of dependence. Thus, while for Schleiermacher the move from primary experience to reflection has the effect of making the

A number of creative reappropriations of the doctrine, published by major theologians, helped to demonstrate the importance of the doctrine of the Trinity for contemporary theology and spirituality. One key trend in this resurgence has been an emphasis on grounding Trinitarian theology in the lived experience of the faithful.

Wolfhart Pannenberg, for example, argues that discussions of the doctrine of the Trinity must begin from the life of the historical Jesus and the kingdom that he preached.[32] Such an approach requires the kind of fundamental revision of traditional monotheism that Trinitarian monotheism suggests, because the in-breaking of divine grace that accompanies Jesus' initiation of the kingdom of God and its continuation in the church animated by the Spirit point explicitly to distinct centers of action in the Godhead. Pannenberg argues that the basis for the doctrine of the Trinity is rooted in the historical revelation of the nearness of the Father's lordship in Jesus' preaching of the kingdom. This revelation is mediated through historical events (particularly, but not exclusively, the Christ event) and is in principle open to all humanity.[33] The mediated form of revelatory experience is prolonged in the Spirit's work of consummating this kingdom throughout history.[34] Thus for Pannenberg, the Christian doctrine of the Trinity is rooted fundamentally, not in a propositional form of revelation either as a biblical mandate or as a dogmatic imperative, but in the lived Christian experience of the living Christ that is mediated through participation in the life of the Spirit and the inaugurated kingdom of God. Such a revelation—given its fundamentally relational quality—is necessarily holistic.[35] It therefore is characterized by both notional and affective elements. Thus Pannenberg, in reflecting on the prayer that Jesus taught, claims that "[t]he aim of the whole message of Jesus is that the name of God should be hallowed by honoring his lordship. All else, especially his message of salvation proceeds from this."[36] As a result, all of the faithful have experienced and are animated by

doctrine of the Trinity remote to experience, in Newman the doctrine of the Trinity is the culmination of a diversity of real spiritual apprehensions grounded in the imagination.

32. Wolfhart Pannenberg, *Systematic Theology: Volume 1* (Grand Rapids: Eerdmans, 1991), 298–99 (hereafter, *ST*).

33. *ST*, 1:196–97. Cf. Wolfhart Pannenberg, "Dogmatic Theses on the Doctrine of Revelation," in *Revelation as History*, ed. Wolfhart Pannenberg (London: Macmillan, 1968), 124–58.

34. *ST*, 1:247–48.

35. Fundamental to Pannenberg's understanding Trinitarian personhood is the development of a relational ontology that emphasizes a dynamic and personalist relation among the Trinitarian persons and their economic activity with all of creation. Cf. Theodore James Whapham, *The Term "Person" in the Trinitarian Theology of Wolfhart Pannenberg* (New York: Peter Lang, 2012), 87–134.

36. *ST*, 1:309.

the same kingdom of God that led to the development of the doctrine of the Trinity.

In the *Grammar*, Newman anticipates the contemporary trend to treat the doctrine of the Trinity as grounded in the faith experience of Christians. His emphasis that each of the propositions that make up the doctrine of the Trinity is grounded in the everyday experience of the faithful and brought forward in the imagination is the crucial move in his argument for the possibility of real assent. The result is a strong emphasis on the experience of the divinity of the Father, Son, and Spirit and the recognition that they are distinct persons. His listing of the particular liturgical feasts that best capture these images (Christmas, Epiphany, Ascension, Corpus Christi) focuses on the life of Christ and his relationship to humanity. In this way, Newman appeals to the experiences of deification, revelation, sanctification, and the sacramental life of the Church among the faithful as the basis for the doctrine of the Trinity. Newman is arguing in effect that if the believer has experienced God's presence in the Eucharist or the connection between God and all of humanity as a result of the incarnation, then that person has experienced the Trinitarian life of God.[37] These experiences are the driving factors for the Christian life. They inevitably result in seeing the world in a different way and motivate believers to have a different understanding of their relationship to the rest of humanity than might otherwise be necessary.

This analysis of Newman and Pannenberg's Trinitarian teaching demonstrates that both scholars emphasize the doctrine of the Trinity as the consummation of the lived experience of the Christian faith, rather than something that is fundamentally an afterthought. Each theologian, while highly engaged in the critical theological discussions of his own day, emphasizes that the Trinitarian Christian faith is fundamental to the lived experience of all Christians. In this way, both scholars emphasize the significance of reflection on Scripture, prayer, and liturgical action as essential elements of Trinitarian spirituality. They also point to the way that persons of faith must conduct themselves in the world.

---

37. Newman says of Christ's coming in the incarnation that "when He came, He too, instead of making and securing subjects by a visible graciousness or majesty, departs;—but is found through His preachers, to have imprinted the Image or idea of Himself in the minds of His subjects individually; and that Image, apprehended and worshipped in individual minds, becomes a principle of association, and a real bond of those subjects one with another, who are thus united to the body by being united to that Image; and moreover that Image, which is their moral life, when they have been already converted, is also the original instrument of their conversion. It is the Image of Him who fulfills the one great need of human nature, the Healer of its wounds, the Physician of the soul, this Image it is which both creates faith, and then rewards it" (*GA*, 359).

The third and final implication of Newman's understanding of the Trinity is that, from the perspective of the individual propositions, the Trinity can be an object of real assent. This corresponds with the emphasis in contemporary Trinitarian theology on the need to speak of the divinity by drawing upon a diversity of images. The realization that the doctrine of the Trinity is a complex of simpler experiential claims about redemption and life in the Spirit leads Newman to claim that the mind cannot bring all of these images to the fore at the same time. He writes:

> [W]hat is presented for the imagination, the affections, the devotion, the spiritual life of the Christian to repose upon with a real assent, what stands for things, not for notions only, is each of those propositions taken one by one, and that, not in the case of the intellectual and thoughtful minds only, but of all religious minds whatever, in the case of a child or a peasant, as well as of a philosopher. . . . We know one truth about Him and another truth,—but we cannot image both of them together; we cannot bring them before us by one act of the mind; we drop the one while we take up the other. None of them are fully dwelt on and enjoyed, when they are viewed in their combination.[38]

Newman argues that this idea is to be taken as a general principle of faith and is connected to the inscrutability of God. One cannot fully fathom the beauty, simplicity, or profundity of either the unity or the Trinity of God. While this fact does not prevent the possibility of real assent to the Trinity, it necessitates humility on the part of the believer and places a limit on the appeal to experience of the divine.

As an extension of the recent emphases upon diversity and plurality, and concerns about overconfidence in one's understanding of the divine, many contemporary theologians argue for the need to broaden the images used to describe the divine. This concern for a greater appreciation of divine inscrutability and calls for drawing more widely upon the diversity of traditional images for the divine has come from a wide variety of theological schools.[39] For example, Pannenberg argues that the doctrine of the Trinity has developed in a way that has given undue influence to the relations of origin

---

38. *GA*, 115–16.

39. A full listing of the authors who have taken an interest in the theme are too numerous to list. However, notable figures include Elizabeth Johnson, John Hick, Eberhard Jüngel, Wolfhart Pannenberg, Elizabeth Mowry LaCugna, Elizabeth Schüssler-Fiorenza, Sallie McFague, and Kevin Vanhoozer.

(Son begotten of the father, Father as unbegotten, and Spirit proceeding from the Father [and the Son]).[40] He holds that this overemphasis on the relations of origin has resulted in a widespread cryptomodalism that fails to recognize the full personhood of the Spirit and tends to subordinate the divinity of the Son to that of the Father.[41] Pannenberg retains the relations of origin among the divine persons, but also wants to expand theological reflection on the relations. This expansion should encompass the full complex nexus of relations among the divine persons to include the Son's work in establishing the kingdom, the Spirit's work of bringing the kingdom to fulfillment, and the Father's receiving the kingdom from the Spirit and the Son in the fullness of time.[42] According to Pannenberg, widening reflection on the relations among the Trinitarian persons will also help to underscore the full personhood of the Spirit and ward off subordinationism.[43]

Newman's emphasis on the need to rely upon multiple images to hold to the fullness of revelation anticipates the contemporary insistence that traditional images for the divine alone are insufficient for theology or for the spiritual life. On the contrary, one of the values of the doctrine of the Trinity is that it asks believers to continually stretch their notions of God as they attempt to hold together diverse experiences of the divine—experiences that echo the experiences of all the faithful. In this way, Newman encourages his readers to develop a doctrine of the Trinity that is rooted in a personal encounter with the divine in all the manifest ways God is revealed in creation.

This study of Newman's presentation of the doctrine of the Trinity has emphasized a variety of ways that his Trinitarian theology is at the core of his

---

40. Pannenberg's use of the traditional titles Father, Son, and Spirit is retained in this context for the sake of simplicity. He argues that while a great diversity of images and metaphors have been used (and should continue to be used) in Scripture and throughout history, certain titles have greater prominence than others. He argues the concept of fatherly care and the father's role as head of the family are grounded in Jesus' message of the nearness of the rule of God. However, he argues that the sexual definition of the father's role plays no part in its meaning and to introduce sexual differentiation into the godhead would mean polytheism (*ST*, 1:260–61).

41. Ekeh suggests that Newman himself has this tendency in his understanding of the Trinity. See Ekeh, "Newman on the Trinity," 208–11.

42. *ST*, 1:320.

43. *ST*, 1:324–25. Pannenberg argues that through the act of creation the Father (in particular) places his own divinity at risk. Thus when the kingdom is handed over to the Father by the Son and the Spirit in the fullness of time, the Father will also receive his own divinity from the activity of the Son and the Spirit. As a result, each of the divine persons clearly receives their divinity from each of the other persons. The full personhood of the Spirit is also emphasized in the work of the Spirit as the principle of unity both in creation and the inner life of the Trinity.

own distinctive theology. In Newman's efforts to demonstrate the possibility for real assent to Trinitarian Christian faith among all believers, he relies upon the imagination as a semi-rational mental capacity that is at the root of all knowledge and is lively enough to animate the will and drive fully human action. Thus the imagination lies at the root of the lived Christian faith, which expresses itself in worship and morality. The imagination brings faith to life and prevents it from becoming a mere abstraction. The particular expression of this lived Trinitarian spirituality will naturally differ from individual to individual. For one, it may result in deep passion to work for justice; in another, it may express itself as a search for whatever is most true. Regardless of the ways that the imagination brings this Trinitarian faith to life, it is significant that this faith is not first and foremost an abstract notional concept.

This presentation of the imagination and the ways in which the doctrine of the Trinity can be present to it is directly related to the seminal quality of Newman's work. It has also demonstrated that a portion of the enduring influence of Newman's Trinitarian theology is that it is an essential component of his spirituality open to the lived realties of all believers, not only experts and specialists. His emphasis on the root of faith in the Trinity as lying in the lived experience of believers stands in radical opposition to the nineteenth-century tendency to view Trinitarian theology as impractical and unnecessary. Finally, his work encourages all to be mindful of the inscrutability of the divine and the need to constantly reflect upon the diversity of divine images.

6

Marked by Christ's Presence
Newman's Incarnational Spirituality

Danielle Nussberger

INTRODUCTION

What does it mean to be a Christian presence in contemporary society? In a 2009 interview with Craig Ferguson, Archbishop Desmond Tutu described the influence of authentic Christian discipleship in South Africa's "Truth and Reconciliation Commission" as a matter of evidencing and nurturing Christ-like, selfless love, mercy, and forgiveness in a lost and broken world. He explained the power of grace-filled compassion that can rise out of our human vulnerability if only we would acknowledge that fragility as it is cradled in the arms of God. And, while doing so, his countenance shone brightly with a welcoming smile that never left his face, and his sparkling eyes danced with joy and wonder at the resilience of the human spirit. Clearly, this is a man whose holiness is marked by the presence of Christ, someone who spends his life responding to the holiness of God's presence as it manifests itself in the lives of the oppressed, the poor, and the needy ones who reach out to us for truth, sustenance, and strength. Despite, and indeed, because of the horrors he witnessed during South Africa's apartheid, he is able to praise humanity's God-given treasures of compassion and forgiveness that shine so brightly in the face of the darkness of human sin.[1] Tutu's faith in humanity, which is dependent upon his faith in a saving God, sparks the following question: "How do we become a people so obviously marked by Christ's

---

1. For Tutu's explanation of his remarkable outlook on humanity's God-given capacity to transform suffering and pain into joy, consult Desmond Tutu and Douglas Abrams, *God Has a Dream: A Vision of Hope for Our Time* (New York: Image Doubleday, 2005).

holy presence, acknowledging our wounds and our brokenness, and forever receiving and promoting the resurrected life God has created from out of our pain and suffering?" Tutu embodies the answer to the question he engenders by consciously meeting Christ in those around him and sharing in their suffering so as to "bear the marks of Jesus on his body" (Gal. 6:17).

Like Archbishop Tutu, the nineteenth-century pastor and theologian, John Henry Newman, also practiced an incarnational spirituality that affirmed Christ as the Incarnate one, the God–Man who became one of us so as to redeem us and make us holy by leaving his mark upon us. In Newman's sermons on the Incarnation, on Mary, and on the Eucharist, we find a bond between these three themes that explains how Christ's past presence in the world through the event of the incarnation continues as a dynamic, current presence in our daily lives. We will now work our way through these three foci as they appear in Newman's sermons in order to trace their interrelationship, beginning with his articulation of the doctrine of the Incarnation, then proceeding to his theology of Mary's unique proximity to the Word that flows out of the Incarnation's veracity. Lastly, we will arrive at the Incarnation's ever-present reality through the Lord's Eucharistic sacrifice that draws us into his holiness and unites us to Mary in her ongoing, transformative embrace of our fallen, yet redeemed, world. At every step along the way, Newman will be teaching us how we become a holy people marked by Christ's presence when we acknowledge the redemptive power of the incarnation, when we see how Mary's unique intimacy with Christ betokens our graced relationship with him, and when we receive the crucified and risen Christ in the Eucharist so as to bear the marks of his body in our simultaneously broken and resurrected lives.

Newman on the Incarnation

It is through the incarnation that all humanity and everything in the world are marked by the presence of Christ. Newman recounts the narrative of salvation by beginning where Genesis begins, with the human fall from grace in the context of Israel's ever-faithful God who promises the restoration of humanity's union with God. Steeped in patristic exegesis of the Old Testament account that relies on typologies to express the forward-looking glance of Israel's covenant to its fulfillment in Christ, Newman presumes the Fathers' utilization of Paul's Adam-Christ typology. In Paul's words: "So, too, it is written, 'The first man, Adam, became a living being,' the last Adam a life-giving spirit. But the spiritual was not first; rather the natural and then the spiritual. The first man was from the earth, earthly; the second man, from heaven. As was the earthly one, so also are the earthly, and as is the heavenly one, so also are the heavenly. Just as we have borne the image of the earthly one, we shall also bear the image of the heavenly one" (1 Cor. 15:45-49). Newman presupposes this Adam-Christ correlation, because, like his mentor Athanasius, he sees Paul gesturing toward God's restoration of our union with God through the incarnation's indestructible union between human and divine in Christ.[2] In Newman's words, "Christ communicates life to us, one by one, by means of that holy and incorrupt nature which he assumed for our redemption; how, we know not; still, though by an unseen, surely by a real communication of Himself."[3] Though Paul does not use the doctrinal language of Christ's assumption of human nature, verses 48–49 of 1 Corinthians 15 are the seeds for this later doctrinal development. We are all like Adam in our created nature. We are all becoming like Christ in our newly redeemed selves that are destined to return to the heaven from which the Son was sent to be our Savior. In order for our humanity to be raised from Adam and Eve's fallen state, we needed God to bring our humanity into perfect intimacy with God's self. Becoming human, the Son of God accomplishes this through his person. As we participate in the first Adam's fallen humanity, so too do we participate in the second Adam's elevation of humanity through the union of his human and divine natures. For this reason, Newman tells us, "Let us not deny Him the glory of His life-giving holiness, that diffusive grace which is the renovation of our whole race, a spirit quick and powerful and piercing, so as to leaven the whole mass of human corruption, and make it live."[4]

When we query after the possibility of holiness rising up from out of our fallenness, we recognize our kinship with Adam and Eve and confront the severity of our sinfulness that cries out for mercy and forgiveness. Given what God has done for us, our confrontation with the darkness of our own sin cannot end in desolation and capitulation to the forces of temptation that still besiege us. God has indeed responded to our sin which has separated us from God's love—God has responded by conquering it: the Son obediently adopted our human nature by which he sinlessly suffered the effects of sin so as to purify us and unite us to the Father through the salvific grace of his death and resurrection. God's very presence with humanity in Christ's incarnation, suffering, death, and resurrection is the means of our redemption and therefore

---

2. In Newman's eyes, Athanasius stands out as a hero who upholds orthodox doctrine, and is therefore an example of what Newman tries to do in his nineteenth-century context. See Newman's *The Arians of the Fourth Century*, ed. Rowan Williams (Notre Dame: University of Notre Dame Press, 2001).

3. John Henry Newman, *Parochial and Plain Sermons* (San Francisco: Ignatius, 1997), 2:320 (hereafter, *PPS*).

4. *PPS*, 2:320–21, "Christ, a Quickening Spirit."

the source of our holiness in the Spirit. We are one with God in Christ, because Christ is God who made himself one with us in all things except sin. Just so, Newman exclaims:

> He [the Son], indeed, when man fell, might have remained in the glory which He had with the Father before the world was. But that unsearchable love which showed itself in our original creation, rested not content with a frustrated work, but brought Him down again from His Father's bosom to do His will, and repair the evil which sin had caused. And with a wonderful condescension he came, not as before in power, but in weakness, in the form of a servant, in the likeness of that fallen creature whom He purposed to restore. So he humbled Himself; suffering all the infirmities of our nature in the likeness of sinful flesh, all but a sinner,—pure from all sin, yet subjected to all temptation,—and at length becoming obedient unto death, even the death of the cross.[5]

In the incarnation, God the Son came to meet us in our sinfulness by establishing the strongest possible bond of intimacy with us, so that we might cling to that grace-filled union and live out of its stores of infinite compassion. As Newman tells us:

> It is the peculiar blessedness of the Christian . . . to be "partaker of the Divine Nature." We believe, and have joy in believing, that the grace of Christ renews our carnal souls, repairing the effects of Adam's fall. Where Adam brought in impurity and unbelief, the power of God infuses faith and holiness. Thus we have God's perfections communicated to us anew, and, as being under immediate heavenly influences, are said to be one with God. And further, we are assured of some real though mystical fellowship with the Father, Son, and Holy Spirit, in order to this: so that by a real presence in the soul, and by the fruits of grace, God is one with every believer, as in a consecrated Temple.[6]

It is Christ, the New Adam, who has left his mark upon us in order that we might be "partakers of the Divine Nature." Our oneness with God is made possible through Christ's union with us in the incarnation, a union that leaves

---

5. *PPS*, 2:246–47, "The Incarnation."
6. *PPS*, 2:249, "The Incarnation."

his presence in our souls and consecrates us to himself as the temples of his Holy Spirit.

There are times and events, like Desmond Tutu's context of South African apartheid, however, that threaten to damage our union with Christ and to erase the mark he has left upon us. Over and over again, we are reminded of just how far we can fall into the abyss when we choose to separate ourselves from each other's needs and from God's love. The incarnation reveals to us the depths of our brokenness. The Word made Flesh blesses us with contrite hearts that long for God's mercy: "The truth is that our Saviour has shown us in all things a more perfect way [to repent] than was ever before shown to man. As He promises us a more exalted holiness, an exacter self-command, a more generous self-denial, and a fuller knowledge of truth, so He gives us a more true and noble repentance. The most noble repentance (if a fallen being can be noble in his fall), the most decorous conduct in a conscious sinner is an *unconditional surrender* of himself to God—not a bargaining about terms, not a scheming (so to call it) to be received back again, but an instant *surrender* of himself in the first instance."[7] One way we make this unconditional surrender sacramentally is when we are baptized; humble and contrite, we are moved by the Spirit into the water to be cleansed of our sin through the blood of Christ's sacrifice. Out of the water's tomb, we emerge anew, clothed with Christ and transformed into his image. Throughout our lives, we renew our baptismal promises, converting ourselves to him over and over again so that we might be a sign of his continued presence in the world.

Newman on Mary

In Mary, Newman finds an exemplar for what it means to live within the miraculously restored bond between God and humanity that occurs in the incarnation. As Mother of the Lord, Mary's immediate bond with her son makes his union with humankind possible; at the same time, she also receives the gift of redemption that is bequeathed to all humankind as a result of the suffering, death, and resurrection of her child. Newman explains:

> Thus He [the Son] came into this world, not in the clouds of heaven, but born into it, born of a woman; He the son of Mary, and she (if it may be said) the mother of God. Thus He came, selecting and setting apart for Himself the elements of body and soul; then, uniting them to Himself from their first origin of existence, pervading them,

7. *PPS*, 3:545–46, "Christian Repentance."

hallowing them by His own Divinity, spiritualizing them, and filling them with light and purity, the while they continued to be human, and for a time mortal and exposed to infirmity. And, as they grew from day to day in their holy union, His Eternal Essence still was one with them, exalting them, acting in them, manifesting Itself through them, so that He was truly God and man, One Person . . .[8]

The Son "unites body and soul, pervades, hallows, spiritualizes, purifies and exalts them" inside his mother's womb. As the event of the incarnation takes place within her, she possesses an unequaled intimacy with Christ that is particular to mother and son. Yet, within the uniqueness of her maternal bond lies the working out of an all-encompassing union between human and divine that she participates in alongside other human beings. She is set apart by the Father to bear his Son; and she is made holy again through her proximity to the Savior. Employing patristic exegesis as before, Newman reminds us that Mary is the new Eve; her obedient and free acceptance of her role as Christ's mother plays a crucial part in the process of our restoration to the fullness of covenantal union with the triune God.[9]

Just as Christ's obedience to the Father's will undoes the first Adam's disobedience, so too Mary's yes to God's invitation to be the Lord's mother nullifies Eve's disregard for God's command to avoid the fruit from the tree in the middle of the garden. However, Newman's utilization of the Eve/Mary comparison goes much further than this. Because Mary gives birth to the Son of God made human, she reverses the curse of sorrowful childbirth pronounced on Eve, and she becomes the condition for the possibility of our transformation in Christ. In his sermon on "The Reverence Due to the Virgin Mary," Newman announces:

> Eve was doomed to bear children in sorrow; but now this very dispensation, in which the token of Divine anger was conveyed, was made the means by which salvation came into the world. Christ might have descended from heaven as He went back, and as He will come again. He might have taken on Himself a body from the ground, as Adam was given; or been formed, like Eve, in some other divinely-devised way. But, far from this, God sent forth His

---

8. *PPS*, 2:247–48, "The Incarnation."

9. See John M. Todd, "The New Eve," *Worship* 27, no. 6 (1953): 273–78. See also Roderick Strange, "The Development of Newman's Marian Thought and Devotion," *One in Christ* 16, no. 1–2 (1980): 114–26.

Son (as St. Paul says), "made of a woman." For it has been His gracious purpose to turn *all* that is ours from evil to good. Had He so pleased, He might have found, when we sinned, other beings to do Him service, casting us into hell; but He purposed to save and to change *us*. And in like manner all that belongs to us, our reason, our affections, our pursuits, our relations in life, He needs nothing put aside in His disciples, but all sanctified.[10]

Through Mary, Christ makes his mark upon us, saving and converting every aspect of our human being, thinking, and acting so that we might be made more fully human by being conformed to him. Mary's role as Christ's mother makes her the mother of our new humanity, because her son takes on flesh in her womb in order to raise human beings back up to their created status of those who bear God's image.

Newman explains that in order for Mary to be the mother of the world's Savior, she had to be marked by the Word's sacred life long before the Holy Spirit overshadowed her to prepare her womb to bear the Incarnate One. The doctrine of the Immaculate Conception stems from Mary's identity as the *Theotokos*, or God-bearer; she is pure and free from original sin, because the Father set her apart for the particular mission of bringing God's Son into the world: "She who was chosen to supply flesh and blood to the Eternal Word, was first filled with grace in soul and body. . . . It was fitting, for His honour and glory, that she, who was the instrument of His bodily presence, should first be a miracle of His grace; it was fitting that she should triumph, where Eve had failed, and should 'bruise the serpent's head by the spotlessness of her sanctity.'"[11] Newman appreciates Mary's uniqueness as someone who "is a specimen, and more than a specimen, in the purity of her soul and body, of what man was before his fall, and what he would have been had he risen to his full perfection."[12] This means that Mary's freedom from sin—though this makes her unique among human beings—indicates the authentic essence of all human beings who are meant to be in an ever-graced relationship with their creator God. For all conceived in original sin, this relationship is restored through Christ's death and resurrection and perpetuated through the sanctifying grace of the Holy Spirit. In her present role as Queen of Heaven, Mary beckons us to embrace our identity as children of God, marked out by Christ to participate

---

10. "The Reverence Due to the Virgin Mary," in *Mary: The Virgin Mary in the Life and Writings of John Henry Newman*, ed. Philip Boyce (Grand Rapids: Eerdmans, 2001), 117–18 (hereafter, *Mary*).
11. *Mary*, 141–43, "The Glories of Mary for the Sake of Her Son."
12. *Mary*, 141, "The Glories of Mary for the Sake of Her Son."

in his divine sonship. On this subject, Newman movingly preaches, "And now thy very face and form, dear Mother, speak to us of the Eternal; not like earthly beauty, dangerous to look upon, but like the morning star, which is thy emblem, bright and musical, breathing purity, telling of heaven, and infusing peace. O harbinger of the day! O hope of the pilgrim! Lead us still as thou has led; in the dark night, across the bleak wilderness, guide us on to our Lord Jesus, guide us home."[13]

This prayer to Mary not only refers to our journey heavenward. In praying to Mary thusly, we are also asking her to show us the way back to that place within us that is marked by the presence of Christ from our baptism onwards. How often have we lost sight of the fact that Christ's incarnation is an event that involves us in the here-and-now? How frequently do we feel distanced from Christ and from one another, believing that we are alone in our endeavors to become better persons of faith and love? Mary's role as our mother through Christ's adoption of our flesh reminds us that we are forever embraced by the loving arms of one who can show her son to us by pointing to his seal upon our heart. She also shows us who we are called to be: human beings in graced union with God, purified and salvifically freed from sin in order to bring Christ to the world in ever new and unique ways when we respond to the needs of those around us.

Newman foregrounds Mary's communion with her Son, understanding it to be a communion with all of humanity because Christ has united us all to himself. We are participants through salvific grace in the Son's relationship with the Father, just as Mary's maternal oneness with her son gives her an unprecedented intimacy with the Godhead. He knows that if our increased knowledge of this biblical and patristic imagery (of Christ as the New Adam and Mary as the New Eve) is to be successful in encouraging our awareness of the reality toward which it points—it must come alive directly before our eyes in the sacramental life of the Church. Otherwise, we may emphasize Mary's unique sanctity without likewise seeing our potential for holiness through our graced proximity to Christ in the Eucharist. Our devotion to Mary is not meant to set us apart from her; rather, she encourages us to approach Christ with a humble posture of thanksgiving for the unending compassion that Jesus pours out upon us so that it might continue to pour forth upon the world through our Christ-like words and actions.

---

13. *Mary*, 144–45, "The Glories of Mary for the Sake of Her Son."

Newman on the Eucharist

Newman's biblical and patristic interpretations of the event of the incarnation and of Mary's role within it are designed to make the past a present reality. It is through participation in the Eucharist that Christians living today are continually marked by the presence of Christ. Scripture itself, in the very words of Christ (John 6:50), attests to the everlasting presence of God in Christ's passion, death, and resurrection, that continues to empower us as individuals, as communities, and as the world that is being re-created in the Spirit. In his *Plain and Parochial Sermon* on the Eucharistic presence, Newman interprets the Bread of Life discourses in John's Gospel; for him, they attest to Christ's sacrifice, offered once-for-all on the cross and now presently offered again with Jesus' gift of himself to us in the Eucharist. The event of the incarnation is ours to experience again and again as we truly receive Christ's flesh and blood. In Newman's words,

> Let us pray Him then to give us such a real and living insight into the blessed doctrine of the Incarnation of the Son of God, of His birth of a Virgin, His atoning death, and resurrection, that we may desire that the Holy Communion may be the effectual type of that gracious Economy. No one realizes the Mystery of the Incarnation but must feel disposed towards that of Holy Communion. Let us pray Him to give us an earnest longing after Him—a thirst for His presence—an anxiety to find Him—a joy on hearing that He is to be found, even now, under the veil of sensible things,—and a good hope that *we* shall find Him there.[14]

The salvific grace that is ours in Christ's suffering, death, and resurrection is perpetually bestowed upon us to make us one with Christ, and therefore one with the Father through Christ and the Spirit. As Mary was holy through her unbreakable bond with the Son, so we are sanctified through our union with the crucified, risen, and Eucharistic Lord who communes with us and lives within us.

We come to the altar of infinite mercy, compassion, and forgiveness, having been baptized into Christ's body and now struggling to remain faithful to our identity as Christ's disciples who are made strong in their weakness, courageous in their vulnerability and in their dependence upon God. Newman stresses our need to receive the Eucharist frequently, because this is one of the

---

14. *PPS*, 6:1281, "The Eucharistic Presence."

major means through which Christ communes with us and leaves his mark upon us today. Newman implores those who would rob themselves of repeated meetings with their Eucharistic Lord:

> You have sustained an irretrievable loss—and what a loss! Not a loss like any thing else in this world—but a loss of approaching the Word Incarnate, Christ the Son of God in a way unlike any other way which God has given—higher, more mysterious, more sublime. Suppose yourself to have your eyes wrapt round and to be carried aloft by Angels to the third heaven and laid at the foot of God's throne—Suppose . . . that God was there—and Jesus on His right hand . . . with the same flesh and blood, though spiritualized (made immortal and spiritual), which He had on earth—with the marks of the nails on it and of the spear—and supposing, though you felt it not, He drew near to you, and placed His hand upon you, sealing you on the forehead with His Father's name, or placing His cross upon your shoulders or on your breast . . .[15]

Newman compares Eucharistic communion with Christ to our eschatological union with him in heaven. He does this in order to emphasize the Eucharist's efficacy in making Christ tangibly present to us: "O what a strange and precious gift it is, to carry Christ within us . . . This was the gift of those Saints and Martyrs in ancient times, whom we so little resemble—thus it was that men born sinners, such as we are, yet by grace were ennobled and changed, till they bore all suffering the most cruel as though it were their ordinary day's work."[16] Though Newman regrets that we are often unlike the saints and martyrs, he is adamant that we too receive the Lord's body and blood sacrificed for us. We are at once marked with his cross and graced with the power of his resurrection.

Elsewhere, Newman refers to the Lord's Supper as a fourfold feast: "a feast of joyful commemoration" that "Christ our Passover is sacrificed for us" (1 Corinthians 5), "a feast upon a sacrifice" that fulfills the covenant between God and human beings and that promises that we have reaped the salvific benefits of Christ's sacrificial death. It is "a feast of inward and spiritual strength" that gifts us with the sanctifying grace of the Holy Spirit, and finally, "a feast of charity" that unites us all to one another in our mutual reliance upon God's mercy for

---

15. Sermon 18, no. 459, in *John Henry Newman Sermons 1824-1843, Volume 1: Sermons on the Liturgy and Sacraments and on Christ as Mediator*, ed. Placid Murray, OSB (Oxford: Oxford University Press, 1991), 131.

16. *John Henry Newman Sermons*, 138–39, Sermon 19, no. 348.

our redemption and sanctification.[17] In this "feast of charity," we give our lives to Christ and to one another, responding to our Savior's sacrifice of body and blood with a resolve to be obedient to Christ in imitation of him. In Newman's words, "And, while partaking of the bread and wine is the seal of the covenant made to us on *God's* part, it is equally certain, it is on our part too a promise to perform our engagements to Him. . . . In partaking the Lord's supper we obviously make a profession of our dependence on Him, we thank Him while commemorating His death, and we openly and in the sight of the world bind ourselves to serve Him."[18]

Christian holiness, therefore, is participation in the joy of divine self-offering. That the Christian community receives the self-gift of Christ in the Eucharist means that they are being made into his image and likeness through an offering of the same gift to one another. We are not asked to give what we lack. We are holy through the act of self-offering to God and to each other, because God has made us holy in the blood of the Lamb. Newman explains that Christ's blood has restored us to union with God; and it is our daily life-blood as a result of our ongoing communion with the crucified and risen, Eucharistic Lord: "Now to eat Christ's body and drink His blood, what can it imply but our becoming *one with Him*?—our substance is to be sustained nourished invigorated by His substance—the life's blood (so to say) of our souls is to be drawn from Him . . ."[19] Our graced union with Christ in the Eucharist anticipates our eschatological union with him when we will join Mary and the Communion of Saints in the everlasting chorus of hosannahs to our Lord and King. Inspired by this vision of future happiness that belongs to the holy ones of God, Newman quotes Rev. 7:15-17: "They serve Him day and night in His temple, and He that sitteth on the throne shall dwell among them. . . . The Lamb which is in the midst of the throne shall feed them, and shall lead them unto living fountains of waters."[20]

Our weekly experiences of Eucharistic celebrations and their aftermath vary. Sometimes we approach the exuberance of guests at the eschatological banquet; and at other times we lose interest and focus inwardly upon our future tasks. On some occasions, we may sense the vast import of the Eucharistic liturgy, fervently participating in every moment of the celebration. Consequently, we may depart from the assembly with a renewed commitment to being Christ for others in every aspect of our lives, allowing the sacrament

---

17. *John Henry Newman Sermons*, 150, Sermon 20, no. 172.
18. *John Henry Newman Sermons*, 148, Sermon 20, no. 172.
19. *John Henry Newman Sermons*, 147, Sermon 20, no. 172.
20. *PPS*, 1:7, "Holiness Necessary for Future Blessedness."

to "sacramentalize" our daily activities. On other occasions, we may feel far removed from what we perceive to be a staid ritual, afterward stepping outside the chapel doors and returning to life's monotony unaltered. The previous options suggest that we experience one or the other extreme of complete involvement or utter disinterest. It is more likely that we find ourselves somewhere in the middle: we want to live differently due to having received sacramental grace and yet become frustrated every time that we fall back into our old patterns of behavior when liturgical time ends and customary time begins again. Another possibility still remains, and it is frightening in its consequences. What if we were to deceive ourselves into believing that our transition from liturgical to customary time did not call for any improvement on our part? What if we were to ignore the disjunction between self-offering and destructive self-aggrandizement that disrespects the integrity and freedom of others?

As a clergyman, Newman anticipates such diversity in our Eucharistic experiences. The community's sacramental transformation is a long-term process that includes many twists and turns in every member's spiritual development. Of course, there are some who will refuse to see the incommensurability between Eucharistic deportment and a prideful posture capable of all kinds of abuses, including denying and injuring others' dignity. What is the source of our hope in these circumstances? Newman tells us that, over time, the mark of Christ's love penetrates us so deeply that we cannot help but be in awe of its effects upon us: "It is plain—this union of the soul with Christ is the work of years, and the object of His favor scarcely dare believe his own happiness, till in course of time his power over the world is evidence to himself of it. His power to resist temptation, to command himself, to do God's will, give him a hope that he is really living in the grace of Him who died for him, and who has from his infancy desired his salvation."[21] Those who already exhibit such happiness in their union with Christ have a profound affect on us. They take seriously the spiritual and moral implications of what happens on and around the altar, and they endeavor to treat everyone with the same Christ-like compassion that responds to ignorance and abuse by not returning like for like. Taking part in the Eucharistic sacrifice with all those who have gone before us in the Communion of Saints reminds us that we are meant to humbly stumble forward in grace, inevitably taking others along with us as fellow strugglers. With Newman's help, our enhanced understanding of the Eucharist's sacramental meaning and its relationship to the incarnation can only

---

21. *John Henry Newman Sermons*, 142, Sermon 19, no. 348.

serve to heighten our appreciation of the liturgy's gifts, which can and should be given again to the world that extends outside of the church's walls.

Marked by Christ's Presence

This chapter began with the following question: "How do we become a people so obviously marked by Christ's holy presence, acknowledging our wounds and our brokenness, and forever receiving and promoting the resurrected life God has created from out of our pain and suffering?" This question arose from coming face-to-face with the saintly personage of Archbishop Desmond Tutu, whose life of self-giving and concern for others showed that he was a person truly marked by the presence of Christ. So often we find ourselves incapable of doing as he has done—responding to hatred and violence with unconditional love and forgiveness. And yet, Desmond Tutu reminds us that such compassion and self-sacrifice is the hallmark of Christian discipleship. Newman practices a similar incarnational spirituality that demonstrates our belief in the God of Jesus Christ who has given us what we need to meet the challenges of our faith; in Christ and the power of the Holy Spirit, we are endowed with the grace to stretch beyond our limitations, allowing our weaknesses to reveal the strength of the God of salvation.

Newman's incarnational spirituality functions on the basis of our present experience of the central realities of our Christian faith. He narrates the drama of salvation in his theologies of the Incarnation, Mary, and the Eucharist, in such a way that we too are actors in the drama because of our participation in Christ. In this way, all Christians are marked by the presence of Christ. When we are contributing to the sorrow and pain of others, we are acting as sinners who must repent and seek forgiveness. When we are ameliorating the suffering of others, we are acting as redeemed ones who have accepted God's grace to grow in love of Christ and one another. We are aware that on this side of the eschaton we will keep reaching out to God to help us heed Jesus' exhortation to "turn away from sin and believe in the gospel" (Mark 1:15), words that we hear repeated year after year in the Roman Catholic, Ash Wednesday liturgy. The power of Christ's presence in our lives is what gives us the courage and the strength to confront our failings honestly and to strive to become the holy people that Mary shows us we are destined to be.

According to Newman, the key to personal, faith-filled commitment to the kind of love and compassion that Desmond Tutu exhibits and promotes is the salvific will of God achieving our redemption in Christ through the power of the Holy Spirit. His incarnational spirituality attunes our minds and hearts to the objective reality of the gift of salvation given to us for the sake of our transformative action in cooperating with God to re-create the world. We understand ourselves more fully due to the narrative of salvation making sense of the experiences that constitute the agony and the ecstasy of our lives. From the suffering caused by hatred and division, to the peace resulting from humility and forgiveness, we intuit when we are being less than who we are called to be and when we have been lifted up to where we belong.

Newman's presentation of the narrative of salvation suggests that these experiences are not accidental or inevitable; we are free to choose discord or peace, but every choice changes us, either making us more prone to one or the other. When we find ourselves trapped in the cycle of violence set off by our initial decisions in favor of separation instead of communion, we find ourselves lost in sin. Once the cycle spins out of control, we have known the helplessness of being unable to stop it. We rejoice at the grace of a transformation that occurs when the Word is made flesh in order to put an end to our divisions and the violence that perpetuates them. Christ's permanent presence in our lives—through the incarnation, through his mother's role as caretaker of our renewed humanity, and through the Eucharist's gift of the Savior's body and blood to us—is the cause of our rebirth into the community of his disciples who communicate his presence to the rest of the world. However, when we struggle with maintaining our closeness to Christ, sometimes we find ourselves in a pre-resurrection darkness. At those times, we may look upon our distance from Mary and the saints and argue that they are unique and that we are part of the masses who will never attain such proximity to Christ. Newman reminds us that we *are* like Mary due to our undivided communion with our Lord and Savior in the Eucharist. In this memorial of Christ's sacrifice on the cross, we are drawn into the drama of salvation to experience the fulfillment of God's covenantal promises and to dedicate ourselves to God anew by living within the glorious life of Christ that we have received.

Newman is certain that we can reap spiritual benefits from entering into the narrative of salvation from the doorways of the Word's incarnation, Mary's unique union with her son that signifies our universal human destiny, and the sacrament of the Eucharist as our means for nurturing our intimacy with Christ, which demands that we become his representatives to a world in need. Therefore, may we join Newman in taking seriously the sinful darkness that we enter into when we turn away from God and divide ourselves from God's grace. May we also take seriously the actions of our saving God who marks us with God's holiness by giving God's own self to us unreservedly in the incarnation. May we reiterate our belief in the God who becomes one with us in Christ and shows us our common destiny of participation in Christ's holiness, which we find perfected in Mary. May we experience that the Son's incarnation is ours as we turn to the altar of mercy and forgiveness with contrite hearts and receive the crucified and risen, Eucharistic Lord who transforms the darkness of sin and death into the wondrous new life of re-creation in the Spirit. Finally, may such recollection and grateful reception of God's saving grace restore our amazement and wonder at the glory of our life in Christ, which we can and must share as his disciples.

7

Newman's Mariology
A Model for a Spirituality of Reception

Ryan Marr

The last five decades in the life of the Catholic Church have been determinatively shaped by the reforms of the Second Vatican Council. Despite the great optimism that surrounded this important religious event, the years following the Council have not been without difficulties. In a 1985 interview with the Italian journalist Vittorio Messori, for instance, Cardinal Joseph Ratzinger pointed out the contrast between the expectations of the Council fathers and the practical consequences of the Council in the two decades following its conclusion: "What the Popes and the Council fathers were expecting was a new Catholic unity, and instead one has encountered a dissension which—to use the words of Paul VI—seems to have passed over from self-criticism to self-destruction. There had been the expectation of a new enthusiasm, and instead too often it has ended in boredom and discouragement."[1] From Ratzinger's perspective, the Second Vatican Council was supposed to initiate a vibrant springtime in the life of the Church, but, instead, we are experiencing a long, harsh winter.[2]

As we all know, these feelings of disillusionment with the postconciliar era are shared by many Catholic intellectuals on the left, albeit for different

---

1. Joseph Cardinal Ratzinger, with Vittorio Messori, *The Ratzinger Report: An Exclusive Interview on the State of the Church*, trans. Salvator Attanasio and Graham Harrison (San Francisco: Ignatius, 1985), 29–30.

2. While some might see in Ratzinger's analysis the latent frustrations of a disaffected conservative, similar diagnoses have been set forth by theological commentators on the left, though (obviously) they have different ideas than does Ratzinger about what might free us from this ecclesial "deep-freeze." See, e.g., Paul Lakeland, *Catholicism at the Crossroads: How the Laity Can Save the Church* (New York: Continuum, 2007).

reasons. In a 2009 article in *Commonweal*, for example, John Wilkins writes that, as "a child of Vatican II," he today feels himself orphaned in light of the current trajectory of the hierarchy. Toward the end of this article, Wilkins rhetorically asks, "Were those like me deceived when we saw a vision of what the church truly was at Vatican II and followed it? Was the council a flash in the pan, a hiccup in the church's life, as it were, before the Catholic organism, challenged, closed back in on itself?"³ In a similar vein, Terrence Tilley charges "restorationists" in the Church of seeking to "evacuate *aggiornamento* of any meaning."⁴ In Tilley's view, these restorationists "appear to be deliberately constructing a fictional countertradition that masks the power relationships they seek to restore: a triumphalist attitude, a clericalist mentality, and a juridicist ecclesiology."⁵ In our present ecclesial context, hope for an end to the cold, harsh winter that Ratzinger described in 1985 appears bleak.

The above quotations sufficiently demonstrate that the process of receiving the Second Vatican Council remains an ongoing one.⁶ While numerous approaches could be utilized for navigating this task, the following chapter looks back to John Henry Newman's Mariology as an instructive image for receiving and applying the teachings of Vatican II. To be clear, the goal of this chapter is not to settle the dispute between right and left regarding the interpretation of the Council, nor is the goal to offer concrete interpretations of specific teachings set forth in the conciliar documents. The aim, rather, is to draw upon Newman's Mariology so as to establish a framework for understanding the way in which theologians and the laity might fruitfully contribute to the reception of Vatican II. To this end, the first section of the chapter will focus on Newman's fifteenth Oxford University Sermon, in particular, his construal of the Blessed Virgin Mary as "our pattern of Faith, both in the reception and in the study of Divine Truth."⁷ The second part will show how Newman's notion of Mary as the pattern of faith provides Catholic theologians and the laity with a model of spirituality based on reflective

---

3. John Wilkins, "Why I Became Catholic: A Witness to Vatican II," *Commonweal* 136 (February 27, 2009): 16–19.

4. Terrence Tilley, "Aggiornamento Adjourned," *Commonweal* (April 11, 2008): 35.

5. Tilley, "Aggiornamento Adjourned," 35.

6. For an insightful examination of the task of reception, see Ormond Rush, *The Reception of Doctrine: An Appropriation of Hans Robert Jauss' Reception Aesthetics and Literary Hermeneutics* (Rome: Gregorian University Press, 1997). Cf. Gilles Routhier, *La Réception d'un Concile* (Paris: Cerf, 1993).

7. John Henry Newman, "The Theory of Developments in Religious Doctrine," Sermon XV in *Fifteen Sermons Preached Before the University of Oxford Between A.D. 1826 and 1843*, ed. James David Earnest and Gerard Tracey (Oxford: Oxford University Press, 2006), 211 (hereafter, *US*).

acceptance of God's revelation and church teaching. This Marian mode of interpretation can serve as the basis for a spirituality of reception in relation to the ongoing process of receiving the teachings of the Second Vatican Council.

Newman's Construal of Mary as the Pattern of Faith

In John Henry Newman's spiritual journey from Anglicanism to Roman Catholicism, Mariology played an indispensable role. As an Anglican, Newman possessed a profound devotion to Mary that was somewhat uncharacteristic within his cultural context.[8] After becoming a Roman Catholic, Newman's reverence for the Blessed Virgin Mary unsurprisingly deepened, and he consistently incorporated theological images of Mary into his preaching and writings.[9] Newman's gradual acceptance of Marian devotion laid the foundation for one of his more original contributions to Mariology—namely, his vision of Mary as the pattern of faith for all Christians. This imagery shows up most explicitly in the fifteenth Oxford University Sermon. In this sermon—best known for its succinct explication of the theory of doctrinal development—Newman begins with a profound reflection on Mary's reception of Divine Truth: "Little is told us in Scripture concerning the Blessed Virgin, but there is one grace of which the Evangelists make her the pattern, in a few simple sentences,—of Faith . . . Mary's faith did not end in a mere acquiescence in Divine providences and revelations: as the text informs us, she 'pondered' them."[10] Through her humble *fiat* in response to God's call, as well as her interior contemplation on the mystery of salvation, Mary has provided *the* model of faithful reception of the Divine Word. Further along in the sermon, Newman elaborates upon this point:

> Thus St. Mary is our pattern of Faith, both in the reception and in the study of Divine Truth. She does not think it enough to accept, she dwells upon it . . . not enough to assent, she develops it; not enough

---

8. See Philip Boyce's "Introduction" to *Mary: The Virgin Mary in the Life and Writings of John Henry Newman*, ed. Philip Boyce (Grand Rapids: Eerdmans, 2001), 17–32.

9. Newman's fullest treatment of Mariology is his *Letter Addressed to the Rev. E. B. Pusey on Occasion of His Eirenicon*, in *Certain Difficulties Felt by Anglicans in Catholic Teaching Considered*, vol. 2 (London: Burns, Oates, & Co., 1875) (hereafter, *Diff*). In terms of the secondary literature, a few landmark studies are Francis Friedel, *The Mariology of Cardinal Newman* (New York: Benziger Brothers, 1928); Lutgart Govaert, *Kardinal Newmans Mariologie und sein persönlicher Werdegang* (Salzburg und München: Universitätsverlag Anton Pustet, 1975); and, Nicholas Gregoris, *"The Daughter of Eve Unfallen": Mary in the Theology and Spirituality of John Henry Newman* (Mount Pocono, PA: Newman House, 2003).

10. *US*, 211.

> to submit the Reason, she reasons upon it; not indeed reasoning first, and believing afterwards, with Zacharias, yet first believing without reasoning, next from love and reverence, reasoning after believing. And thus she symbolizes to us, not only the faith of the unlearned, but of the doctors of the Church also, who have to investigate, and weigh, and define, as well as to profess the Gospel . . .[11]

This quotation brings into sharp relief the key components of Newman's vision of Mary as the Christian pattern of faith. For Newman, Mary's faith serves as an example for us along two main lines. First, Mary's example definitively rules out a fideistic approach to revelation, that is, approaching the content of Christian truth in an unreflective manner, as if it somehow stood outside the bounds of rational inquiry.[12] Within the Gospels, Mary does not merely accept and assent to divine truth, but dwells upon and develops it. Possessing a humble and obedient faith, in other words, does not mean eschewing serious intellectual engagement.

Alongside ruling out fideism, Mary's example equally precludes a rationalistic mode of theological reflection. Throughout his life, but especially during his years as a Roman Catholic, Newman stood in fierce opposition to the rationalism that was growing in influence—not only in the realm of philosophical inquiry, but also (and most disturbingly, for Newman) in the fields of biblical studies and theology.[13] In Tract 73, Newman describes rationalism as

> a certain abuse of Reason; that is, a use of it for purposes for which it never was intended, and is unfitted. To rationalize in matters of Revelation is to make our reason the standard and measure of the doctrines revealed; to stipulate that those doctrines should be such as to carry with them their own justification; to reject them, if they come in collision with our existing opinions or habits of thought, or are with difficulty harmonized with our existing stock of knowledge.

---

11. *US*, 211–12.

12. Olli-Pekka Vainio defines fideism as "a mode of thought or teaching according to which reason is more-or-less irrelevant to (religious) belief, or even that faith is strengthened, not undermined, if one judges that reason is unable to give it support." See Vainio, *Beyond Fideism: Negotiable Religious Identities* (Burlington, VT: Ashgate, 2010), 2.

13. In the face of increasing skepticism, Newman somberly prophesied "that the trials which lie before us are such as would appal [*sic*] and make dizzy even such courageous hearts as St. Athanasius, St. Gregory I, or St. Gregory VII." See Newman, *Faith and Prejudice and Other Unpublished Sermons* (New York: Sheed & Ward, 1956), 117.

And thus a rationalistic spirit is the antagonist of Faith; for Faith is, in its very nature, the acceptance of what our reason cannot reach, simply and absolutely upon testimony.[14]

From Newman's vantage point, imitation of Mary constitutes the most potent antidote to this temptation. Yes, Mary reasoned upon divine truth, but her reflection on this truth began with her *fiat*, or submission to God's will. In short, Mary prioritized faith over reason—or, to put it more aptly, her reasoning process started from the assent of faith.

Mary's Example as the Antidote to Rationalism

The final point from the above section deserves further elaboration, as it has significant implications for a key issue in Newman's theology—namely, his conception of the relationship between faith and reason. For Newman, theological inquiry, especially that undertaken in the context of the university, always runs the risk of succumbing to rationalism.[15] From Newman's perspective, rationalism represents the archetypal sin in the exercise of human reason. Properly understood, faith is not opposed to reason, but builds on and perfects it. Rationalism undermines this symbiosis, by enshrining human reason as "the standard of doctrines revealed."[16] The struggle, of course, is not between faith and reason *qua* reason, but between faith and a rationalistic spirit. In Avery Dulles's words, "The rationalist errs by taking himself, rather than the Creator, as his own center. For the rationalist faith is never more than an opinion."[17] Whereas faith rests upon an "acceptance of mystery" mediated through the testimony of others, the rationalistic spirit demands evidence gleaned from human experience—or, to use biblical language, it wishes to walk not by faith but by sight.[18]

Ironically, after articulating his theory of doctrinal development, Newman himself had to face the charge of introducing rationalist principles into theological investigation. Newman readily recognized that he was walking a

---

14. Published in John Henry Newman, *Essays Critical and Historical*, vol. 1 (London: Longmans, Green, & Co., 1907), 30–99. For a helpful overview of Newman's critique of rationalism as well as his constructive epistemological approach, see Avery Dulles, *Newman* (New York: Continuum, 2002), 36–45.

15. Dulles, *Newman*, 142.

16. This wording derives from Tract 73, "On the Introduction of Rationalistic Principles into Revealed Religion," in *Essays Critical and Historical*, vol. 1 (New York: Longmans, Green, & Co., 1907), 30.

17. Dulles, *Newman*, 36.

18. Dulles, *Newman*, 36–37. Also see 2 Cor. 5:7.

fine line on this matter, and in the 1878 edition of the *Essay on Development* he took time to address this concern. In his view, while the process of doctrinal development is susceptible to rationalism, it need not fall into this trap.[19] The safeguard against rationalism—as we might expect from the above discussion—is patterning our theological reflection after the example of Mary. Clearly, Mary did not commit a sin by reasoning upon and developing the divine truth conveyed to her by the angel Gabriel. How could the Immaculata be accused of rationalism? In terms of the theological task, then, it is significant that "Mary's faith did not end in a mere acquiescence in Divine providences and revelations."[20] Mary remained free, one could say, from the rationalist tendency by prioritizing faith above reason. Mary employed her reason to gain a deeper understanding of the Word entrusted to her, but her starting point—and ultimate standard of truth—was faith ("not indeed reasoning first, and believing afterwards, with Zacharias, yet first believing without reasoning, next from love and reverence, reasoning after believing . . ."[21]).

Around the time that Newman was revising his *Essay on Development*, he also published his most famous treatment of ecclesiology: his 1877 Preface to *The Via Media of the Anglican Church*. In the 1877 Preface, Newman suggests that the Church possesses three distinct offices—a prophetical office, a priestly office, and a regal office—which "[stand] in a dialectical relationship of mutual tension and mutual support."[22] As Newman frames the matter, "Christianity . . . is at once a philosophy, a political power, and a religious rite: as a religion, it is Holy; as a philosophy, it is Apostolic; as a political power, it is imperial, that is, One and Catholic. As a religion, its special center of action is pastor and flock; as a philosophy, the Schools, as a rule, the Papacy and its Curia."[23] The Church runs into problems, Newman infers, whenever one of the offices oversteps

---

19. Newman writes: "The process of development, thus capable of a logical expression, has sometimes been invidiously spoken of as rationalism and contrasted with faith. But, though a particular doctrine or opinion which is subjected to development may happen to be rationalistic, and, as is the original, such are its results: and though we may develope erroneously, that is, reason incorrectly, yet the developing itself as little deserves that imputation in any case, as an inquiry into an historical fact, which we do not thereby make but ascertain,—for instance, whether or not St. Mark wrote his Gospel with St. Matthew before him, or whether Solomon brought his merchandise from Tartessus or some Indian port. Rationalism is the exercise of reason instead of faith in matters of faith; but one does not see how it can be faith to adopt the premisses, and unbelief to accept the conclusion." Newman, *An Essay on the Development of Christian Doctrine* (New York: Longmans, Green, & Co., 1949), 177.

20. *US*, 211.

21. *US*, 212.

22. This latter phrase comes from Avery Dulles, SJ, "The Threefold Office in Newman's Ecclesiology," in *Newman after a Hundred Years*, ed. Ian Ker and Alan G. Hill (Oxford: Clarendon, 1990), 378.

its boundaries, thereby throwing into disequilibrium the relationship between itself and the other two offices. In his own day, Newman was concerned that the regal office was threatening to choke out the life of the prophetical office.[24] In response to this danger, he sought to return theology to its proper place within the functioning of the Church's life. In Newman's estimation, "Theology is the fundamental and regulating principle of the whole Church system. It is commensurate with Revelation and Revelation is the initial and essential idea of Christianity."[25] In light of this fact, the prophetical office "has in a certain sense a power of jurisdiction over [the regal and sacerdotal] offices," which "are far more liable to excess and corruption."[26] Put differently, the Church remains always in need of theologians to keep "within bounds both the political and popular elements in the Church's constitution."[27] The content of the deposit of faith tames the excesses to which devotionalism is prone, while the magisterium of the Church, in the practical exercise of its office, is accountable to tradition.[28]

After making these points, Newman quickly adds that theology has dangers unique to its task. In his words, "theology cannot always have its own way; it is too hard, too intellectual, too exact, to be always equitable, or to be always compassionate . . ."[29] As noted above, theological inquiry unmoored from the content of revelation inevitably devolves into rationalism. Elsewhere in his writings, Newman claims that theology can stave off the error of rationalism by fostering a Marian modality. Interestingly, there seems to exist a connection between venerating Mary and imitating her as the pattern of faith,

---

23. John Henry Newman, *The Via Media of the Anglican Church*, ed. H. D. Weidner (Oxford: Clarendon, 1990), 25 (hereafter, *VM*).

24. See, for instance, §2, section 6 of the Preface, *VM*, 27–28. Earlier in the essay, Newman writes, "It is so ordered on high that in our day Holy Church should present just that aspect to my countrymen which is most consonant with their ingrained prejudices against her, most uncompromising for their conversion . . ." This remark is most likely a veiled reference to Ultramontanist understandings of the papal office, which were the target of Newman's criticism throughout the latter decades of his life.

25. *VM*, 29.

26. *VM*, 29.

27. *VM*, 29.

28. According to George Weigel, during the Second Vatican Council Pope Paul VI suggested that *Lumen Gentium* include the statement that the Pope is "accountable to the Lord alone." The Council's Theological Commission rejected this proposal, noting that "the Roman Pontiff is also bound to revelation itself, to the fundamental structure of the Church, to the sacraments, to the definitions of earlier councils, and other obligations too numerous to mention." See Weigel, *Courage to Be Catholic: Crisis, Reform, and the Future of the Church* (New York: Basic Books, 2002), 117–18.

29. *VM*, 30.

that is to say, between Marian devotion and the preservation of orthodoxy. Thus, in his most elaborate treatise on Mary, the *Letter to Pusey*, Newman writes:

> Now I say plainly, I never will defend or screen any one from your just rebuke, who, through false devotion to Mary, forgets Jesus. But I should like the fact to be proved first; I cannot hastily admit it. There is this broad fact the other way;—that, if we look through Europe, we shall find, on the whole, that just those nations and countries have lost their faith in the divinity of Christ, who have given up devotion to His Mother, and that those on the other hand, who had been foremost in her honour, have retained their orthodoxy.[30]

Cultivating piety toward the Mother of God, in other words, anchors the prophetical office, helping to secure the orthodoxy of theological reflection amidst the currents of rationalism and heresy.

From this perspective, what Newman calls the sacerdotal office—or, devotional aspect of the Church's life—possesses an inherently Marian dimension.[31] By habitually meditating upon the mystery of salvation, including Mary's role within it, we are in a certain sense imitating her reception of Divine Truth. In doing so, we create the ideal conditions for fruitful theological work. To come at the issue from another angle, the prophetical office depends upon the sacerdotal office to remain healthy. While devotion may be prone to superstition, reasoning, Newman observes, "tends to rationalism,"[32] and, consequently, theology needs a properly functioning sacerdotal office to prevent it from being drawn into skepticism.[33] Newman expresses this point even more forcefully in the *Essay on Development*: "The contempt of mystery, of reverence, of devoutness, of sanctity," he writes there, "are . . . notes of the heretical spirit."[34] While we might assume that the regal office serves the primary role in restraining the excesses of theology, a robust devotional life remains equally, if not more, important for the overall health of the prophetical office. Here, too, Mary provides us with an invaluable example, in that her life

---

30. *Diff*, 2:92.

31. Hans Urs von Balthasar expresses a similar idea when he speaks of "the Marian mold of the Church." See, e.g., Hans Urs von Balthasar and Joseph Ratzinger, *Mary: The Church at the Source*, trans. Adrian Walker (San Francisco: Ignatius, 2005), 125–44.

32. *VM*, 25.

33. VM, 25.

34. Newman, *An Essay on the Development of Christian Doctrine*, ed. Ian Ker (Notre Dame: University of Notre Dame Press, 1989), 354.

offers the preeminent model of one who properly ordered theological reflection to faith. This Marian dimension to spirituality, then, remains essential to the theological endeavor.³⁵

Newman's Mariology and the Ecclesial Vocation of the Theologian

One unexplored, but potentially fruitful, avenue for further investigation is the way in which Newman's construal of Mary as our pattern of faith might shed light on the relationship between theologians and the magisterium. Nearly two and a half decades ago, the Congregation for the Doctrine of the Faith addressed this topic at length in *Donum Veritatis*, on the ecclesial vocation of the theologian. In Newmanesque fashion, *Donum Veritatis* holds up Mary as our exemplar in the exercise of faith:

> The Virgin Mary is Mother and perfect Icon of the Church. From the very beginnings of the New Testament, she has been called blessed because of her immediate and unhesitating assent of faith to the Word of God (cf. *Lk* 1:38, 45) which she kept and pondered in her heart (cf. *Lk* 2:19, 51). Thus did she become a model and source of help for all of the People of God entrusted to her maternal care. She shows us the way to accept and serve the Word. At the same time, she points out the final goal, on which our sights should ever be set, the salvation won for the world by her Son Jesus Christ which we are to proclaim to all [people].³⁶

The language here sounds strikingly similar to Newman's remarks in the fifteenth Oxford University Sermon, though with one significant difference. Whereas the Congregation of the Doctrine for the Faith's imagery construes Mary's faith in primarily passive terms, Newman emphasized that alongside her submission to revelation Mary also played an active role in developing what she had received.³⁷ As the biblical record indicates, Mary did not operate as a

---

35. Something of this same idea might be behind the famous remark of Karl Rahner relayed by Cardinal Suenens: "At the 1971 Congress of the Marian Ecumenical Society . . . I mentioned that I had once asked Rahner why trendy Christians are so indifferent to Mary, and I quoted his reply: 'For too many people, Christianity has become another "ism," an ideology, an abstraction—and abstractions have no need of mothers.'" See Leon Joseph Cardinal Suenens, *Memories and Hopes*, trans. Elena French (Dublin: Veritas, 1992), 240–41.

36. *Donum Veritatis*, §42, accessed June 20, 2013, at http://www.vatican.va/roman_curia/congregations/cfaith/documents/ rc_con_cfaith_doc_19900524_theologian-vocation_en.html.

merely passive participant in God's plan; to the contrary, her *cooperation* with grace made possible the conception of divine life within her, thereby opening the door to salvation for the whole world.[38]

Newman found confirmation of the biblical testimony in the Mariological reflections of various Church Fathers. In his *Letter to Pusey*, for instance, after setting forth quotations from Justin, Tertullian, and Irenaeus, Newman remarks, "Now, what is especially noticeable in these three writers, is, that they do not speak of the Blessed Virgin merely as the physical instrument of our Lord's taking flesh, but as an intelligent, responsible cause of it."[39] This insight has significant implications for understanding the vocation of the theologian vis-à-vis the ecclesiastical magisterium. In an imbalanced ecclesiological arrangement, the hierarchy can assume that the role of theologians consists merely in restating doctrinal truths authoritatively expounded by the magisterium.[40] But, just as Mary played an active role in developing the truth entrusted to her, so also theologians are active—though *not* autonomous—participants in the reception, application, and development of Church teaching. This all-important task of theologians particularly comes into play whenever an ecumenical council promulgates binding doctrinal pronouncements. In a letter from 1871, Newman strongly affirmed that the responsibility of interpreting conciliar teaching falls in a special way upon the shoulders of the *schola theologorum*, who work to "assimilate and harmonize" new pronouncements within the broader context of continuous Church tradition.[41] Patterning themselves after the example of the Blessed Virgin Mary,

---

37. Although *Donum Veritatis* does acknowledge "freedom of inquiry" as indispensable to the theological task (§12), it stresses preeminently submission to the magisterium. Certainly, Catholic theologians need to foster an appropriate docility toward the magisterium, but, in turn, magisterial authorities ought to guard against a counterproductive heavy-handedness in their relationship to theologians. *Donum Veritatis* could have highlighted the vital role that theologians play in the process of doctrinal development by drawing attention to the active character of Mary's reasoning upon Divine Truth, as does Newman.

38. See, e.g., *Diff*, 2:36: "[A]s Eve was a cause of ruin to all, Mary was a cause of salvation to all; that as Eve made room for Adam's fall, so Mary made room for our Lord's reparation of it; and thus, whereas the free gift was not as the offence, but much greater, it follows that, as Eve co-operated in effecting a great evil, Mary co-operated in effecting a much greater good." Cf. Boyce, "Introduction," 66; Dulles, *Newman*, 78.

39. *Diff*, 2:35.

40. For a critique of this viewpoint, see Richard Gaillardetz, "Reflections on Key Ecclesiological Issues Raised in the Elizabeth Johnson Case," in Gaillardetz, ed., *When the Magisterium Intervenes: The Magisterium and Theologians in Today's Church* (Collegeville, MN: Liturgical, 2012), 284–87. Cf. Aidan Nichols, *The Shape of Catholic Theology* (Collegeville, MN: Liturgical, 1991), 29–31.

theologians properly undertake an active role in the development of Church teaching.⁴²

Newman's Mariology and the Laity

Significantly, Newman did not limit this role to the work of professional theologians, but firmly believes that all the members of Christ's body, including the lay faithful, are called to participate in the preservation and transmission of doctrine. Newman's fullest treatment of this topic is also his most controversial—namely, his 1859 *Rambler* article, "On Consulting the Faithful in Matters of Doctrine." Within this essay Newman asserts that, in the preparation of a dogmatic definition, the episcopate, or teaching church (*ecclesia docens*), has a duty to consult the sense of the faithful (*sensus fidelium*) regarding the doctrine under discussion. "Why?" Newman asks. "[B]ecause the body of the faithful is one of the witnesses to the fact of the tradition of revealed doctrine, and because their *consensus* through Christendom is the voice of the infallible Church."⁴³ As Edward Miller points out, the keystone of Newman's perspective on this matter is his firm conviction that the Church, when healthy, operates not according to the guidance of the clergy alone, but also takes into account the outlook and opinions of the laity, or "learning Church" (*ecclesia discens*). In Miller's words, "Just as Newman insists that the whole person thinks—not only one's intellect but also one's feelings, memories, etc.—he also insists that the whole ecclesial body is involved in discerning and living out the revealed truth. The laity have their rightful role in church affairs just as the clergy do, and the process by which religious doctrines come to expression involves theologians as importantly as it involves episcopal authorities."⁴⁴ When the clergy forget this truth, they fall into the error that Saint Paul condemns in 1 Corinthians

---

41. Letter to William Maskell dated 12 February 1871, *The Letters and Diaries of John Henry Newman*, ed. C. S. Dessain and Thomas Gornall (Oxford: Clarendon, 1973), 25:284 (hereafter, *LD*). Cf. *LD*, 25:447, Newman's letter to Sir William Henry Cope dated 10 December 1871, in which Newman notes that following the conclusion of a Council, theologians "settle the force of the wording of . . . dogma, just as the courts of law solve the meaning and bearing of Acts of Parliament." Cf. Ian Ker, *Newman and the Fullness of Christianity* (Edinburgh: T. & T. Clark, 1993), 74–76.

42. On the role of the *schola theologorum* in the reception of conciliar teaching, see Michael J. Pahls, "Development in the Service of Rectification: John Henry Newman's Understanding of the *Schola Theologorum*," in *Authority, Dogma, and History: The Role of the Oxford Movement Converts in the Papal Infallibility Debates*, ed. Kenneth L. Parker and Michael J. Pahls (Bethesda, MD: Academica, 2009), 195–211.

43. John Henry Newman, *On Consulting the Faithful in Matters of Doctrine*, ed. John Coulson (New York: Sheed & Ward, 1961), 63. Italics in original (hereafter, *Cons*).

12: assuming that as the "head" they have no need for other parts of the body. To the contrary, the body of Christ is at its strongest when its various parts are working together and toward the same ends.[45]

In articulating this position, Newman's ecclesiological outlook stood in stark contrast with the more popular perception that the laity's primary roles were to pray, pay, and obey—perhaps most memorably captured in the dismissive remark of Monsignor Talbot to Archbishop Manning: "What is the province of the laity? To hunt, to shoot, to entertain. These matters they understand, but to meddle with ecclesiastical matters they have no right at all, and this affair of Newman is a matter purely ecclesiastical. . . . Dr. Newman is the most dangerous man in England, and you will see that he will make use of the laity against your Grace."[46] While the *Rambler* controversy was at its height, Newman confronted a similar form of this prejudice in an impassioned conversation with Bishop Ullathorne, Newman's ordinary in the diocese of Birmingham. During a meeting on the 22 May 1859, Ullathorne complained to Newman that Newman's appeal to the sense of the faithful was "too disturbing for Catholic taste."[47] When Newman retorted that the Bishops lacked an adequate comprehension of the state of the laity, Ullathorne "said something like, 'Who are the laity?,'" to which Newman replied, "The Church would look foolish without them."[48] The fact that Bishop Ullathorne was a relatively moderate member of the British episcopate provides some sense of just how much Newman was swimming against the ecclesiological stream of his time.

To capture the kind of cooperation between the laity and bishops that he had in mind, Newman employed the phrase *pastorum et fidelium conspiratio*.[49] As an ideal example of the pastors and faithful working together in harmony, he pointed to Pope Pius IX's consultation of the whole Church prior to his promulgation of the dogma of the Immaculate Conception. In his 1849 encyclical *Ubi Primum*, Pope Pius IX asked the bishops of the world to report back to him on the faith of their flocks as related to the Blessed Virgin Mary's

---

44. Edward Jeremy Miller, *John Henry Newman on the Idea of Church* (Shepherdstown, WV: Patmos, 1987), 59.

45. Newman expounds upon this and other key passages related to ecclesiology in a sermon from his Anglican period, "The Unity of the Church." See Newman, *Parochial and Plain Sermons* (San Francisco: Ignatius, 1997), 7:1550–57.

46. Quoted in Wilfrid Ward, *The Life of John Henry Newman: Based on His Private Journals and Correspondence*, vol. 2 (New York: Longmans, Green, & Co., 1921), 147.

47. This description of Ullathorne's concern comes from Coulson's introduction to *Cons*, 18.

48. *LD*, 19:141.

49. *Cons*, 104.

conception: "It is Our earnest wish that you make known to Us as soon as possible what devotion your clergy and faithful people entertain toward the Conception of the Immaculate Virgin, and what may be their disposition to see this matter defined by the Holy See."[50] Over a century later, at the Second Vatican Council, the bishops of the world gave an official stamp of approval to the process of consulting the faithful by providing the theological rationale behind recourse to this measure:

> The entire body of the faithful, anointed as they are by the Holy One, cannot err in matters of belief. They manifest this special property by means of the whole people's supernatural discernment in matters of faith when "from the Bishops down to the last of the lay faithful" they show universal agreement in matters of faith and morals. That discernment in matters of faith is aroused and sustained by the Spirit of truth. It is exercised under the guidance of the sacred teaching authority, in faithful and respectful obedience to which the people of God accepts that which is not just the word of men but truly the word of God. Through it, the people of God adheres unwaveringly to the faith given once and for all to the saints, penetrates it more deeply with right thinking, and applies it more fully in its life.[51]

Notably, at the beginning of this paragraph from *Lumen Gentium*, the council fathers observe that "[t]he holy people of God shares also in Christ's prophetic office."[52] Although the document does not cite Newman's writings, upon reading this remark students of Newman's theology cannot help but recall his vision of the dynamic interrelationship that exists between the three offices of the Church, with the prophetical office having "in a certain sense a power of jurisdiction over [the regal and sacerdotal] offices."

Of course, this high view of the place of the lay faithful in the life of the Church correspondingly places serious demands on the laity in terms of their spiritual and intellectual development. Even before the publication of his *On*

---

50. Pope Pius IX, *Ubi Primum*, in *The Papal Encyclicals, 1740-1878*, ed. Claudia Carlen (Wilmington, NC: McGrath, 1981), 292.

51. *Lumen Gentium*, 12, accessed July 3, 2013, at http://www.vatican.va/archive/hist_councils/ii_vatican_council/documents/vat-ii_const_19641121_lumen-gentium_en.html. For a detailed discussion of the historical and theological issues related to the *sensus fidelium*, see Daniel J. Finucane, *Sensus Fidelium: The Use of a Concept in the Post-Vatican II Era* (San Francisco: International Scholars, 1996).

52. *Lumen Gentium*, 12.

Consulting the Faithful, Newman was highlighting the importance of having a well-instructed, theologically sophisticated laity:

> I want a laity, not arrogant, not rash in speech, not disputatious, but men who know their religion, who enter into it, who know just where they stand, who know what they hold, and what they do not, who know their creed so well, that they can give an account of it, who know so much of history that they can defend it. I want an intelligent, well-instructed laity; I am not denying you are such already: but I mean to be severe, and, as some would say, exorbitant in my demands, I wish you to enlarge your knowledge, to cultivate your reason, to get an insight into the relation of truth to truth, to learn to view things as they are, to understand how faith and reason stand to each other, what are the bases and principles of Catholicism . . .[53]

Both theologians and the laity ought to pattern themselves after the example of the Blessed Virgin Mary, whose faith did not end in a mere acquiescence to divine truths, but who proceeded to reason upon these truths and also to develop them. In our own day, the primary locus of this activity is the ongoing reception of Vatican II, the subject to which we now turn.

THE MARIAN MODEL AND THE RECEPTION OF VATICAN II

This concluding section will put Newman's Mariology to the test, so to speak, by exploring its usefulness for the ongoing task of receiving the Second Vatican Council. Newman himself recognized that "Councils have ever been times of great *trial*."[54] During the course of Vatican I and afterwards, as Newman sought to calm the consciences of troubled souls, he consistently counseled his correspondents to practice patience in the face of present difficulties and to have faith in God's providential care for the Church.[55] Regarding these challenges, Newman's image of Mary as our pattern of faith proves particularly instructive. In our own, sometimes disorienting, historical context, some theologians

---

53. John Henry Newman, *Lectures on the Present Position of Catholics in England: Addressed to the Brothers of the Oratory in the Summer of 1851* (Notre Dame: University of Notre Dame Press, 2000), 390.

54. *LD*, 25:158.

55. See, for instance, Newman, *LD*, 25:310: "I know that a violent reckless party, had it its will, would at this moment define that the Pope's powers need no safeguards, no explanations—but there is a limit to the tyrannical—Let us be patient, let us have faith, and a new Pope, and a re-assembled Council may trim the boat."

suggest that what the contemporary Church most needs is a definitive interpretation of Vatican II's documents—some word of clarity that will forever dispel the disputes that presently buffet the body of Christ. This tendency can be seen, for example, in the outlook of Monsignor Brunero Gherardini, who ends his 2011 work, *The Ecumenical Vatican Council II: A Much Needed Discussion*, with a fervent appeal to the pope to "offer some clarity by responding in an authoritative manner to the question about the Council's continuity with the other councils . . . and about its fidelity to the ever rigorous tradition of the Church."[56] While such an intervention could open an avenue for fruitful dialogue, Newman's paradigm sets forth something else as first in the order of priority: Newman challenges all of us, theologians and the laity, to cultivate a certain kind of posture in relation to Church teaching, one modeled after Mary's response to God's call.

To put the matter in somewhat homiletical terms, have Catholic theologians in tandem with the laity sufficiently reflected upon and internalized the teachings of the Second Vatican Council? Newman's image of Mary as our pattern of faith shifts the discussion: in a certain sense, it demands conversion. Newman's Marian mode of interpretation requires taking seriously the originality of the council, dwelling upon the content of its documents, and faithful acceptance of the ethos bequeathed to us by the council.[57] Rather than being preoccupied with guaranteeing that a particular interpretation becomes enshrined as definitive, we are faced with the challenge of allowing the Council's teaching and its vision to shape the way we live out the demands of the gospel. If Church Councils are truly guided by the ministry of the Holy Spirit, as we confess they are, then in the most recent Council God has spoken a word to us, in a way analogous to the Angel Gabriel's message to Mary. Typologically, we face today the same task that confronted Mary: we must not think it enough to accept the Council's teaching, we must dwell upon it; not enough to assent, we must develop it; not enough to submit our reason, we must reason upon it.

Alongside the demands placed upon theologians, the magisterium bears the responsibility to leave sufficient space for theologians to conduct their work. In response to Benedict XVI's recent criticisms of a hermeneutic of discontinuity,[58] some theologians and historians have expressed concern that the contemporary hierarchy is attempting to turn back the clock, by undoing the

---

56. Gherardini, *The Ecumenical Vatican Council II: A Much Needed Discussion*, trans. Franciscans of the Immaculate (Frigento: Casa Mariana Editrice, 2011), 297.

57. For the centrality of the concept of ethos to Newman's thought, see James Pereiro, *Ethos and the Oxford Movement: At the Heart of Tractarianism* (New York: Oxford University Press, 2008).

reforms initiated at Vatican II.[59] This anxiety can be seen, for instance, in a 2007 collection of essays, edited by David Schultenover—*Vatican II: Did Anything Happen?* In his contribution to this work, John W. O'Malley cautions that an overemphasis on continuity can end up obscuring the concrete achievements of the Council. "While always keeping in mind the fundamental continuity in the great tradition of the Church," O'Malley writes, "interpreters must also take due account of how the council is discontinuous with previous practices, teachings, and traditions, indeed, discontinuous with previous councils."[60] While I would not frame the issue in quite the same way, O'Malley here captures a legitimate concern. Certainly, something significant took place at Vatican II, and any hermeneutic employed in interpreting the Council must adequately take its originality into account.

What Newman provides us with, however, is not a specific kind of interpretation—whether conservative or progressive—but a *mode* of interpretation: what we might call a Marian modality with which to approach the entire process. In this respect, following Mary as our pattern of faith will not necessarily guarantee the ultimate success of our chosen interpretations of the Council documents. Rather, it revolutionizes the very way in which we navigate the questions. The reception of the teachings of the Second Vatican Council is an ongoing process. In the process both theologians and the laity have a contribution to make. For now, theologians offer a specific (and indispensable!) service to the Church in their work of interpreting and applying conciliar teaching. The laity exercise their active role in the process of the reception of Vatican II through the *sensus fidelium*. Their role in the ongoing reception of the teachings of the Second Vatican Council must be an active one, patterned on Mary's model of reception as reflective acceptance. Concerning the concrete demands that this model places upon both theologians and the laity, Newman's theology remains an invaluable resource. In this instance, his word to us is simple, yet profound: "Behold thy Mother."

---

58. See Benedict XVI's 2005 "Christmas Address to the Roman Curia," accessed May 20, 2013, http://www.vatican.va/holy_father/benedict_xvi/speeches/2005/december/documents/hf_ben_xvi_spe_20051222_roman-curia_en.html.

59. For a sustained critique of the procedures of recent magisterial interventions, see the collection of essays in Gaillardetz, ed., *When the Magisterium Intervenes.* Cf. Tilley, "Aggiornamento Adjourned," 35.

60. John W. O'Malley, "Vatican II: Did Anything Happen?," in *Vatican II: Did Anything Happen?*, ed. David G. Schultenover (London: Continuum, 2007), 56.

8

Newman's Vision of Holiness in This World

John R. Connolly

In his early years as an Evangelical Anglican, Newman tended to emphasize the unseen world over the visible world. His view of holiness during this period of his life could be described as an "other-worldly holiness." As Newman moved away from his Evangelical period to high church Anglicanism, and later to Roman Catholicism, his emphasis shifted. Through his readings of the early Christian writers, his deepening consciousness of the sacramental principle, and his sermons on the indwelling of the Holy Spirit, Newman began to emphasize the visible signs of God's presence in this world. He began to see holiness as a quest to discover and encounter the invisible world in the visible world. Newman came to realize that holiness is an affirmation of this world and that it can be found in and through the ordinary actions of daily life. After analyzing Newman's vision of this worldly holiness, this chapter will point out the significance of Newman's view of holiness for a Catholic lay spirituality today.

THE VISIBLE WORLD AND THE INVISIBLE WORLD

Newman's conception of the relationship between the visible world and the invisible world is crucial to understanding his vision of holiness. In the sermon, "The Invisible World" (16 July 1837), Newman begins his description of the two worlds by quoting the following scriptural passage: "while we look not at the things which are seen, but at the things that are not seen; for the things which are seen are temporal, but the things which are not seen are eternal" (2 Cor. 4:18).[1] Drawing upon this passage, Newman distinguishes the two worlds on the basis of sight and time. The visible world is "the world we see" and is temporal; the invisible world is "the world we do not see" and is eternal.[2] Newman goes on to stress that the invisible world, even though we do not see it, is as real as the visible world.[3]

Awareness of the visible world comes through sight and empirical verification. We know that the visible world exists because we see it. Our eyes and senses give us proof that this world exists. We are born into a world of sense, "of real things which lie all around us."[4] The visible world is seen "through our bodily organs, our eyes, ears, and fingers."[5] Not only do we know the visible world through sense perception, but also we are conscious of our perception of the things in the visible world. "They [objects of the visible world] act upon us, and we know it; and we act upon them in turn, and know we do."[6]

On the other hand, the invisible world is one that is not visible to the human eye and sense experience. The realities of the invisible world are known through revelation. As Newman says, Scripture tells us that this world exists.[7] The invisible world cannot be seen; it can only be known through faith.[8] Although the phenomena of the invisible world cannot be seen with the human eye, they are all around us, "coming and going, watching, working or waiting."[9] The realities in the invisible world include God, God's revelation, the souls of the dead, and the angels.[10] Newman calls the invisible world a "world of spirits."[11] Even though the invisible world cannot be seen, we do hold communion with it and take part in it. However, we are not conscious of doing so. Newman states that the invisible world acts upon us without "impressing us with the consciousness that it does so."[12]

---

1. John Henry Newman, *Parochial and Plain Sermons* (San Francisco: Ignatius, 1997), 4:860–68. This edition includes all eight volumes (hereafter, *PPS*).

2. *PPS*, 4:860.

3. *PPS*, 4:860.

4. *PPS*, 4:860.

5. *PPS*, 4:860.

6. *PPS*, 4:861.

7. PPS, 4:861.

8. *PPS*, 4:860.

9. *PPS*, 4:861.

10. *PPS*, 4:861–62. Here Newman states that God is not ordinarily among the realities that can be seen in the visible world. However, he goes on to mention that the incarnation of God in Jesus is one exception in which God was seen in the visible world.

11. *PPS*, 4:863.

12. *PPS*, 4:861.

Without negating the basic goodness of this world, Newman clearly gives priority to the invisible world. The invisible is said to be a "more wonderful" world than the visible world, if for no other reason than we do not see it.[13] Although Newman refuses to say that the things of the invisible world are "vastly more important" than the things of the visible world, he does say that the invisible world is a much higher world.[14] All the wonderful and beautiful things in the visible world "proceed from a centre of love and goodness, which is God himself; but they are not His fullness; they speak of heaven, but they are not heaven; they are but as stray beams and dim reflections of His Image; they are but crumbs from the table."[15] The visible world is temporal and will pass away. Christians look forward to the second coming of Christ when the visible world will fade away and the invisible world "will shine forth."[16] The invisible world is a beginning and a promise of something beyond it, but it is not enough and it does not satisfy us. After giving a very inspiring imaginative description of his vision of the invisible world, Newman concludes that it is really so great and so beyond the visible world that human words cannot adequately describe it.[17] "Earthly words are indeed all worthless to minister to such high anticipations. Let us close our eyes and keep silence."[18]

NEWMAN'S OTHER-WORLDLY HOLINESS

Newman's efforts to work out the relationship between the visible and the invisible world during his evangelical Anglican years resulted in what can

---

13. *PPS*, 4:860.

14. *PPS*, 4:861. Newman refuses to say that the things in the invisible world are "vastly more important" than the things of the visible world because the human person exists in the visible world and there is nothing created that is "more precious and noble" (*PPS*, 4:861).

15. *PPS*, 4:867.

16. *PPS*, 4:866.

17. *PPS*, 4:867–68. Here are some quotes from Newman's vision of the invisible world. "Who can imagine by a stretch of fancy the feelings of those who have died in faith, wake up to enjoyment! The life then begun, we know, will last for ever. . . . We may indeed increase for ever in knowledge and in love. . . . When we find ourselves after long rest gifted with fresh powers, vigorous with the seed of eternal life within us, able to love God as we wish, conscious that all trouble, sorrow, pain, anxiety, bereavement, is over for ever, blessed in the full affection of those earthly friends whom we loved so poorly, and could protect so feebly, while they were with us in the flesh, and above all, visited by the immediate visible ineffable Presence of God Almighty, with his Only-begotten Son our Lord Jesus Christ, and His Co-equal Spirit, that great sight in which is the fullness of joy and pleasure for evermore,—what deep, incommunicable, unimaginable thoughts will be then upon us! what depths will be stirred up within us! what secret harmonies awakened, of which human nature seemed incapable!"

18. *PPS*, 4:868.

be described as an other-worldly holiness. The visible world—although not evil—was viewed as an obstacle to experiencing the graces of the invisible world. In order to experience the glories of the invisible world, one somehow had to overcome the desires and distractions of this world. The positive experience of the things of this world was looked upon with suspicion. Shortly after his 1816 conversion, Newman developed a suspicious and somewhat Puritanical attitude toward the visible world.[19] This view is expressed in the following poem that Newman wrote in the same year, "O may I scorn each mundane joy, / And meditate on Thee. / May heaven all my thoughts employ, / Then happy shall I be."[20]

Toward the end of 1816, he wrote a prayer in Latin in which he asked God to save him from such attractions of the world as parties and dances. He condemns these festivities on the grounds that St. Paul and St. John had taught him to avoid the wicked joys of the world and to flee from the eyes and the flesh, and the pride of life.[21] During the Christmas vacation of 1821, Newman decided not to attend plays anymore.[22] He also considered it a sin to write a letter on Sunday.[23]

Newman's disdain for the excessive drinking at Trinity College is well known. There is his famous statement that "drink, drink, drink," seems to be a qualification for admission into Trinity College.[24] He refused to attend the College's annual "Gaudy" at which, he states, the sole purpose of drinking was to get drunk.[25] Newman refers to the actions of his fellow students on this occasion as the "apostasies of the many." For him, the students' quest for drunkenness was a violation of their commitment and service to God.[26] Perhaps these reactions are understandable in a young sensitive religious man; yet, his disdain for drinking at times seems to approach the fanatical. In a conversation

---

19. Hilda Graef, *God and Myself: The Spirituality of John Henry Newman* (London: Peter Davies, 1967), 14.

20. John Henry Newman, *Autobiographical Writings*, ed., with an introduction by Henry Tristram (New York: Sheed & Ward, 1957), 151 (hereafter, *AW*).

21. *AW*, 153.

22. *AW*, 181. After reading W. Wilberforce's *Practical Christianity*, Newman said that he decided to avoid going to plays.

23. Graef, *God and Myself*, 22.

24. *AW*, 32.

25. Graef, *God and Myself*, 17. The Gaudy was celebrated on the Monday after Trinity Sunday.

26. *AW*, 38. Newman writes, "O how the Angels must lament over the whole Society throwing off their allegiance and service to their Maker, which they have pledged the day before at His Table, and showing themselves true sons of Belial" (*AW*, 38).

with one of his fellow students, Newman states that "getting drunk, was, in the sight of God, nearly as great a crime as murder."[27]

Newman's suspicions of the pleasures and accomplishments of this world also extended to another aspect of his life at Trinity College. In his studies, Newman went through a phase in which he saw the desire for academic success as an obstacle to his religious commitment to God. When applying for a scholarship at Trinity, Newman wrote on 18 May 1818, "Let me not be lead [*sic*] away from Thee by the hope of it . . . grant it not to me, if it is likely to be a snare to me, to turn me away from Thee."[28] In an 1820 letter to his brother Francis, Newman prays that he not be granted any honors in his examinations, "if they are to be the least cause of sin in me."[29] Unfortunately, in this case his prayers were answered. On his Mediterranean cruise with Hurrell Froude and Hurrell's father, Newman felt a certain reluctance to enjoy and take pleasure in the beauties of nature, because they tended to take his focus off God and the invisible world.[30] In a letter to his mother on 19 December 1832, he wrote, "For what are all these strange sights but vanities, which bring no sensible good . . . attended too, as they ever must be by all who wish to do their duty with anxious and jealous watchfulness, lest the heart be corrupted by them."[31] These encounters with nature and new places through his travels were viewed as distractions from his commitment to live fully and completely in the invisible world.[32]

Newman's intense enthusiastic and sometimes fanatical spirituality at this time was a source of distress to both his mother and father. His mother thought that he was being overly righteous and was verging upon enthusiasm.[33] In 1822 his father warned him that he was becoming too religiously extreme. His father warned him to "[t]ake care. . . . Have a guard. . . . You are encouraging a nervousness and morbid sensibility, and irritability, which may be very serious. . . . You are on dangerous ground. The temper you are encouraging may lead to something alarming. . . . Do nothing ultra."[34] Although his fanatical tendencies did upset his parents, Newman was always respectful of their views.[35]

---

27. *AW*, 182.
28. *AW*, 157–58.
29. *AW*, 159.
30. Graef, *God and Myself*, 36–37.
31. John Henry Newman, *The Letters and Diaries of John Henry Newman*, ed. Charles Stephen Dessain (London: Nelson, 1961–77), 3:155 (hereafter, *LD*).
32. Graef, *God and Myself*, 38.
33. *AW*, 175.
34. *AW*, 179.

In responding to his father's criticism, Newman said that he was sorry that he had neglected to pray against fanaticism. When he left home to return to Oxford in January 1822, he took his father's words to heart—"Do not show any ultraism in any thing."[36]

Although Newman went through this period of other-worldly holiness that bordered on the fanatical, Graef cautions against overstating the case.[37] She reminds us that during this period Newman did enjoy some of the pleasures of life. He spoke with great enthusiasm and pleasure about his first meal at Oxford.[38] He enjoyed playing the violin. In the midst of the financial crisis caused by the failure of his father's bank, Newman prayed for assistance, and thanked God for all the temporal blessing he had received.[39]

THE THEOLOGICAL BASIS OF NEWMAN'S OTHER-WORLDLY HOLINESS

The theological basis for Newman's other-worldly holiness can be found in the *Parochial and Plain Sermons*, particularly the earlier ones. In the sermon, "The World Our Enemy" (8 March 1929), Newman set out to clarify the scriptural meaning of the term "the world," and to explain how we are to "understand the information and warnings of the sacred writer concerning it."[40] The scriptural passage that Newman selected as the theme for this sermon is 1 John 5:19, "We know that we are of God, and the whole world lieth in wickedness." In his explanation of the meaning of the term "the world," Newman made a distinction between two possible senses.

In the first sense, the world means "the present visible system of things, without taking into consideration whether it is good or bad."[41] Here Newman simply defines the world as an orderly system.[42] Elaborating further Newman says, "By the world, then, is meant this course of things, which we see carried on by means of human agency, with all its duties and pursuits."[43] Newman again stresses that the world is not a "sinful system," because it was created by God and "cannot be otherwise than good."[44] Yet he cautions that, even in this

---

35. *AW*, 153. Newman writes that he respects his parents' beliefs and is ready to obey them even if they command that he act against his own judgment.
36. *AW*, 179–80.
37. Graef, *God and Myself*, 16.
38. *AW*, 31–32.
39. *AW*, 190, 196, and 205.
40. *PPS*, 7:1436.
41. *PPS*, 7:1436.
42. *PPS*, 7:1440.
43. *PPS*, 7:1437.

sense, Christians are counseled not to love the world. The world in this sense is an enemy to our souls; the love of it is dangerous. Newman's rationale for this warning is that the possession and pursuit even of the good things of the visible world can be distractions that prevent a person from dedicating oneself fully and completely to the things of the invisible world. Even though the world is "fair and excellent," Newman states that "it is very likely to seduce our wayward hearts from our true and eternal good."[45] Attention to the things of this world "may lead us to neglect those interests which will endure when itself [the visible world] has passed away."[46] The things we do in this world, even those that are good, honest, and right in themselves are to be approached with caution because they might seduce us. Even those actions in the world that are done for the well-being of others, e.g., science, good government, acquiring wealth, preventing and relieving poverty, are especially dangerous, because they fix "our exertions on this world as an end, they go so far as to persuade us that they have no other end."[47] Such things make us think too much of success in this life and on temporal prosperity. Part of Newman's suspicion of the world here is rooted in the power of sight over faith. The visible world is known through sight, whereas the invisible world is known through faith. Consequently, there is the ever-present tendency that the visible world will distract us from the invisible world which is lasting, crucial to salvation, and, therefore, immensely more important.[48]

In the second sense, Newman defines the world in terms of its actual concrete historical existence, "the world as corrupted by man, the course of human affairs viewed in connexion with the principles, opinions, and practices, which actually direct it."[49] Understood in this sense, the world is not only dangerous, it is, as Newman says, "positively sinful."[50] Newman again insists that the world is intrinsically good because it was created by God, but, because of the Fall, the sin of Adam, the whole world has been contaminated and made evil. The infection of sin has spread throughout the whole system. Although the framework [of the world] is good and divine, the spirit and life within it are evil. As a result of the Fall, the whole world has been "plunged and steeped" in a "flood of sin."[51] No part of the world remains as God originally created it

---

44. *PPS*, 7:1437.
45. *PPS*, 7:1437.
46. *PPS*, 7:1437.
47. *PPS*, 7:1438.
48. *PPS*, 7:1438.
49. *PPS*, 7:1440.
50. *PPS*, 7:1438.

or is free from the corruption of sin. "Evil has preoccupied the whole of it, and holds fast its conquest."[52] Evil seems to have gotten the upper hand. "Evil had the start of good by many days; it filled the world, it holds it; it has the strength of possession, and it has its strength in the human heart."[53] The last few words of this quote hold the key to what Newman is saying. The sinful condition of the whole world is due more to the sinful will and weakness of humans, rather than to any lack of effectiveness in the work of God through Christ. It is human persons who love and encourage what is sinful. Once sin was set up in the world, its place was secured by human beings' unwillingness to relinquish it. So, understood in this second sense, Newman says that this world is actually a "sinful world."[54]

Newman holds that the Scriptures are warning us against the world understood in both senses. The world is an enemy of our souls in both senses. In the first sense, Christians are told to shun the world "because, however innocent its pleasures, and praiseworthy its pursuits may be, they are likely to engross us, unless we are on our guard."[55] The world is our enemy in the second sense, "because in all its best pleasures, and noblest pursuits, the seeds of sin have been sown; an enemy hath done this; so that it is most difficult to enjoy the good without partaking of the evil also."[56]

Illustrations of Newman's other-worldly holiness can be found in three of his *Parochial and Plain Sermons*, "Temporal Advantages" (23 January 1825), "The Danger of Accomplishments" (18 October 1831), and "The Danger of Riches" (1 February 1835). In the first sermon, "Temporal Advantages," Newman argues against the pursuit of temporal advantages. To begin with, the acquisition of worldly goods never fully satisfies us. There is always something beyond them for which we are striving. Since the soul was made for "religious employments and pleasures . . . no temporal blessings, however exalted or refined, can satisfy it."[57] They take time away from God and the pursuit of religious interests. To the extent that our attention is given to the pursuit of temporal advantages, our concern will be withdrawn from God and the things of the invisible world. The pursuit of temporal advantages leads us to "love the world" and to "trust in the world."[58] Although Newman admits that temporal

---

51. *PPS*, 7:1438.
52. *PPS*, 7:1438–39.
53. *PPS*, 7:1439–40.
54. *PPS*, 7:1440.
55. *PPS*, 7:1440.
56. *PPS*, 7:1440.
57. *PPS*, 7:1455–56.

advantages are not intrinsically evil, because they come from God, he still says that they are dangerous and bad for us, particularly if we seek them as ends in themselves.[59]

In the sermon, "The Danger of Accomplishments" (18 October 1831), Newman raises questions about the value of accomplishments in this world. By "accomplishments" Newman means overzealousness in "the elegant arts and studies, such as poetry, literary composition, painting, music, and the like."[60] Newman's suspicion of accomplishments is a further illustration of his otherworldly holiness. This is evident from the list of suggestions he makes toward the end of the sermon. He offers the following cautions: 1, avoid giving too much time to lighter occupations; 2, never read works of fiction or poetry, or interest ourselves in the fine arts for the mere sake of things in themselves; 3, avoid the abuse of the poetical talent; 4, singing is dangerous because of using words that have a light, or bad, meaning; and 5, the professions of stage-players and orators are dangerous ones.[61]

In another sermon, "The Danger of Riches" (1 February 1835), Newman warns his congregation of the dangers that surround the possession and the pursuit of material things. The root of the danger of riches is that they focus our attention and efforts on the visible world and distract us from God and the things of the invisible world. Riches become "a substitute in our hearts for that One Object to which our supreme devotion is due."[62] "They [riches] are present; God is unseen."[63] To Newman the greatest danger lies in the quest for riches, "desiring and pursuing them."[64] In the pursuit of riches one makes objects of this world ends in themselves, thwarting the gospel claim that Christians have no objective, end, pursuit, or business that is merely of this world. Referring to these objects as "excitements," Newman warns that their pursuit casts us out of "our serenity and stability of heavenly faith," and focuses our attention on things that fall short of what is "infinitely high and eternal."[65] Although excitements are not evil in themselves, Newman insists that "it is plainly unchristian, a manifest foolishness and sin" to seek them out.[66]

---

58. *PPS*, 7:1457.
59. *PPS*, 7:1461.
60. *PPS*, 2:461.
61. *PPS*, 2:466.
62. *PPS*, 2:447.
63. *PPS*, 2:447.
64. *PPS*, 2:449.
65. *PPS*, 2:449.

In Newman's vision of other-worldly holiness, not only is the emphasis placed upon the invisible world, but the visible world is viewed as an obstacle to the believer's pursuit of the things of the invisible world. The "world," the visible world, although good in itself and not evil, is both dangerous and sinful. It is dangerous because the possession and pursuit of the good things of this world are distractions that take one's attention away from the pursuit of the things of the invisible world. Because of the overwhelming presence of sin in the visible world, due to the Fall and human weakness, it is impossible to enjoy the positive goods of this world without also participating in the evil in this world. Newman warns against the pursuit of temporal advantages, accomplishments, and riches because they take our attention away from God and the pursuit of the things of the invisible world. In this vision of other-worldly holiness the visible world is an enemy to the pursuit of holiness because it leads the believer to love this world and trust in this world, rather than the next. Holiness comes through the denunciation and rejection of the things of the visible world.

THE TRANSITION TO A THIS-WORLDLY HOLINESS

As Newman moves away from his evangelical Anglican views, he also gradually discards this vision of other-worldly holiness, and moves toward a form of this-worldly holiness. This transition was a gradual, evolving, and uneven process that occurred between the years 1828 and 1845. The start of this period is marked by the beginning of Newman's reading of the early Christian writers during the long vacation of 1828.[67] Through his reading of the early Christian writers, two notions were integrated more fully into his theological thinking: one is the sacramental principle; the second is the Christian teaching on the indwelling of the Holy Spirit. Both of these topics figure significantly in the development of Newman's this-worldly holiness. The end-point of this period, 1845, coincides with the writing of the *Essay on the Development of Christian Doctrine*. Hilda Graef points out that, by the time of the *Essay on the Development of Christian Doctrine*, Newman's view of holiness had clearly changed.[68] Jose

---

66. Newman tells his congregation that "[a] life of money-getting is a life of care; from the first there is a fearful anticipation of loss in various ways to depress and unsettle the mind; nay to haunt it, till a man finds he can think about nothing else, and is unable to give his mind to religion, from the constant whirl of business in which he is involved" (*PPS*, 2:451). To this he adds that the pursuit of gain is detrimental to the spiritual life of the Christian because "it fixes the mind upon an object of this world; yet others remain behind" (*PPS*, 2:452).

67. *AW*, 84.

Morales maintains that Newman's transition from an other-worldly to a this-worldly holiness "becomes visible especially from 1845 onwards."[69]

THE SACRAMENTAL PRINCIPLE

In the *Apologia Pro Vita Sua* Newman discusses the sacramental principle in three places.[70] In the first instance he associates it with his reading in 1825 of Joseph Butler's work, *The Analogy of Religion*. Newman states that one of the things he learned from Butler is that there is an analogy between the separate works of God that "leads to the conclusion that the system which is of less importance is economically or sacramentally connected with the more momentous system."[71] Here Newman maintains that there is a sacramental connection between the things in the visible world and those in the invisible world. Newman's second mention of the sacramental principle in the *Apologia* can be found in his summary of the influence that John Keble had upon his thinking. From reading Keble's book of poems, *The Christian Year*, 1827, Newman states that one of the things that was "brought home" to him was the sacramental system, that is, "the doctrine that material phenomena are both the types and the instruments of real things unseen."[72] Again, Newman affirms that this is the same principle that he had learned from Joseph Butler, but that it had been "recast in the creative mind of my new master [Keble]."[73] In the

---

68. Graef, *God and Myself*, 98–99. Graef states that by this time Newman had come to see that Christianity's home is in this world, that his one-sided moralistic outlook of the earlier years was gone, that the incarnation was the central aspect of Christianity, and that he had developed a more positive attitude toward human nature. As evidence for this view Graef quotes the following passage from the *Essay on the Development of Christian Doctrine*, "Its home [Christianity's] is in the world; and to know what it is, we must seek it in the world . . ." John Henry Newman, *An Essay on the Development of Christian Doctrine*, forward by Ian Ker (Notre Dame: University of Notre Dame Press, 1989), 4 (hereafter, *Dev*).

69. Jose Morales, "Newman's Ideal of Holiness in This World," 148–51, in *Christliche Heiligkeit als Lehre und Praxis nach John Henry Newman*, ed. Gunter Biemer and Heinrich Fries (Sigmaringendorf: Regio-Verlag Glock und Lutz, 1988), 153.

70. John Henry Newman, *Apologia Pro Vita Sua*, ed. A. Dwight Culler (Boston: Houghton Mifflin, 1956) (hereafter, *Apo*). In the *Apologia* Newman uses a number of terms to refer to the sacramental principle. He calls it the "sacramental economy" (*Apo*, 31), the "sacramental system" (*Apo*, 39), the "mystical or sacramental principle" (*Apo*, 46), and he connects it with the principle of analogy that he learned from Joseph Butler (*Apo*, 31 and 39).

71. *Apo*, 31. The full title of Joseph Butler's work is *The Analogy of Religion: Natural and Revealed, to the Constitution and Course of Nature* (1736).

72. *Apo*, 39.

73. *Apo*, 39.

third reference to the sacramental principle in the *Apologia,* Newman asserts that his reading of the early Christian writers, which began in 1828, reaffirmed his acceptance of the sacramental principle. With great enthusiasm, he writes that he was carried away by reading the works of Clement and Origen which, he states, were "based on the mystical and sacramental principle," namely, "that the exterior world, physical and historical, was but the manifestation to our senses of realities greater than itself."[74] Newman's acceptance of the sacramental principle enabled him to focus on the connection between the invisible world and the visible world, rather than on the opposition between the two. Through the sacramental principle the things in this world can be viewed in a more positive way, because they are actually seen as vehicles for entering and experiencing the invisible world.

The sacraments and the prayer life of the visible Church provide the believer with an entrance into the invisible world.[75] Through its sacramental and liturgical life the Church enables the Christian to encounter the invisible world. In the sermon, "The Visible Church an Encouragement to Faith" (14 September 1834), Newman tells his congregation, "He who comes to Church to worship God, be he high or low, enters into that heavenly world of Saints of which I have been speaking. For in the Services of worship we elicit and realize the invisible."[76] Even the "ordinances we behold," "the very disposition of the building," "the altar with its fine adornments," are "figures of things unseen."[77] Newman adds that Sunday attendance at Church itself can give the believer "a glimpse of things unseen."[78] Through its sacramental and prayer life, the Church, as it were, becomes the steward of the mysteries of the invisible

---

74. *Apo,* 46–47. Newman goes on to speak about the various "Economies and Dispensations of the Eternal" such as divine dispensations for non-Christians and Jews. He speaks about how the "sacramental principle" allows for a gradual divine revelation: "And thus room was made for the anticipation of further and deeper disclosure of truths still under the veil of the letter, and in their season to be revealed" (*Apo,* 46). Geoffrey Wainwright suggests that Newman's notion of the sacramental principle raises systematic and ecumenical questions in three areas, the material reality of the Christian Sacraments, the value of other religions for salvation, and the historical and eschatological scope of the ecclesial dispensation. Geoffrey Wainwright, "Dispensations of Grace, Newman on the Sacramental Mediation of Salvation," in *Newman and Faith, Louvain Theological and Pastoral Monographs,* ed. Ian Ker and Terrence Merrigan (Louvain: Peeters/Grand Rapids: Eerdmans, 2001), 148.

75. Graef, *God and Myself,* 62. Graef says that, for Newman, sacraments introduce the Christian into the invisible world.

76. *PPS,* 3:641.

77. *PPS,* 3:642.

78. *PPS,* 3:642.

world.[79] As Newman says, the invisible Church is "gradually moulded and matured in the visible Church."[80]

THE INDWELLING OF THE HOLY SPIRIT

The second element that plays a major role in the development of Newman's this-worldly holiness is his understanding of the indwelling of the Holy Spirit. From his evangelical conversion in 1816, through the years of the Oxford Movement, through the crisis of his doubts about the Anglican Church, through his years as a Catholic, and up to the moment of his death, Newman had a special devotion to the Holy Spirit.[81] Charles Dessain maintains that this Christian teaching was an inspiration and support for Newman during the whole of his long career up to his death.[82] In 1828, after reading the early Christian writers, the doctrine of the indwelling of the Holy Spirit was given a more central role in Newman's theology. The notion of the indwelling of the Holy Spirit is so central in Newman's thought that it becomes the foundation of his understanding of Christian spirituality. For Newman, spirituality is the ongoing effort to live in the presence of the indwelling Spirit and the process of realizing the presence of the Spirit in this world.[83]

---

79. Graef, *God and Myself*, 64. Graef quotes a passage from Newman's sermon, "The World's Benefactors" (November 30, 1830), to support her view. See *PPS*, 2:235.

80. *PPS*, 3:636.

81. John Henry Newman, *Meditations and Devotions of the Late Cardinal Newman* (New York: Longmans, Green, & Co., 1903), 398.

82. Charles S. Dessain, *The Spirituality of John Henry Newman* (Minneapolis: Winston, 1980), 79. Dessain maintains that, although the doctrine of the indwelling remained the support of Newman's life throughout his years as a Catholic, on becoming a Catholic he wrote little on the subject. "The atmosphere of the times was not propitious, and as a convert he did not wish to set up as a dogmatic and mystical teacher" (Dessain, *Spirituality*, 94–95). Dessain also points out that when Newman reissued the *Parochial and Plain Sermons* as a Catholic, he did not retract any of the things that he had said about the indwelling of the Holy Spirit (Dessain, *Spirituality*, 96–97). Further evidence that Newman never abandoned the doctrine of the indwelling of the Holy Spirit as a Catholic can be found in the Catholic work, *Meditations and Devotions*, 396–411.

83. For an in-depth analysis of Newman's notion of the Indwelling of the Holy Spirit and its role in his understanding of spirituality see chapter two. It also is around this time that Newman begins to move away from an evangelical understanding of justification, and the indwelling of the Holy Spirit plays a pivotal role in his revised understanding of justification. As an evangelical, Newman held a radical understanding of justification by faith alone. Justification is not brought about through the sacrament of baptism, but only by the acceptance of the gospel through faith. Righteousness is imputed to all those who are justified by faith. At this point in his understanding, Newman makes a radical distinction between justification and regeneration. Justification is an instantaneous and extrinsic gift. Regeneration, on the other hand, is a gradual internal change within the person that leads the person toward a more

The indwelling of the Holy Spirit provides the Christian with an entrance into the next world.[84] It enables the believer living in the visible world to encounter the things of the invisible world. In the sermon, "The Gifts of the Spirit" (November 1835), Newman speaks of the indwelling of the Holy Spirit as an illumination.[85] Reminding us that illumination comes through baptism, Newman states that it provides the Christian with "a personal entrance into the next world," and "a portion of heavenly glory."[86] In fact, those who have received the indwelling of the Holy Spirit can be said to be in heaven: "They are in Heaven, in the world of the spirits, and are placed in the way of all manner of invisible influences." Immediately following this, Newman adds, "'Their conversation is in heaven'; they live among the angels, and are within the reach (as I may say) of the Saints departed."[87] Remarking on the mysterious nature of this amazing gift, Newman says, "I myself, who speak, am at this moment in Heaven too, even in my human nature."[88] This theme is repeated in the sermon, "Mental Prayer" (13 December 1829), when Newman states that "the new birth of the Holy Spirit sets the soul in motion in a heavenly way."[89] Through the indwelling of the Holy Spirit, Newman adds, "the true Christian pierces through the veil of this world and sees the next."[90]

Awareness of the presence of the indwelling of the Holy Spirit comes through prayer and meditation. Prayer, for Newman, is entering into conversation and communion with the indwelling Spirit. According to James Keating, the indwelling Spirit was the touchstone for Newman and his prayer life. To this Keating adds, "For Newman, to pray was to enter within, to

---

complete moral holiness. Newman develops his new understanding of justification in the 1834 sermon, "The Indwelling Spirit." Here the emphasis is placed on the indwelling of the Holy Spirit, not on the moment of justification. Regeneration is understood to be instantaneous, rather than a gradual process. It effects a real change in the believer. It is not simply the imputation of God's righteousness. Also, baptism does not merely impute righteousness, but actually brings about a real change in the believer through the indwelling of the Holy Spirit. Both justification and regeneration are effected simultaneously through the indwelling of the Holy Spirit. The presence of the Holy Spirit within the person is the author of both faith and renewal (*PPS*, 2:365–74). Newman also presents his revised view of justification in his *Lectures on the Doctrine Justification* (London: Longmans, Green, & Co., 1900).

84. Graef, *God and Myself*, 64.

85. *PPS*, 3:650. Graef, *God and Myself*, 64. Graef says that illumination is a term frequently used by the early Christian writers as a synonym for baptism.

86. *PPS*, 3:650.

87. *PPS*, 3:650.

88. *PPS*, 3:650–51.

89. *PPS*, 7:1539.

90. *PPS*, 7:1540.

converse with the indwelling Spirit."[91] Vincent Blehl maintains that, for Newman, "prayer is the breadth and pulse of the spiritual life within us, the new life implanted by the Holy Spirit."[92] Prayer forms and nourishes the believer's communion with God in and through the indwelling Spirit. Keating states that prayer, for Newman, is "*a state of communion*, of being at peace in the presence of God."[93] Through prayer Newman came to the reality of the Spirit dwelling within him.[94] So important is the life of prayer to Newman that, without it, the indwelling of the Holy Spirit could never become a reality.[95] Mental prayer (meditation), for Newman, is an essential and necessary part of every believer's prayer life. It is through meditation that a notional assent to the doctrine of the indwelling Spirit can become a real assent. Meditation leads to an experience of the inner presence of God and the invisible world that is not merely intellectual and notional, but one that engages the entire person in the depths of one's being.[96] For Newman, prayer and meditation are essential elements in the ongoing quest to realize the presence of the indwelling Spirit and to grow in the spiritual life.[97] Through prayer and meditation the invisible world becomes present in the visible world.

Newman's This-Worldly Holiness

"You men of Galilee, why stand you looking up into heaven?"

–Acts 1:12

"You cannot see the unseen world all at once."

–PPS, 7:1542

---

91. James Keating, "Newman: Theologian of Prayer," *Downside Review* 122 (January 2004), 12.

92. Vincent Ferrer Blehl, SJ, *The White Stone: The Spiritual Theology of John Henry Newman* (Petersham, MA: St. Bede's, 1993), 137.

93. Keating, "Newman," 7.

94. Keating, "Newman," 4.

95. Zeno, *John Henry Newman: His Inner Life* (San Francisco: Ignatius, 1987), 274.

96. Zeno, *Newman: Inner Life*, 274–75.

97. Keating, "Newman," 4.

The sacramental principle and the doctrine of the indwelling of the Holy Spirit enable Newman to look at this world more positively and to see the visible world as a vehicle for entering into the invisible world. The visible world becomes a window to the invisible world. The invisible world, through the sacramental principle and the indwelling of the Holy Spirit, is present in this world and can be encountered in this world. Consequently, Newman's holiness can be described as a this-worldly holiness. In his work, *Historical Sketches*, Newman states that "Christianity is a religion for this world."[98] From the perspective of a this-worldly holiness, a Christian holiness begins with an engagement of this world, not with its rejection.

The pursuit of the things of the invisible world is no justification for abandoning the tasks and duties of this world.[99] In the sermon, "Doing Glory to God in Pursuits of the World (1 November 1836), Newman states that those who place their exclusive attention on the next life "are apt to undervalue this life altogether, and to forget its real importance."[100] What is even worse, Newman says, is that Christians sometimes think that the unseen world ought to take their attention away from this world. "Men come to fancy that to lose taste and patience for the businesses of this life is renouncing the world and becoming spiritually-minded.'"[101] Sometimes Christians come to think that the ordinary business of this world is something beneath them. They think that having a spiritual mind means renouncing all worldly employments, claiming to take no interest in them, and despising the natural and ordinary pleasures of life.[102] Newman severely criticizes this view: "In various ways does the thought of the next world lead men to neglect their duty in this; and whenever it does so we may be sure that there is something wrong and unchristian . . . in their manner of thinking of it [the next world]."[103]

The true Christian, Newman says, "will see Christ revealed to his soul amid the ordinary actions of the day, as by sort of a sacrament. Thus he will take his worldly business as a gift from Him, and will love it as such."[104] In Newman's

---

98. John Henry Newman, *Historical Sketches* (London: Longmans, Green, & Co., 1912), 2:94. See also Jose Morales, "Newman's Holiness," 151.

99. Morales, "Newman's Holiness," 151–52. Morales states that this is a possibility that Newman severely criticizes.

100. *PPS*, 8:1656.

101. *PPS*, 8:1657. Newman says that this is the temptation to which Christians in all ages have been exposed.

102. *PPS*, 8:1658.

103. *PPS*, 8:1656.

104. *PPS*, 8:1662.

this-worldly spirituality, holiness is to be found by throwing oneself completely into the duties of one's daily life and performing them as well as one can. Newman states that God is best served "when men are not slothful in business, but do their duty in that state of life which it has pleased God to call them."[105] In a letter to George Ryder (2 December 1850), Newman writes that the greatest mortification of the Christian "is to do well the ordinary duties of the day."[106] It is important to stress that in Newman's vision of this-worldly holiness, holiness is to be found in and through the performance of one's duties in this world, not in trying to escape from this world in order to get to the next. While in the world, Newman says, the Christian glorifies God, "not *out* of it [the visible world], but in it, and by means of it."[107] In the sermon, "Rising with Christ" (1836 or 1837), Newman tells his congregation that "I am not calling you to go out of the world, or to abandon your duties in the world, but to redeem time."[108] Perfection is to be found in performing the daily duties of one's life. "[I]f we would aim at perfection, we must perform well the duties of the day. I do not know anything more difficult, more sobering, so strengthening than the constant aim to go through the ordinary day's work well."[109] In Newman's this-worldly holiness, the world and its duties are the normal locus in which Christians live out their vocation.[110]

Significance of Newman's This-Worldly Holiness

Newman's vision of this-worldly holiness has a number of spiritual lessons to offer Catholic laywomen and men living in the Church and the world of the twenty-first century. Jose Morales points out that Newman was one of the first Catholic thinkers to view the temporal work of the laity in the world as an aspect of the Church's mission.[111] Newman understood the layperson's role

---

105. *PPS*, 8:1658.
106. *LD*, 14:153.
107. *PPS*, 8:1658.
108. *PPS*, 6:1323.
109. Placid Murray, OSB, ed., *Newman the Oratorian: His Unpublished Oratory Papers* (Dublin: Gill & Macmillan, 1969), 235. This citation is from Newman's Oratory Paper, no. 10, 11 December 1850. See also Murray, *Newman the Oratorian*, 359, where in a 27 September 1856 Chapter Address, Newman says, "It is the saying of holy men that, if we wish to be perfect we have nothing more to do than to perform the ordinary duties of the day well."
110. Morales, "Newman's Holiness," 153. Morales thinks that Newman is not just suggesting that temporal tasks are only a means to an eternal end, but that they have value in themselves and should be performed also for their own sake. Morales, "Newman's Holiness," 152.
111. Morales, "Newman's Holiness," 158–59.

in the Church as a "Christian living in the World," in a positive way.[112] In the Second Vatican Council, the Catholic Church embraced and accepted the temporal vocation of the laity in the world. The *Decree on the Lay Apostolate* states that the laity exercise their apostolate in the Church by "penetrating and perfecting the temporal order through the spirit of the Gospel."[113] To this the document adds, "Since this is a characteristic of their state of life, to live in the midst of the secular business of the world, they are called by God to exercise their apostolate in the world like a leaven, with the ardor of the spirit of Christ."[114]

In his vision of this-worldly holiness Newman offers the laity today a model for living out their temporal vocation in the world. It is through the performance of one's daily duties in this world that one will encounter God and the things of the invisible world. "The employments of this world, though not in themselves heavenly, are, after all, the way to heaven."[115] God is found in all the things that one experiences in daily life. The true Christian, Newman says, will see God in all things: "[I]n whatever comes upon him, he [the Christian] will endeavour to discern and gaze (as it were) on the countenance of the Saviour."[116] Quoting 1 Cor. 10:31, which states that whatever we do, whether we eat or drink, everything should be done for the glory of God, Newman says that it appears that nothing is too slight or trivial to glorify God.[117] Newman tells his congregation that the mark of a truly spiritual person is that he or she is consistent in a "jealous carefulness about all things little and great."[118] In the sermon, "Secrecy and Suddenness of Divine Visitation" (2 February 1831), Newman reminds his congregation "how mysteriously little things are in this world connected with great; how single moments, improved or wasted, are the salvation or ruin of all-important interests."[119] For the Christian, "true contemplation of the Saviour lies *in* his worldly business."[120] Christ is seen in "the employments which he puts upon His chosen, whatever they may be."[121]

---

112. Morales, "Newman's Holiness," 159.

113. Second Vatican Council, *Decree on the Apostolate of the Laity, Apostolicam Actuositatem* (Washington, DC: National Catholic Welfare Conference, 1965), no. 2 (hereafter, *AA*).

114. *AA*, no. 2.

115. *PPS*, 8:1656.

116. *PPS*, 8:1662.

117. PPS, 8:1656.

118. *PPS*, 2:329, "Saving Knowledge" (Monday, Easter Week, 1835).

119. *PPS*, 2:299–300. See also Ian Ker, *John Henry Newman: A Biography* (Oxford: Oxford University Press, 1988), 93.

120. *PPS*, 8:1662.

121. *PPS*, 8:1662.

For Newman true holiness permeates the entire life of the believer. As he tells his congregation in the sermon "Mental Prayer," "A man cannot be religious one hour, and not religious the next. . . . A man who is religious, is religious morning, noon, and night; . . . He sees God in all things, every course of action he directs towards those spiritual objects which God has revealed to him; every occurrence of the day, every event, every person met with, all news which he hears, he measures by the standard of God's will."[122]

Since Newman's this-worldly holiness permeates the entire life of the believer in this world, it would be a mistake to interpret it as a merely individual personal piety. Clearly, Newman was not a liberation theologian in the contemporary sense, but his this-worldly holiness is a vision of holiness that is open to the transformation of society, as well as individuals. Following in the spirit of the Second Vatican Council, Newman's vision of holiness can comfortably be extended to the social dimension. In speaking of the temporal mission of the laity, the Second Vatican Council says that preeminent among the works of the laity is Christian social action.[123] The Council describes the apostolate of the laity in the social dimension as the "effort to infuse the Christian spirit into the mentality, customs, laws, and structures of the community in which one lives."[124] In their role of building up society, the laity "strive to discharge their domestic, social and professional responsibilities with Christian generosity."[125]

The primary objective of Newman's this-worldly holiness is to live daily life in the presence of the indwelling Spirit and to work to make the Spirit present in all things in this world. This would include not only self but others and the structures of society, both in Church and state. When speaking of seeing God in all things, Newman makes a reference to Christ being seen in the poor, the persecuted, and in children.[126] In speaking of poverty in the sermon, "Mental Prayer," Newman says that it seems clear that, according to the Gospel, the absence of wealth is a more blessed and more Christian state than the possession of it.[127] Furthermore, the indwelling of the Holy Spirit has

---

122. *PPS*, 7:1536–37. Here Newman is speaking about a person's duty to pray based upon reason and conscience (*PPS*, 7:1536). Newman states that a person with this awareness of the presence of God can be said to be praying without ceasing (*PPS*, 7:1537). Everything one does is a prayer.

123. *AA*, no. 7.

124. *AA*, no. 13.

125. *AA*, no. 13.

126. *PPS*, 8:1662, "Doing Glory to God in Pursuits of the World" (1 November 1836). In the sermon, "Christ Hidden from the World" (25 December 1837), Newman states that "[a]gain: He has made the poor, weak, and afflicted, tokens and instruments of His Presence . . ." (*PPS*, 4:893).

implications for Catholic Social Teaching. Not only does the indwelling of the Holy Spirit enhance the dignity of the human person that comes through creation, but it unites all those in whom the Spirit dwells. Imagine what effect the realization that God dwells in each human person would have upon the believer in approaching issues of injustice, like poverty, racism, various forms of oppression, war, discrimination, and women's rights. The indwelling of the Holy Spirit makes us "realize how intricately we are connected to the rest of the world and that our righteousness is meant to spread to the far corners of the Earth and not just to our immediate needs."[128] It is common among some liberation theologians today to see a connection between daily life experience and the social responsibility of Christians. Ada Maria Isasi-Diaz, a contemporary U.S. Latina liberation theologian, speaks about the daily life experience, "*lo cotidiano*," as a source of theology.[129] It is in their daily life, their work, their need for food and shelter, their relationship with family and friends, their encounters with authority, their experiences of faith such as in praying and in the liturgy, that defines the reality of Latinas. It is the "stuff" of their reality.[130] The only way to make the Spirit fully present in their daily lives is to work to overcome all forms of oppression—personal and structural.

When the laity receive their apostolate from Christ through baptism, they are incorporated into the Church as the People of God. As a result, the temporal vocation of the laity is also a participation in the mission of the Church. The *Constitution on the Church* of the Second Vatican Council teaches that the lay apostolate is a participation in the mission of the Church itself. According to this document, every layperson is "a witness and a living instrument of the mission of the Church itself."[131] For Newman as well, the temporal vocation of the laity is a participation in the salvific mission of the Church. It is through baptism that one receives the Holy Spirit and is incorporated into the Church. For Newman, sacrament and the indwelling of the Holy Spirit come together in the Church. What constitutes the Church for Newman is the indwelling of the Holy Spirit. In the sermon, "The Church Visible and Invisible" (25 October 1835), Newman tells his congregation that the "Church would cease to be the

---

127. *PPS*, 2:447.

128. Magali Del Bueno Riancho, "Veni Sancte Spiritus: The Indwelling of the Holy Spirit in John Henry Newman's Theology," an unpublished paper given at Loyola Marymount University, 2011.

129. Ada Maria Isasi-Diaz, *Mujerista Theology: A Theology for the Twenty-first Century* (Maryknoll, NY: Orbis, 1996), 66.

130. Isasi-Diaz, *Mujerista Theology*, 66–67.

131. Second Vatican Council, *Constitution on the Church*, *Lumen Gentium* (Washington, DC: National Catholic Welfare Conference, 1964), no. 33 (hereafter, *LG*).

Church, did the Holy Spirit leave it; and it does not exist at all except in the Spirit."[132] Gerald Dolan maintains that, for Newman, the gift of the Holy Spirit cannot be "dissociated from the constitution and mission of the Church."[133] In his sermon, "The Gift of the Spirit," Newman calls the dispensation under which the Church exists "the ministration of the Spirit."[134] It is through its sacraments that the Church makes the indwelling Spirit present in the world. The Church's sacraments are the instruments that the Holy Spirit uses to bring about salvation.[135] Through the indwelling of the Spirit in the Church, the laity are empowered to live in the Spirit in their daily lives and to work to make the Spirit present in the world. By doing so, the invisible world becomes present in the visible world.[136]

Newman's this-worldly holiness challenges Catholic laywomen and men to live their faith at its most fundamental level. Faith is not a product that needs to be correctly branded. For Newman faith is not a notional assent, but a real assent. Faith is a personal relationship with God through Christ mediated in and through the indwelling of the Holy Spirit. Catholic laity are called to live in the presence of the indwelling Spirit and to work to make God's Spirit of love present in the Church and the world. In the sermon, "Ventures of Faith" (21 February 1836), Newman says that it is of the very essence of faith to make "present what is unseen."[137] As a result, the vocation of Catholic laymen and women is a secular one. They are called to embrace the world and all things human, and to participate with God in the Spirit in the transformation of the world by working to facilitate the presence of the indwelling of the Holy Spirit in this world, and making heaven present on earth.

---

132. *PPS*, 3:625. In the sermon, "Unreal Words" (2 June 1839), Newman says that if the seductions of the world eat out this divine inward life, the outward Church is "but a hollowness and a mockery," like the "whited sepulchers" of which Christ speaks (*PPS*, 5:984–85). When this happens, Newman says that we still trust that the Holy Spirit has not totally deserted the Church, "yet we may say that in proportion as it approaches to this state of deadness, the grace of its ordinances, though not forfeited, at least flows in but a scanty or uncertain stream" (*PPS*, 5:985).

133. Gerald Dolan, OFM, "The Gift of the Spirit According to Newman (1828–1839)," *Franciscan Studies* 30 (1970): 98. He adds that, for Newman, the distinguishing grace of the gospel dispensation is the indwelling of the Holy Spirit in individual Christians and in the whole Church (96).

134. *PPS*, 3:644.

135. *PPS*, 3:626.

136. *PPS*, 3:637. In the sermon, "The Visible Church an Encouragement to Faith" (14 September 1834), Newman states, "The Holy Spirit has vouchsafed to take up His abode in the Church, and the Church will ever bear, on its front, the visible signs of its hidden privilege."

137. *PPS*, 4:923.

9

John Henry Newman and the Communion of Saints

Brian W. Hughes

As an Oratorian, Newman embodied and professed the spiritual values and charism of St. Philip Neri in his life's work and spirituality. Concerning Newman, St. Philip is usually discussed in reference to the historical foundations of the oratory, his Rule (compiled later by Oratorians, not St. Philip), and religious maxims. Certainly, he and other Birmingham and London Oratorians referenced these historical and practical elements during Newman's life. Such details remain significant in expanding any serious portrait of Newman and any nuanced view of Oratorian spirituality. Yet, it seems to me that scholars' historical focus upon St. Philip Neri is overly narrow. It overlooks Newman's lived experience of St. Philip, theologically and spiritually, which appears throughout his writings and letters.[1] This gap in scholarship raises a question: Does Newman's relationship to St. Philip tell us anything significant theologically for Christian life today? I believe it does.

A focus upon saints more generally seems all the more pressing today. In our modern, highly technological and yet more self-alienating world, it becomes a challenge for Christians to maintain their faith in the living reality of God. If institutional affiliation is some evidence of religious commitment, Catholic Christianity in the United States continues to be in trouble. This past year, the Pew Research Center reports that strong Catholic identity has been in

1. No mention of the spiritual relationship between Newman and St. Philip is made by biographers Ian Ker, *John Henry Newman* (Oxford: Oxford University Press, 1988); Sheridan Gilley, *Newman and His Age* (London: Darton, Longman, & Todd, 1990); Avery Cardinal Dulles, SJ, *Newman* (New York: Continuum, 2002); or Frank M. Turner, *John Henry Newman: The Challenge to Evangelical Religion* (New Haven: Yale University Press, 2002). Exceptions include Dr. Zeno, *John Henry Newman: His Inner Life* (San Francisco: Ignatius, 1987), 134–35.

decline, as has mass attendance, for over thirty years.[2] This decline accompanies an increasing segment—one in five!—of American society that religiously self-identifies as "none."[3] It cannot be denied, however, that in the context of these changing religious attitudes, talk of the "saints" might seem quaint, almost naïve, perhaps conjuring comforting or kitsch images from bygone ages but hardly relevant to the self-disclosure of God in people's lives today.[4] David Matzko McCarthy crystallizes the problem: "Our modern problem is not that God has made himself a distant monarch, but that our lives, especially our social roles and personal space, have become distant from what we presume to be an ever-present and loving God. We have difficulty mapping out the meaning of things."[5]

Newman's relationship with St. Philip Neri certainly can demonstrate to contemporary seekers and Christians the meaning of a saint in human life. Newman's own spiritual journey provides a case study for Christians who desire to understand a personal and theological interpretation of the communion of saints. Embodied holiness can attract and orient in ways far richer than what institutional organizations seem to be offering today. Specifically, this essay will touch on three areas: 1) St. Philip and the method of personal influence; 2) how Newman understands the doctrine of the communion of saints; and 3) what St. Philip's relationship to Newman meant as patron and friend. My hope, after considering these areas, is to suggest how they interconnect and provide some insight for Christians seeking a better way to understand how the communion of saints can be spiritually relevant today.

St. Philip Neri: Method of Influence

St. Philip Neri (1515–1595), known as the Apostle of Rome, arrived there in 1534. He had left his native city of Florence at eighteen. Praying in the Roman catacombs in 1544, Philip had a profound, mystical experience of the Holy Spirit that, according to biographers, inflamed his heart with great love and

---

2. "Strong Catholic Identity at a Four-Decade Low in U.S." The Pew Forum on Religion & Public Life, accessed 19 June 2013 at http://www.pewforum.org/Christian/Catholic/Strong-Catholic-Identity-at-a-Four-Decade-Low-in-US.aspx.

3. "'Nones' on the Rise." The Pew Forum on Religion & Public Life, accessed 19 June 2013 at http://www.pewforum.org/Unaffiliated/nones-on-the-rise.aspx.

4. David Brown remarks that "as contemporary scandals make us increasingly aware of the fallibility of the Church, there has been a corresponding decline in the interesting conventional books about the saints." *Through the Eyes of the Saints: A Pilgrimage Through History* (London: Continuum, 2005), xi.

5. David Matzko McCarthy, *Sharing God's Good Company: A Theology of the Communion of Saints* (Grand Rapids: Eerdmans, 2012), 27.

joy. Ordained in 1551, Philip was close to the Jesuits, especially Francis Xavier, and almost joined them. Before forming the Oratory, he served in hospitals and influenced widely different people through his humility, simplicity, and sense of humor, which was legendary. He is especially known for disdaining and ridiculing all forms of showiness and vanity, dismantling the intentions and excitement of even those who would honor him.[6] Newman points out that though St. Philip deeply admired the radical reformer Girolamo Savanarola—eventually excommunicated, hung, and burned—he understood his mission to be the opposite of Savanarola's, working quietly in the background and avoiding attention.[7] His life's work was pastoral. He was not a scholar either, as he wrote no doctrinal or spiritual treatises.[8] What distinguished him was his character, his person. Philip drew many people to himself through his warm personality, finding a special apostolate as spiritual master and confessor.[9]

Newman, too, was drawn to St. Philip Neri and, subsequently, to the Congregation of the Oratory for a variety of reasons: personality, flexibility, room for study and writing, preference for the Athenian style of religious life over the Spartan (the Spartans are the Jesuits, of course).[10] Surely, one of the reasons was not what Fr. Faber claimed in *The Spirit and Genius of St. Philip Neri*: "[T]he prominent object of the Oratorian is to become an affectionately servile copy of St. Philip, and that his whole spiritual life is to lead that way."[11] One could make a strong case that Newman's intellectual apostolate differed considerably from St. Philip's pastoral one. Like all original thinkers and innovators, Newman borrowed and built upon in order to transform. This point rings true if one examines what Newman refers to as the method of St. Philip, which is nothing less than the way of the saints. In describing St. Philip's

---

6. John Henry Cardinal Newman, *Apologia Pro Vita Sua and Six Sermons*, edited, annotated, and with an introduction by Frank M. Turner (New Haven and London: Yale University Press, 2008), 352.

7. Newman, "The Mission of St. Philip Neri," *Sermons Preached on Various Occasions* (Notre Dame: Gracewing, 2007). Newman says "He did not 'contend nor cry out, nor break the bruised reed, nor quench the smoking flax;' . . . so was it in the beginning, so has it been ever since. After the storm, the earthquake and the fire, the calm, soothing whisper of the fragrant air. After Savanarola, Philip" (219) (hereafter, *OS*).

8. Louis Bouyer writes, "Philip neither taught any special doctrine nor any special devotions." *The Roman Socrates*, trans. Michael Day (Westminster, MD: Newman, 1958), 26.

9. For a more detailed treatment, see Paul Türks, *Philip Neri: The Fire of Joy*, trans. Daniel Utrecht (Edinburgh: T. & T. Clark, 1995).

10. See John Henry Newman, *Rise and Progress of Universities*, intro. by Mary Katherine Tillman (Notre Dame: Gracewing, 2001), 85f.

11. Frederick William Faber, *The Spirit and Genius of St. Philip Neri* (London: Burns & Lambert, 1850), 4.

approach to the difficult problems of his own age—for example, increasing pride, sensuality, love of political intrigue and power, which also accompanied a new fascination with beauty, "classical literature and art"—Newman holds that St. Philip countered this not with aggressive condemnation or "argument" but with the "great counter-fascination of purity and truth."[12] On several occasions, Newman speaks of St. Philip and the Oratorian charism as having a "method." This is the method of personal influence.[13]

An important reference to this method occurs in the context of education. It speaks to both Newman's educational philosophy and the religious charism of the Oratory. Newman contrasts Athens with Rome: Athenian democracy, freedom, and liberality in daily life are quite opposed to Rome's imperial force, system, and strict laws. This distinction between Athens and Rome parallels the differences between the key characteristics of the Oratory and of other religious orders, especially the Jesuits! In each case, Newman distinguishes two important "principles of action in human affairs, Influence and System, some ecclesiastical institutions are based upon System, and others upon Influence." Systems, whether philosophical, theological, or religious, tend toward strict organization, consistency, uniformity, expansion, establishing logical frameworks within which one can think and act.[14] With the principle of influence, other characteristics assume priority. Newman states:

> I repeat . . . it was the absence of rule, it was the action of personality, the intercourse of soul with soul, the play of mind upon mind, it was an admirable spontaneous force, which kept the schools of Athens going, and made the pulses of foreign intellects keep time with hers. Now, I say, if there be an Institution in the Catholic Church, which in this point of view has caught the idea of this great heathen precursor of the Truth, and has made the idea Christian,—if it proceeds from one who has even gained for himself the title of the "Amabile Santo,"—who has placed the noblest aims before his children, yet withal the freest course; who always drew them to their duty, instead of commanding, and brought them on to perform before they had yet promised . . . who in his humility had no intention of forming any Congregation at all, but had formed it before he knew of it, from the beauty and the fascination of his own

---

12. John Henry Newman, *The Idea of a University*, ed. I. T. Ker (Oxford: Clarendon, 1976), 199 (hereafter, *Idea*).

13. See *Idea*, 202; see also Newman, *Rise and Progress of Universities*, 87.

14. Newman, *Rise and Progress of Universities*, 86–88.

saintliness; and then, when he was obliged to recognize it and put it into shape, shrank from the severity of the Regular, would have nothing to say to vows, and forbade propagation and dominion; whose houses stand, like Greek colonies, independent of each other and complete in themselves; whose subjects in those several houses are allowed, like Athenian citizens, freely to cultivate their respective gifts and to follow out their own mission; whose one rule is Love, and whose own weapon Influence . . .[15]

The method of influence as a principle of action is far less constrained, less symmetrical, and far less uniform. In many ways, there is greater freedom for expression, spontaneity, and individual creativity within it. These characteristics can be seen again in another important description of St. Philip. Newman writes that Philip's "weapons should be but unaffected humility and unpretending love. All he did was to be done by the light, and fervour, and convincing eloquence of his personal character and his easy conversation."[16] To a large extent, this is how Newman describes the power of the saints in a draft preface of Faber's *Lives of the Saints* in 1848.[17] It is precisely this power of personal presence, Christian virtue embodied, that Newman already believed was more important to use in confronting the skeptical and sensual climate of his time than any rational argument or evidence. This principle holds true in education, in religious formation, in dealing with people generally.[18] "We consider," writes Newman, "that the Lives of the Saints are one of the main and special instruments, to which, under God, we may look for the conversion of our countrymen at this time."[19]

Now, I am not claiming that Newman learned the significance of personal influence solely from St. Philip Neri. He held it to be paramount in his Anglican years, especially in 1832, the year he delivered his university sermon, "Personal Influence, the Means of Propagating the Truth."[20] In addition, he noted the value of personal influence to Dr. Wiseman just a few years before his

---

15. Newman, *Rise and Progress of Universities*, 86–88.

16. *Idea*, 200.

17. See *The Letters and Diaries of John Henry Newman*, ed. Stephen C. Dessain (London: Nelson, 1962/ Oxford: Clarendon, 1961), 12:399, Appendix 5 (hereafter, *LD*).

18. See the reference to "personal influence" in the scheme for the establishment of the Catholic University of Ireland. Newman to Archbishop Cullen, 11 October 1851, *LD*, 14:383.

19. *LD*, 12:399–400.

20. John Henry Newman, *Fifteen Sermons Preached Before the University of Oxford*, ed. James David Earnest and Gerard Tracey (Oxford: Oxford University Press, 2006), 62–77.

conversion to Catholicism.[21] I am claiming that Newman's conversion to Catholicism and his openness to Catholic piety, devotions, and the life of St. Philip Neri furthered this insight, gave it direction, and nurtured it into different areas: the Oratory, university education, theology, and discipleship.[22] Newman's own Oratorian brethren refer to the principle in their letter to the Archbishops of Ireland warning of the potential harm to the Birmingham community caused by Newman's extended stay in Dublin. "My Lords, none know so well as Bishops the need of a Head for the superintendence of a body of labourers; and assuredly that need is not lessened by their circumstance of its consisting of persons brought together into one House, and subject to a common rule of life;—when too, in addition, they are held together, as is the case in the Oratory, not by any irrevocable vow, but mainly by the personal influence of the individual into whose hands they have freely committed themselves . . ."[23] It does not appear that this method of influence was a secret, interior light of Newman's. His own Birmingham community explicitly acknowledges it in a formal letter. Newman's interpretation of this method of personal influence regarding St. Philip and, by extension, in the Oratorian vocation, is so different from Faber's that one cannot be so surprised at their mutual misunderstanding and distrust.

Communion of Saints

As a doctrine of faith, the communion of saints emerges in the Apostles' Creed. When exactly the communion of saints became an article of faith will likely remain unknown, since the Apostles' Creed's origin is more difficult to date than the Nicene. Scholars think it dates to the beginning of the fifth century.[24] The earliest text of the creed itself is mid-eighth century, in a treatise by Pirminius, though parts of it are found much earlier from Hippolytus's *Apostolic Tradition*, a creed by Marcellus, and in a late fourth-century commentary on the creed by the monk Rufinus.[25] However, we do know that patristic theologians acknowledged a special role of the martyrs for prayer and intercession.[26] As

21. *LD*, 8:298, Newman to Nicolas Wiseman, 14 October 1841.

22. For an early reference on this method in the founding of the Oratory, see *LD*, 12:45, Newman to Mrs. J. W. Bowden, 21 February 1847.

23. *LD*, 18:114, Ambrose St. John et al., "To the Archbishops of Dublin, Armagh, and Cashel," 6 August 1857.

24. Elizabeth Johnson, *Friends of God and Prophets: A Feminist Theological Reading of the Communion of Saints* (New York: Continuum, 2003; reprint 1998). 95.

25. Robert Krieg, "Apostle's Creed," *The HarperCollins Encyclopedia of Catholicism*, ed. Richard P. McBrien (New York: HarperSanFrancisco, 1995), 74–76.

Lawrence Cunningham writes, "In the period after Constantine, the veneration and liturgical [worship] of the sainted martyrs was a well-established part of Christian life."[27] Early on in the fifth century, Theodoret supplies a wonderful corroborating passage. "The philosophers and the orators have fallen into oblivion; the masses do not even know the names of the emperors and their generals; but everyone knows the names of the martyrs, better than those of their most intimate friends."[28] Given these historical markers and early veneration of the martyrs and saints, one becomes confident that the doctrine was an early—not a later—part of the creed since it was so closely attached to ecclesial practices.

Newman's theological vision about the communion of saints emerges early in one of his Anglican sermons, "The Communion of Saints." In his Anglican years, Newman, like other Protestants, took a more critical view of Catholic piety concerning the saints. His sermon bypasses the subjects of veneration or intercession. In the theological context of the Apostles' Creed, Newman reads the communion of saints as a major mission of the Holy Spirit. He starts his treatment by holding that it is the work of the Spirit to create a union between human beings and God.[29] If there is an analogical unity between human beings and God in the order of creation, there is an even "more intimate" unity between the indwelling of God in those in the church effected by the indwelling of the Holy Spirit.[30] The indwelling of the Holy Spirit in the hearts of believers is the promise of Pentecost. Believers share a "mysterious union with things unseen" that configures them together as the "Body of Christ."[31] This unity is real, historical, and transhistorical. The Holy Spirit is the vivifying principle of the Christian Church, connecting the visible and the invisible, the present and antecedent generations of all the faithful together to praise, give thanks, and glorify God.[32]

---

26. Michael Perham, *The Communion of Saints* (London: Alcuin/SPCK, 1980), 12–13.

27. Lawrence S. Cunningham, *A Brief History of Saints* (Malden, MA: Blackwell, 2005), 18–19.

28. Theodoret, *Curatio affectionum graecarum*, 8.67 Patrologia Graeca, 83.1033A as quoted in Peter Brown, *The Cult of the Saints: Its Rise and Function in Latin Christianity* (Chicago: University of Chicago Press, 1981), 50; Suzanne Saïd and Monique Trédé maintain that Theodoret's work dates from no later than 423 ce. See *A Short History of Greek Literature* (New York: Routledge, 1999), 176.

29. John Henry Newman, "The Communion of Saints," *Parochial and Plain Sermons*, vol. 4 (San Francisco: Ignatius, 1997), 839 (hereafter, *PPS*).

30. For a recent treatment of this, see John R. Connolly, "Newman's Notion of the Indwelling of the Holy Spirit in the *Parochial and Plain Sermons*," *Newman Studies Journal* 5, no. 1 (Spring 2008): 5–18.

31. *PPS*, 4:840.

32. *PPS*, 4:840–41.

As one can already discern, Newman places the communion of saints at the deepest intersection of the Holy Spirit and the church. Indeed, the church's truest and richest identity is not the visible, present-day company of believers. It is the company of the eschatological fullness of the blessed and resurrected company of God. Newman points to those lives caught up in God's own triune life and thus perfected. Newman states that the church

> in its nobler and truer character . . . is a body invisible, or nearly so, as being made up, not merely of the few who happen still to be on their trial, but of the many who sleep in the Lord. . . . Well then may the Church be called invisible, not only as regards her vital principle, but in respect to her members. . . . The Church is invisible, because the greater number of her true children have been perfected and removed, and because those who are still on earth cannot be ascertained by mortal eye; and had God so willed, she might have had no visible tokens at all of her existence, and been as entirely and absolutely hidden from us as the Holy Ghost is, her Lord and Governor.[33]

Scholars like Ian Ker observe that Newman stepped away from the idea that the invisible church is the true church. Nonetheless, as a Tractarian and as a Catholic, Newman did maintain an eschatological relationship between the two.[34] The visible church as such does not just have a visible element only, but possesses sacramental and transcendent dimensions. Progress in Christian life, that is, a deepening of faith, love, joy, and peace, entails some consciousness of and living bond to this communion. How, for Newman, one gains knowledge of and participation with the communion of saints comes from "certain outward signs" that are in the visible "Christian Ministry."[35] Here Newman means that the "Bishops and Pastors, together with Christians depending on them, at this or that day is *called* the Church, though really but a fragment of it, as being that part of it which is seen and can be pointed out . . ."[36] Though not the fullness of the real and authentic church, the successors of the apostles and the institutional structures and practices are visible signs of an invisible reality. Newman knew and taught that the creed and the church sacraments do provide one deeper

---

33. *PPS*, 4:841.

34. Ian Ker, "The Church as Communion," *The Cambridge Companion to John Henry Newman*, ed. Ian Ker and Terrence Merrigan (Cambridge: Cambridge University Press, 2009), 137–55; 137.

35. *PPS*, 4:842.

36. *PPS*, 4:843.

contact with the mystical Body of Christ on its journey "into the presence of the great company of Saints."[37] In some ways, there is for Newman, a communion of spirits that transcends space and time but is accessible, nevertheless, through the vivifying power of the Spirit in individual Christians and in the church. This communion foresees, through temporal participation in Christian sacraments, rituals, and actions, an eternal "City of God," Augustine's phrase for the fully realized Communion of Saints.[38] That Newman refers to the heavenly church and its members as "signs" allows one to postulate an implied matrix of symbolic meaning that is not developed in the sermon.

This interpretation seems consonant with Newman's example of baptism, which draws on a latent theology of sacramental presence to which he alludes but does not elaborate. He does say, for instance, that "Baptism admits, not into a mere visible society, varying with country in which it is administered, Roman here, and Greek there, and English there, but *through* the English, *or* the Greek, *or* the Roman porch into the one invisible company of elect souls, which is independent of time and place, and untinctured with the imperfections or errors of that visible porch by which entrance is made. And its efficacy lies in the inflowing upon the soul of grace of God lodged in the unseen body into which it opens . . ."[39] There is a sense here of a transcendent and eternal holiness catching up new and current Christians with the strength of a company of believers who have preceded them. If one takes the Eucharist, praises, and prayers offered during the liturgy, the profession of the creed—these actions are not independent from the heavenly community who shares in the prayers, praise, and thanksgiving of the earthly church. It would be more helpful if Newman provided more specificity to his examples, but his reflection throughout the sermon brushes against speculative limits. The invisible and the eternal connect to the visible and the temporal in a mystical and real way.[40]

Other noteworthy features of the sermon stand out. First, there is little reference to specific saints. He mentions only three: Noah, Job, and St. Paul. He stresses the communal, collective dimension of the doctrine of the Body of Christ as opposed to persons officially canonized as holy exemplars. This view seems so odd for Newman, who later collaborated with Faber on a multivolume

---

37. *PPS*, 4:843–44.
38. *PPS*, 4:844.
39. *PPS*, 4:844.
40. "The unseen world through God's secret power and mercy, encroaches upon this world; and the Church that is seen is just that portion of it by which it encroaches; and thus though the visible Churches of the Saints in this world seem rare, and scattered to and fro, like islands in the sea, they are in truth but the tops of the everlasting hills, high and vast and deeply-rooted, which a deluge covers" (*PPS*, 4:845).

work on English saints.[41] Second, there is a paradoxical tension in Newman's thought. On the one hand, he regards pious and popular interpretations of individual saints engaged in the fantastic, the enthusiastic, and the miraculous with cautious reserve, even disapproval. Toward the end of the sermon, Newman cautions that God wants human beings to think well of the faithful departed saints but not "pay them undue honor" since Christians ought to put their faith in God alone.[42] He advises that undue invocations, unnecessary forms of "honoring," and saintly intercession could lead to idolatry. Moreover, Newman holds that the action of the communion of saints should be understood more as that of a body and "not as an agent, nor in her members one by one."[43] On the other hand, he wants to claim that the saints in heaven are not simply at rest, existing in divine passivity, and doing nothing for us needy pilgrims below.[44] It is here that he struggles. Following St. Paul, Newman agrees that "in coming to the Church, we approach not God alone, nor Jesus the mediator of the New Covenant, nor Angels innumerable, but also, as he [St. Paul] says expressly, 'the *spirits* of the *just* made perfect.'"[45] However, Newman labors to find analogies for how the holy departed energize human life in the day-to-day since, as he puts it, "we know not *how* they are active, or *how* they are at rest, or *how* they can be both at once."[46] They are with us as "holy unseen companions."[47] For Newman, the communion of saints teaches that they are holy companions, truly citizens of heaven, whom one mysteriously encounters in the church's communal life, its prayer, and its liturgy. At the same time, the saints serve as inspiring models who are loved properly in and through the love Christians give to each other.[48] One unites with the community of the living through Christian discipline, and so one is then caught up in mysterious, real ways with the heavenly communion of saints. To sum up, let me cite Newman again.

> There are in every age a certain number of souls in the world, known to God, unknown to us, who will obey the Truth when offered to

---

41. See John Henry Newman, *Lives of English Saints*, intro. Arthur Wollaston Hutton (London: S. T. Freemantle & Picadilly, 1901).
42. *PPS*, 4:848.
43. *PPS*, 4:848.
44. *PPS*, 4:846–48.
45. *PPS*, 4:847.
46. *PPS*, 4:847.
47. *PPS*, 4:846.
48. *PPS*, 4:847–49.

them, whatever be the mysterious reason that they do and others do not. These we must contemplate, for these we must labour, these are God's special care, for these are all things; of these and among these we must pray to be, and our friends with us, at the Last Day. They are the true Church, ever increasing in number, ever gathering in, as time goes on; with them lies the Communion of Saints; they have power with God.[49]

There is, then, a graced bond between the eternal and the temporal, the invisible and the visible, the past and present spirits formed and being formed in greater unity and holiness through the Holy Spirit to love God in mutual discipleship.

St. Philip in Newman's Personal Life: Patron and Friend

Let me turn to the spiritual relationship that one can glimpse between Newman and St. Philip specifically. It is at best incomplete to judge someone's personal devotion to a patron saint simply from their writings. Many moments of emotion, distress, anxiety, hope, joy, and the many conversations Newman must have had with friends and family involving St. Philip are lost to scholars. One cannot represent the multidimensional and lived experience of St. Philip for Newman. Still, scholars are fortunate that Newman left abundant writings that permit robust indications, however fragmentary, of how he conceived of St. Philip in his spirituality and in his work. To establish this more personal relationship clearly, let me lay out some key theological distinctions from Elizabeth Johnson's pioneering work on the communion of saints, *Friends of God and Prophets*.[50]

In her book, Johnson raises the question: How did the early Christians during the patristic era and beyond understand their relationship to the martyrs and to other holy people who died? According to Johnson, two major patterns emerged. The first one is "an egalitarian model that names other companions and friends, the other a patriarchal one that casts certain privileged dead into positions of patronage."[51] The companionship model describes the past dead as a "cloud of witnesses" who are empowered and who thus empower and encourage the living through the Spirit. The group of friends here is one that

---

49. *PPS*, 4:830, "The Visible Church for the Sake of the Elect."
50. Johnson, *Friends of God and Prophets*. See also Brown, *The Cult of the Saints*; Cunningham, *A Brief History of Saints*.
51. Johnson, *Friends of God and Prophets*, 78.

vitally nourishes faith in a dynamic of mutuality and equality. As Johnson puts it:

> To use a spatial metaphor, the saints are not situated *between* God and the living disciples, but are *with* their sisters and brothers through the one Spirit poured out in the crucified and risen Jesus Christ. It is not distance from God, nor fear of "his" judgment, nor impression of "his" cold disinterest, nor need for grace given only in small portions, nor a sense of one's own utter unimportance in the hierarchy of power.... Rather, gratitude and delight in this cloud of witnesses with whom they share a common humanity, a common struggle, and a common faith commend their memory to contemporary interest.[52]

This model sees the support of the saints as horizontal rather than pyramidical or vertical. There is also a deep sense of mutual connectedness and commonality in Jesus' mission through the Spirit. Biblically, what comes to mind is John 15:15 when, after washing the disciples' feet, Jesus says that the disciples are now his friends rather than servants because he has made known to them what he is doing. Masters and servants lack that same relationship due to the inequality in power. Jesus' meaning is not about power but about a communion of self-sacrificial love.

In addition, the holy companion model provides what Johnson gleans from St. Augustine's theology of saints as "lessons of encouragement." Models of holiness become, for the living church, "strong beacons of light."[53] The saints in celebration and memory and festival are sources of inspiration and of teaching, strengthening the community that honors their memory in God. These friends of God are witnesses to faith, hope, and love in multiple and varied ways that sound out the dimensions to human life and holy life, lifting up those coming after who face similar struggles, temptations, and suffering. This meaning is illustrated famously in a scene from Augustine's *Confessions*. In Book 8, Augustine experiences his will as torn between chastity and sensual lust. He narrates a holy vision of Lady Continence who appears to him as the model of ordered desire. He describes what follows: "There were large numbers of boys and girls, a multitude of all ages, young adults and grave widows and elderly virgins. In every one of them was Continence herself, in no sense barren but 'the fruitful mother of children' (Ps. 112:9).... And she smiled on me

---

52. Johnson, *Friends of God and Prophets*, 81.
53. Johnson, *Friends of God and Prophets*, 84.

with a smile of encouragement as if to say: 'Are you incapable of doing what these men and women have done? Do you think them capable of achieving this by their own resources and not by the Lord their God? Their Lord God gave me to them.'"[54] This experience of a group of holy people, of friends as models, is precisely what one lesson of encouragement means in Christian experience. Augustine is shown hope through the possibility of saving grace modeled in the community that transcends time. There is no sense of hierarchy or unequal division of power, simply a holy cloud of witnesses that literally represent courage to Augustine.

The other model of communion of saints is one of patronage. The main shift from the "friend" to "patron" model begins from the third to the fifth century. Johnson describes a shift from saints more as "witnesses" and friends on a more-or-less equal level with Christians to special figures who might bring far greater help than ordinary Christians could get on their own. Christians, as the centuries wore on, became more pessimistic about salvation as their image of God became more hierarchical and unapproachable. Here Johnson holds that Christians turned to the saints as mediators and as more approachable than God as king or judge might have been. There is a greater atmosphere of fear and distance than empathy. What gets lost in this shift is the saints as teachers and exemplars; their role as helpers or patrons becomes dominant. The patron is one who advocates for you but is beyond and not "with" you in the journey.[55]

Various causes, notes Johnson, explain the shift from the community-friendship model to a vertical patron-client one. In the fourth century, the Christian church took over Roman forms of administration, bureaucracy, centralizing authority, and law. In addition, Johnson observes that there was an increased emphasis on the divinity rather than the humanity of Christ after the Arian controversy. This emphasis provided yet more distance in theological literature and devotional practice between Christ's humanity and the humanity of ordinary Christians. Johnson holds that the "net effect of these and other major changes was that the official presence of the Spirit moved out from the community as a whole to rest in more specifically holy hands and places, or, to put it another way, " 'the sacred' migrated from the nave to the sanctuary."[56] Now, Johnson admits the broad generality of her claims, but the main point is the sense of Jesus as friend and brother—which we do see so clearly in the gospel—being offset by a more imperial image of Jesus as judge and monarch surrounded by a "heavenly court."[57] On a court and later feudal model, the

---

54. Saint Augustine, *Confessions*, trans. Henry Chadwick (Oxford: Oxford University Press, 1998), 151.
55. Johnson, *Friends of God and Prophets*, 86.
56. Johnson, *Friends of God and Prophets*, 86.

role of the holy person or "saint" becomes one who can speak on your behalf, advocate for you, plead with your king. A saint is one who helps specifically by her intercession to a stronger, more powerful party on behalf of a weaker, more dependent one.[58]

The "patronage system" generally emerges during periods of social, political, and economic inequality. Such systems parallel social stratifications and follow greater differences in honor and privilege.[59] Patrons are the superior, "clients" the inferior parties in such situations. Sociologically, patrons provide clients material assistance, whether economic or military, in exchange for a client's loyalty, honor, and perhaps further work that patrons deem necessary.[60] The key difference between the companionship model and the patron model turns on perceived social and power inequality between the Christian and the saint. Consciousness of being part of a graced community of equals that provides inspiration, faith, hope, and love shifts to a focus on one's unworthiness, neediness, and desire for an active intercessor. One's patron saint provides protection and assistance in navigating the corridors of God's heavenly kingdom. Signs of power came to include, beyond the expected heroic virtues, specific liturgical honors and spectacular miracles.

Johnson's descriptions of the companionship and the patronage model of the communion of saints illuminate Newman's personal relationship to St. Philip. References to St. Philip Neri—or in Newman's preferred name, simply St. Philip—occur in most of the thirty-one volumes about 975 times. They start in 1846 (that's volume twelve) in a letter to Faber of 1 February.[61] In this reference, Newman claims long "reverence and admiration for the character of St Ph.[Philip] Neri."[62] What emerges as one reviews the many mentions of St. Philip is certainly that Newman regarded him as his patron.[63] Over the years, Newman praises St. Philip for working miracles, his intercessions for him, and for the Oratory. He includes specific actions of protection, healing (Newman

---

57. Johnson, *Friends of God and Prophets*, 86.

58. Johnson, *Friends of God and Prophets*, 87.

59. Johnson, *Friends of God and Prophets*, 87.

60. Johnson, *Friends of God and Prophets*, 87–88.

61. *LD*, 11:105. Newman to F. W. Faber, 1 February 1846,

62. *LD*, 11:105. Newman to F. W. Faber, 1 February 1846. I have not found citations in earlier volumes.

63. *LD*, 11:226, Newman to T. F. Knox, 20 August 1846; *LD*, 12:66, Newman to F. W. Faber, 31 March 1847; *LD*, 13:402, Newman to Edward Caswall, 3 February 1850; *LD*, 14:98, Newman, *Decree Releasing the London Oratorians*, 9 October 1850; *LD*, 15:337, Newman to James Nugent, 28 March 1853.

credits St. Philip with preventing an outbreak of Scarlett Fever), and sustenance, all of which Newman honors.[64]

Notice that Newman's former reserve about saints' intercession and miracles in his Anglican sermon is gone. Indeed, Newman speaks of St. Philip as a living reality to whom he is under obedience and who actively permits and prohibits certain courses of action.[65] On several occasions, the will of St. Philip stands as a focal point for Newman's discernment.[66] These views are not the temporary infatuation or religious fetish that one might find in a new convert soaking in baroque pieties and the practices of Rome during his stay at Propaganda. Newman considered all these dimensions of veneration and honor legitimate into his later years. He mentions the importance of saintly miracles, relics, garments, and the like in the Preface to the Third Edition of the *Via Media* in 1877.[67] Nevertheless, in more reflective passages, Newman does not think that St. Philip's assistance is to be blindly received irrespective of human freedom. Oratorians must be active collaborators in their own good. Newman writes, "So far we have nothing to be anxious about, but there is one thing which ought to make us anxious, because, whatever St Philip may do for us, the issue depends upon our own co-operation with him, not on him solely."[68]

True to the patronage model, there is the dimension of inequality between St. Philip and Newman, but the relationship by no means stands as flat or one-dimensional. It is more complex than that. In this respect, one passage stands out. The context finds Newman complaining to Ambrose St. John about the individuality of the Oratorians, unknown servants in his employ, and the need for lay brothers rather than hired help in the Oratory. After comparing himself to Job and his sufferings, Newman goes on a humorous rant tinged with self-pity and perhaps a bit of irony. He portrays St. Philip as a friend that needs to be doing more.

---

64. *LD*, 20:453, Newman to Emily Bowles, 29 May 1863; *LD*, 24:190, Newman to the Hon. Colin Lindsay, 18 December 1868.

65. *LD*, 17:491, Newman to H. E. Manning, 11 January 1857; *LD*, 17:502, Newman to William Monsell, 18 January 1857; *LD*, 18:377, Newman to Ambrose St. John, 13 June 1858.

66. *LD*, 18:158, Newman to John Stanislas Flanagan, 31 October 1857; *LD*, 17:270, Newman to the Fathers of the Birmingham Oratory, 14 June 1856; *LD*, 17:491, Newman to H. E. Manning, 11 January 1857; *LD*, 23:321, Newman to John Thomas Walford, 24 August 1867.

67. John Henry Newman, *The Via Media of the Anglican Church*, ed. H. D. Weidner (Oxford: Clarendon, 1990), 44–45.

68. John Henry Newman, "Chapter Address," 1 February 1878, in Placid Murray, *Newman the Oratorian: His Unpublished Oratory Papers* (Westminster, MD: Christian Classics, 1969), 387.

But, when I think of St Philip, I argue thus — 'There is just one virtue he asks for "detachment;" [[which at the same time he prevents me having.]] now the only external thing which keeps me from being perfectly detached, is that I have made myself *his* servant. What wish have I for life, or for success of any kind, except that I have got his Congregation upon my hands? *He* has implicated me in the world, in a way in which I never was before, or at least never since my sisters married and my mother died. For his [[St Philip's]] sake I have given up my liberty, and have as far as the temptation [[and trial]] of anxiety goes, done almost as much as if I had married. The one thing I ask of him is to shield me from the temptation to extreme anxiety; and the only way by which I can reconcile myself to the notion that he is doing what I feel I might expect is that he sees in me some very great offences against him.' And, when I complain, I utter inarticulate cries about something too deep for words. I now, (considering our disorganized state, and the malign action of St Philips own people, my sons, upon us,) so far, pity poor Father Dalgairns in his restlessness here, from understanding it better — though I trust I shall never be so unfaithful to St Philip as he was to me. Please God, and I hope not from pride, I will be faithful to St Philip, and then God will reward me, though St Philip does not.[69]

The dramatic swings of human relationships, assorted feelings, mutual give-and-take—all these aspects shape the ongoing, variegated sentiments of Newman toward St. Philip. They have a dynamic rapport.

In addition to St. Philip being a patron, he is also a friend. Returning to some of Johnson's points, the companion or friend model emphasizes discipleship, lessons of encouragement, inspirational exemplarity, and mutual solidarity in Christ. One way this model appears for Newman is in his descriptions of St. Philip's virtues and their importance for the Christian and Oratorian vocation. Writing to T. F. Knox, Newman speaks of the differences between the religious lifestyles of Sulpicians, Jesuits, and Oratorians. Toward the end of the letter, he remarks: "Again if you come to us with the grave, unmoved bearing of a Jesuit, you might be as good a Christian as a disciple of St

---

69. *LD*, 18:377, Newman to Ambrose St. John, 13 June 1858. For another instance of Newman struggling with St. Philip, see Newman, *Meditations and Devotions of the Late Cardinal Newman* (New York: Longmans, Green, & Co., 1907), 386. I doubt that Johnson would argue for a strict separation between patron and friend models in human experience. Peter Brown recounts a complex blending of the two in the life of Paulinus of Nola concerning Saint Felix. Brown, *Cult of the Saints*, 53f.

Philip—but you would not be a Philippian, whose spirit is to conceal seriousness under great cheerfulness, simplicity, modesty, and humour."[70] In another letter, Newman talks about his need to rest during the Achili affair. He tells Sr. Imelda Poole that St. Philip took medical advice when necessary and that he should follow the same path since it would do him good.[71] In another passage, we see Philip as a blend of both patron and friend models. In 1853, he writes to Knox about the bonds between them as friends and about the bonds of the Oratory. "For myself, when I recollect what St Philip has done for us, how wonderfully he has led us forward without or against hope, how he has smooth[ed] all difficulties, and kept us unharmed from dangers, I am both grateful for the past and confident about the future. Let us only resolve, as we do, to please him, and we cannot go wrong. If we act as if he were among us, asking his powerful intercession and advice, we must please ourselves, and please each other; I mean, we shall approve ourselves to God and to our brethren."[72]

In this passage, notice the language of closeness and intimacy with which Newman speaks of St. Philip. Though there are the tropes of patriarchal inequality, St. Philip seems far more a friend who is working to help his brothers. That horizontal dimension comes through when Newman speaks of Philip as "among" them rather than above them. Furthermore, this reference by Newman to imagining or recollecting St. Philip among them is not a throwaway line. In one of his oratory papers, he specifically notes the importance of using the Ignatian exercise of composition of place to bring the presence of a saint—in the instance of the oratory paper, St. Philip—before one.[73] That is precisely a key part of the companion model. Finally, every time Newman mentions St. Philip and one of his maxims, he highlights a lesson of encouragement, whether it is "amare nesciri" or "'Throw yourselves into God's hands, and be sure, that, if He wants any thing of you, He will make you good in all that He wishes to use you for.'" Again, the importance of maxims—lessons, teachings that aid discipleship and holiness—fits the friendship model.[74] Indeed, Newman states that teaching through precept and maxim was how St. Philip himself educated others.[75]

---

70. *LD*, 12:113, Newman to T. F. Knox, 10 September 1847.

71. *LD*, 15:252–53, Newman to Sister Mary Imelda Poole, 9 January 1853.

72. *LD*, 15:441, Newman to T. F. Knox, 30 September 1853.

73. Murray, *Newman the Oratorian*, 257.

74. *LD* 17:49, Newman to Ambrose St. John, 9 November 1855; see also *LD*, 13:300, Newman to A. J. Hanmer, 21 November 1849. For the maxims, see St. Philip Neri, *The Maxims and Counsels of St Philip Neri*, trans. F. W. Faber (Dublin: M.H Gill, 1890).

75. *OS*, 118, "St. Paul's Gift of Sympathy."

Conclusion

In conclusion, I have tried to show only a few ways that St. Philip Neri emerges theologically and personally in Newman's own life. One could easily have discussed St. Philip's mission as one of engagement with rather than separation from the world, his incarnational spirituality, his moderation in ascetical practices, or his insistence on low-key, unobtrusive conversation as an important form of evangelization. As a theological and practical principle, Newman credits St. Philip with providing a clear direction for this method of personal influence upon his vocation, his duties, and his work.[76] This insight in maturity builds upon his own conviction formed during his Anglican years. This method also seems better known to his Oratorian brethren as a religious and spiritual charism of their work and one that should define their mutual relationships. Indeed, it is the method of the saints, the power of embodied holiness. Personally, St. Philip becomes for Newman both a living patron and a friend, though the patronage model becomes more dominant in his letters. What is interesting to note is both that Newman's relationship to St. Philip as a friend fits coherently with the latent communion ecclesiology that undergirds Newman's sermon on the communion of saints.

To this end, let me crystallize Newman's key points for a contemporary Christian spirituality today. First, Christian baptism involves a real connection to the communion of saints, as it is a formal, personal, and sacramental entry into the communion that is the church. In one's daily pattern of commitments, practices, and prayers, the Christian life is a profoundly and radically social existence. Christians come to know who and what they are through their neighbors and through created realities that reveal the incomprehensibility of God. Second, Newman teaches that it is possible and real for Christians today to enjoy a personal, spiritual relation with a particular saint as the primary relationship to the communion of saints. Third, this personal relationship is a friendship that, at times, can be difficult to understand, emotionally dynamic, or ambiguous; sometimes there is a more egalitarian character, yet at others there is a more patron dimension in the bond. It is an adult, complex relationship and not one of immature fantasy. Fourth, this relationship is connected to the relationality that is the indwelling of the Holy Spirit working in daily life. Indeed, the cultivation of the relationship to a particular saint intensifies one's relationship to other people, the church, and society through enhanced self-awareness and discipleship.

---

76. *OS*, 201, "The Mission of St. Philip."

In sum, the sacramental presence of past witnesses and models of Christian faith do support and influence the present-day church vivified through the Spirit's indwelling. Newman encounters this presence of St. Philip through the actions and practice of Christian virtue he exhibits and in his experiences with others. A wonderful passage from his sermon relates well these different yet related points. Of the communion of saints, Newman writes:

> These are inspiring thoughts for the solitary, the dejected, the harassed, the defamed, or the despised Christian; and they belong to him, if by act and deed he unites in that Communion which he professes. He joins the Church of God, not merely who speaks about it, or who defends it, or who contemplates it, but who loves it. He loves the unseen company of believers, who loves those who are seen. The test of our being joined to Christ is love; the test of love towards Christ and His Church is loving those whom we actually see.[77]

In the end, those faithful witnesses and present company of believers are mutually bound up in the incomprehensible mystery that transcends time and place. This incomprehensible mystery also means that salvation, like the church, is a social reality that undergirds what David Matzko McCarthy calls our "social desire" to be with God through the saints.[78] For us, as for Newman, the communion of saints incarnates and mediates the work of the Spirit and helps define our ecclesial communion, contemporary spirituality, and our destiny.

---

77. *PPS*, 848–49.

78. McCarthy, *Sharing God's Good Company*, 9–28.

10

Newman and the Spirituality of the Oratory
Embracing the Presence of the Indwelling Spirit

Kevin Mongrain

INTRODUCTION

Although John Henry Newman's Oratory Papers were originally transcribed and published in the late 1960s, and currently can be found in a complete edition titled *Newman the Oratorian* (Gracewing, 2004), they are not a well-known or widely studied part of his corpus.[1] This is unfortunate because these papers give us a fresh perspective on Newman's thinking about the spiritual life.

In his Preface to the 1968 edition, Placid Murray, OSB remarks that there are three reasons why the Oratory Papers are relevant for studying Newman. First, they help us understand Newman's view of himself as a priest. Second, they give a nineteenth-century example of what became common in the twentieth: the effort to reform a religious order by returning to the original vision of the Founder. Third, they show us that "we need nowadays spiritual reading 'with a difference.' We tire of books which merely teach; we feel that if spiritual reading is to be valid, it cannot be worked out on paper alone—it should be written first of all on the living tissue of men's hearts and lives." And it is in this sense, Murray contends, that the Oratory Papers gain significance beyond the walls of the Birmingham Oratory and become

---

1. John Henry Newman, *Newman the Oratorian: Oratory Papers (1846-1878)*, ed. Placid Murray, OSB (Herefordshire, UK: Gracewing, 2004). This edition is a reprint from the first edition, published in Dublin, Ireland by Gill & Macmillan in 1968.

"immediately relevant to the life of the Church today."[2] It is this third point that I would like to pick up and develop in this chapter.

Picking up on Murray's point, how then do we begin to interpret the apparently disparate and miscellaneous collection of texts that make up the complete Oratory Papers? Murray provides many clues to their internal coherence, and they are quite helpful. But I would depart from him and suggest an approach that can help not only to identify their inner coherence but also place them in the wider context of Newman's thought. For instance, it would be beneficial to begin reading the Oratory Papers keeping in mind an intriguing claim Newman makes in his *Apologia Pro Vita Sua*. In that text he declares: "[I]f I am asked why I believe in a God, I answer that it is because I believe in myself, for I feel it impossible to believe in my own existence (and of that fact I am quite sure) without believing also in the existence of Him, who lives as a Personal, All-seeing, All-judging Being in my conscience."[3] In his Oratory Papers we find a vast reservoir of spiritual theology that, while formulated in and for a particular religious community, crystallizes Newman's basic point about belief from the *Apologia*. For Newman, all genuine spirituality is marked by a strong personal engagement in one's own process of becoming the person one already is in the eyes of God. This means for him playing the role God assigns in life with an almost artistic sensibility in creating a masterpiece of one's own life and selfhood. So this line from the *Apologia* can function like an external lens on the Oratory Papers.

We also can find an internal lens within the Oratory Papers, which—for reasons that will become clear later—can be brought to bear with the external lens to illuminate some of the inner coherence of these texts on spiritual theology. This internal lens comes from Oratory Paper No. 31, given on February 20, 1858, where Newman puts forward the following claim: "Every one in this world has to play a part, the part which the great Lord and Master of all assigns him. This is my consolation: I must take my part whether it is high or low; as in the cast of characters in a drama."[4] This chapter will explore Newman's Oratory Papers through the two lenses just identified, arguing that they help us see that for Newman the unity of one's personal identity with one's institutional role in the Church was the surest path away from depersonalizing practices in religion and toward habits that foster genuine spiritual freedom and authenticity.

---

2. "Preface" to *Newman the Oratorian*, xiii–xiv.

3. John Henry Newman, *Apologia Pro Vita Sua*, ed. Phillip Hughes (New York: Image-Doubleday, 1956), 287.

4. Newman, *Newman the Oratorian*, 368.

Two Predominant Themes in the Oratory Papers

I have already spoken of two lenses. There are also two particularly predominant themes in the texts. The two lenses mentioned above can help us see how these two themes work together within the texts and how they suggest some things about Newman's overall spiritual vision.

The first theme is that Newman preferred the Oratory of St. Philip Neri because it uniquely embodied, in his time, the faith of the early church. Newman tells his listeners in Oratory Paper No. 6 (given February 9, 1848) that the Oratory is "in some sense . . . a return to the very first form of Christianity, as it existed in the lifetime of the Apostles."[5] A little further on in this same paper, he asserts that "in the sixteenth century, after heresies and schisms innumerable, St Philip comes forward to bring back all who will listen to him to primitive times, not by undoing what the Church had grown into, but by cultivating those inward tempers and moulding that special character to which in the Apostolic age such especial and prominent attention was given . . ."[6] Newman continues for several pages, making the case that the Oratory was designed by St. Philip to resemble what he likes to call "the primitive Church."

The primitive Church for Newman—as we will see in more detail in a moment—was characterized by a high level of personal autonomy and hence did not need many rules, creeds, or many of the other general structures we have come to associate with institutional religion. Notice, for example, this passage from Oratory Paper No. 6: "It was St Philip's object therefore, instead of imposing laws on his disciples, to mould them, as far as might be into living laws, or, in the words of Scripture, to write the law on their hearts. This is what the great philosopher of antiquity had considered the perfection of human nature; this is what is so frequently brought before us in Scripture, especially in St Paul's Epistles. It is what the holy Patriarchs of the Regulars, St Benedict, St Dominic, St Francis, St Ignatius, and the rest, had felt to be beyond them, (and which is, humanly speaking, impossible when any extended body is concerned; but) which in primitive times was possible in separate communities, and which St Philip revived, or rather reformed, reducing into something like system what in the case of the early monks silence and contemplation for the most part superseded."[7] Newman's criticism here of "the Regulars" is surprising, and quite illuminating too. In contrast to the monastic orders—in which, Newman asserts, the monks are like "slaves"[8]—he contends that the Oratorian, under the lead and

---

5. Newman, *Newman the Oratorian*, 203.
6. Newman, *Newman the Oratorian*, 203.
7. Newman, *Newman the Oratorian*, 206–7.

example of St. Philip, possesses "the free spirit of St Paul, and walks forward to [his] work, with the law written on the heart, not so much by external precepts, as by the light and truth within it."[9]

The kind of criticism of the Regular Orders presented in the last quotation leads to the second, closely related predominant theme of the Oratory Papers: the explicit contrast between the Oratory and the Society of Jesus as diametrically opposed religious types. Certainly, Newman does aver at one point that he considered for a time joining the Jesuits when he first became a Catholic; while he venerated them, he did not feel drawn to them.[10] Yet in many other places in the texts we see something other than veneration in Newman's comments. The Society of Jesus provides a heuristic foil for Newman to highlight what is admirable and truly "Apostolic" about the Oratory. He mentions the Jesuits almost thirty times in the Oratory Papers, and most of these are negative contrasts with the Oratory.

In his critical comparison of the Oratory and the Jesuits, Newman insists that they are almost reverse images of each other. He describes the Jesuit "type" as "imposing," "military," "staid," "abstracted," and "grave."[11] The Jesuits are strict in their "mechanical obedience" to their superiors, whereas the Oratorian "seems to be acting at his own discretion—he acts from himself—the laws on which the community moves are not external but within—it is selfmoved."[12] The Jesuits as a group are like a clockwork machine, a military organization; they are men who live by, for, and of their rules and regulations. Jesuits do not think or act freely, but simply obey. As a group, the Jesuits are analogous to the ancient Greek Spartans.[13] As individuals, Jesuits "are often little more than mechanical instruments" and incapable of dealing with others—friend or enemy—with discretion or prudence because all they understand is obedience, compulsion, and power.[14]

According to Newman, the Oratorian, on the other hand, is "tactful," "gentle," "merry," with "sparkling eyes," "pleasant, bright faced," "modest."[15]

8. Newman, *Newman the Oratorian*, 218.

9. Newman, *Newman the Oratorian*, 206. In contrast to Jesuits and traditional monastics, here is Newman's Oratorian: "He sits in an easy chair, in a lounging posture, one hand stretched on a table, with bright sparkling eyes and a merry countenance. Here you have a type of the exterior of an Oratorian compared with a regular." *Newman the Oratorian*, 207.

10. Newman, *Newman the Oratorian*, 391.

11. Newman, *Newman the Oratorian*, 207–9.

12. Newman, *Newman the Oratorian*, 208.

13. Newman, *Newman the Oratorian*, 210–11.

14. Newman, *Newman the Oratorian*, 209.

15. Newman, *Newman the Oratorian*, 207–08.

The Oratory is not a rigid machine or a beehive but a "living principle" in which the unity of the whole comes from each member following his own heart and mind.[16] The Oratorians are like the ancient Athenians in that they "have no need of laws, but perform from the force of inward character those great actions which others do from compulsion."[17] Oratorians, Newman explains, establish personal spiritual habits and live from Christ within their hearts, and hence do not need to exalt obedience and external rule-following. Newman goes on to contend that, unlike the process of following St. Ignatius' *Exercises*, which requires one to make choices that are "high, powerful, tragic, and decisive," the process created by St. Philip is "gentle and amiable" and requires simply that one "attempt a gradual and imperceptible change" with the slow, quiet aid of divine grace that works more like "dew drops on the grass" than a flood.[18] Newman develops this theme in Oratory Paper No. 25, given in March 1856. Here he argues that the Oratory does not require vows of any kind because "the perfection of the Oratory" does not "lie in *anything external*."[19] The life of the community and each individual in it is dependent on "supernatural grace" not "rigid forms and burdensome externals," Newman insists.[20] This line of thinking follows the point he had made earlier in Oratory Paper No. 6: "Thus to shift for oneself, to depend upon's own resources, consideration, fellow feeling, knowledge of character, tact, good judgement are the characteristics of an Oratorian whereas the Jesuit does not know what tact is, cannot enter into the minds of others, and is apt to blunder in most important matters from this habit of mechanical obedience to a Superior and a system."[21]

What are we to make of Newman's rhetorical contrast of the Oratorians and the Jesuits? He himself admits that he may be "exaggerating the contrast" but nevertheless holds to his point as "substantially true."[22] Placid Murray offers a comment in his Preface that gives a somewhat psychological reading of Newman's basic aversion to the Jesuits. He avers that Newman was "safeguarding his own personality" and that of his brother Oratorians from what appeared to him to be a depersonalizing, individual-crushing, rigidly uniform way of religious life that essentially shut God out of the heart and replaced grace with general human laws, imposed by men on men through sheer willpower,

---

16. Newman, *Newman the Oratorian*, 208.
17. Newman, *Newman the Oratorian*, 210.
18. Newman, *Newman the Oratorian*, 212.
19. Newman, *Newman the Oratorian*, 332, italics in original.
20. Newman, *Newman the Oratorian*, 338–39.
21. Newman, *Newman the Oratorian*, 209–10.
22. Newman, *Newman the Oratorian*, 208.

dominance, and control.²³ There may be a point in Murray's psychological reading, but it also runs the risk of overlooking what Newman's rhetoric tells us not simply about his own fears but, more importantly, his theology. There is a theological coherence to Newman's thinking that leads him to this stark, either/or manner of thinking, irrespective of whether he is factually accurate about the Society of Jesus. It is to this coherence that we now turn.

Newman on the "Primitive" Church and Its Theology of Salvation as Deification

As we have seen, Newman believed that St. Philip was more faithful to the tradition of the ancient or primitive Church than any of the contemporary religious orders he knew in his time. True Christianity, he tells his listeners, is "beyond" the other orders' ability or understanding. What then is Newman's view of the "primitive" Church? This is obviously a huge question. Nevertheless, it is possible to offer a sketch of the basic outlines of Newman's view of its distinctive characteristics, the ones that St. Philip had the "genius" to recognize and retrieve. There are many places where Newman discusses the distinctive characteristic of the "primitive" Church. For the sake of simplicity, I will focus on his book *The Arians of the Fourth Century*, as well as his *Lectures on Justification*, to highlight the gist of his thinking about what the early Christians got absolutely right.²⁴ The great wisdom of the early Christians, Newman believes, was that they understood salvation as *theosis* (θέωσης) or *theopoiesis* (θεοποιεσης) and they ordered their religious life accordingly.²⁵ But what does

---

23. Murray, "Preface," Newman, *Newman the Oratorian*, 80–81.

24. Interested readers would find relevant Newman's two long essays, "The Church of the Fathers" and "Primitive Christianity," which were originally written for the *British Magazine* between 1833 and 1836 and published as a single work in 1840. Both essays have been recently republished in the single volume *The Church of the Fathers*, ed. Francis McGrath (Notre Dame: University of Notre Dame Press, 2002).

25. A persuasive case for the influence of Greek patristic theologies of deification in Newman's thought has been made by Charles Stephen Dessain in a two-part essay, "Cardinal Newman and the Doctrine of Uncreated Grace," *Clergy Review* 47 (1962): 207–25 and 269–88. See also Dessain, "Cardinal Newman and the Eastern Tradition," *Downside Review* 94 (1976): 95–96. I accept his basic thesis and presume much of Dessain's conclusions in what follows. As John Connolly has observed, Newman preferred to speak of the indwelling of the Holy Spirit instead of using terms like *theosis*, deification, or divinization. See John Connolly, "Newman's Notion of the Indwelling of the Holy Spirit in the Parochial and Plain Sermons," *Newman Studies Journal* 5, no. 1 (Spring 2008): 5–18. When Newman did use the term "deification," it was usually in reference to Athanasius' theology. See John Henry Newman, *The Letters and Diaries of John Henry Newman* (Oxford: Clarendon, 1979), 22:160–61 (hereafter, *LD*); *LD*, 28:197; see also John Henry Newman, *Select Treatises of St. Athanasius* (London: Longmans, Green,

this mean? Let us begin with the ordering of religious life, and then move to deification as Newman understands it.

In his fascinating and fascinated discussion of the Church of Alexandria in *Arians of the Fourth Century*, Newman can barely conceal his delight with this "illustrious" model of primitive Christianity at its best.[26] This Church preserved the "esoteric" core of the faith wrapped in a sophisticated "exoteric" discourse designed both to protectively conceal the mysteries of revelation and suggestively allure the genuinely interested to them. The system of sequential catechesis moved from "the simple truths of Natural Religion" to the concrete exercise of "moral truths" to "spiritual knowledge" for the "competent" and "elect."[27] The Alexandrian Christians did justice to all three phases of the Christian life, not short-changing or confusing any of them. They understood, Newman explains, that the deeper truths, the sacred mysteries, of the gospel are revealed to Christians in proportion to one's proficiency to receive and understand them. Moral training was therefore both indispensable for preparing one for the deeper life of mystical prayer, but also not to be confused for the ultimate goal of Christian faith. The Alexandrians therefore illustrate the general consensus in the "primitive" Church that humans can help each other prepare to be taught mystical truth by the God of Love, but they cannot—and absolutely should not—substitute their preparatory training in listening to God's voice for God's voice itself.

This is a truth Newman thinks most contemporary Christians have lost in their zeal to refute nonbelievers with rational arguments and then plant faith in hearts with crude attempts to whip up the emotions of neophytes. The Alexandrians certainly practiced exoteric theology for the skeptical outsiders, but they, unlike many contemporaries, knew the meaning of "reserve," and hence they knew how to refrain from throwing the pearls to swine. The point of being a Christian, they understood, according to Newman, was "higher wisdom," and only those with "habitual piety" and a "conscientious disposition" were prepared to receive it.[28] The preparation had to move in the right order, unfolding the path to mystical truth gradually, without prematurely disclosing God's secret wisdom to those not ready for it.[29] The Alexandrians understood

---

1903), "Deification," 88–90, "The Divine Indwelling," 193–95, and "μετουσία," 424–25, and John Henry Newman, *Tracts Theological and Ecclesiastical* (London: Longmans, Green, 1908), 361.

26. John Henry Newman, *The Arians of the Fourth Century*, 5th ed. (London: Pickering, 1883) (hereafter, *Ari*).

27. *Ari*, 44–45.

28. *Ari*, 46–47.

29. *Ari*, 50–51.

very well that there is no need to overly theorize and formalize the faith for beginners; only God can teach God—or as Newman puts it, "God can defend and vindicate His own command"[30]—and the task of the Church is simply to prepare people to be learners in God's own schoolroom. This set of assumptions and practices about the "secret wisdom" known only to those who were trained properly to be mystically adept Newman calls the *Disciplina Arcani*, and he believes that it is the defining characteristic of the primitive Church.[31] The *Disciplina Arcani* is what allowed the Alexandrians—and the primitive Christian authenticity they epitomized—to create an elaborate system of exoteric religion while at the same time guarding that system from idolizing itself.

The next question is this: What is the "secret" esoteric wisdom of Alexandrian Christianity that Newman was so keen to retrieve as the Oratorian spiritual path? The answer begins with this line from Oratory Paper No. 1, June 1846: "The one object to practice and promote[is] the loving adoration of the mysteries of Religion—especially that of the most Sacred Trinity."[32] Note that Newman says here "adoration" not simply "understanding." He points out several times in the Oratory Papers that historically the Oratory, unlike many other religious orders, has not been involved in doctrinal controversies. Instead, it is more concerned making "use" of the doctrines.[33] For Newman, then, the doctrine of the Blessed Trinity connotes first all a spiritual discipline. It is of course directly connected to the whole point of the *Disciplina Arcani*. A true Christian learns to become receptive to the indwelling of the triune God in the depths of the heart.

As Newman argues in many places—particularly in his *Lectures on the Doctrine of Justification*—the belief in the indwelling Trinity is core and fundamental to everything about the life of faith. This is why for Newman salvation and justification must necessarily involve sanctification: to be saved is to become one with God in a process the Church Fathers called *theosis* and/or *theopoigsis*. There is no way to adequately put this doctrine into words; it can only be prepared for, accepted in one's life, and expressed in holiness. In *The Lectures on Doctrine of Justification* he explains, "[J]ustification consists in an *unknown, unrevealed, mysterious* union with Christ; if we do not allow that there is a mystery, then we shall be bound to say what that union does consist in."[34] To be saved is to embrace the "inward gift" of God's presence, and this act of

---

30. *Newman the Oratorian*, 46.
31. *Ari*, 50–54, 56, 59, 64–65.
32. *Newman the Oratorian*, 149.
33. *Newman the Oratorian*, 198.

embracing both deepens its roots in the heart and leads to the bearing of fruit in righteousness, or works of love. This is an inherently mystical view of Christian salvation. Newman is unashamed to state that bluntly and defend it vigorously:

> If this notion of the literal indwelling of God within us, whether in the way of nature or of grace, be decried as a sort of mysticism, I ask in reply whether it is not a necessary truth that He is with and in us, if He is everywhere? And if He is everywhere and dwells in all, there is no antecedent objection against taking Scripture literally, no difficulty in supposing that the truth is as Scripture says,—that as He dwells in us in one mode in the way of nature, so He is in us in another in the way of grace; that His infinite and incomprehensible Essence, which once existed by and in itself alone, and then at the creation so far communicated itself to His works as to sustain what He had brought into existence, and that according to the different measures of life necessary for their respective perfection, may in the Christian Church manifest itself in act and virtue in the hearts of Christians, as far surpassing what it is in unregenerate man, as its presence in man excels its presence in a brute or a vegetable. And those who without any antecedent difficulty still refuse to accept the literal interpretation of Scripture, should be reminded, that, since the promise expressly runs that we shall be made one *as* the Father and the Son are one, we are necessarily led either to think highly of the union of the Christian with God, or to disparage that of the Father and the Son; and that such schools of religion as maintain that the former is but figurative, will certainly be led at length to deny the real union of our Lord with His Father, and from avoiding mysticism, will fall into what is called Unitarianism.[35]

To be Trinitarian is to be mystical. This is clear in several of his *Parochial and Plain Sermons*, such as of course "The Indwelling Spirit."[36] Note also this remarkable line from volume five of this set of Sermons, "Shrinking from Christ's Coming," where Newman declares—or celebrates might be a more apt term—that,

---

34. Newman, *Lectures on the Doctrine of Justification*, 9th edition (London: Longmans, Green, 1908), 134, "Lecture Six: The Gift of Righteousness" (hereafter, *Ljc*).

35. *Ljc*, 145–46.

36. Newman, *Parochial and Plain Sermons*, vol. 2 (London: Longmans, Green, 1908), 217–31 (hereafter, *PS*).

> if we be [Christ's] the inward support of His Spirit too, carries us on towards Him, . . . God is mysteriously threefold; and while He remains in the highest heaven, He comes to judge the world;—and while He judges the world, He is *in us also,* bearing us up and going forth in us to meet Himself. God the Son is without, but God the Spirit is within,—and when the Son asks, the Spirit will answer. That Spirit is vouchsafed to us here; and if we yield ourselves to His gracious influences, so that He draws up our thoughts and wills to heavenly things, and becomes one with us, He will assuredly be still in us and give us confidence at the Day of Judgment.[37]

The Oratory could not and would not be a form of shrinking from this truth. Unlike the other orders, which Newman categorizes as "religions," the Oratory is a "quasi-religion, or a sort of Religion" because it is about letting God be God in the self instead of substituting a human system of ideas or practices for God's indwelling.[38] To embrace this Indwelling and allow it to rule one's life from within is the very essence of the Oratory, which is itself a retrieval of the *Disciplina Arcani* of the primitive Church.

The "perfection" of the Oratory, Newman therefore repeatedly insists, is nothing more than "to perform the ordinary duties of the day well."[39] It sounds oddly minimalistic to characterize a life of mystical union with the Trinity in this way. But then again, the indwelling God comes into the mundane and ordinary to hallow it from within. The receivers need not make themselves holy saints, but merely allow themselves to be made holy saints slowly, gradually, in God's time. Here is Newman again on the "perfect" life of the Oratorian from Oratory Paper 28, September 1856:

> There are no *short* ways to perfection, but there are *sure* ones. I think this is an instruction which may be of great practical use to persons like ourselves who make a profession of aiming at perfection. It is easy to have vague ideas what perfection is, which serve well enough to talk about it, when we do not intend to aim at it—but as soon as a person really desires and sets about seeking it himself, he is dissatisfied with any thing but what is tangible and clear, and constitutes some sort of direction towards the practice of it. We

---

37. *PS*, 5:46–57.
38. Newman, Oratory Paper No. 25, *Newman the Oratorian*, 327.
39. Newman, *Newman the Oratorian*, 359.

must bear in mind what is meant by perfection—it does not mean any extraordinary service, anything out of the way, or especially heroic in our obedience (not all have the opportunity of heroic acts, sufferings) but it means what the word perfection ordinarily means. By perfect we mean that which has no flaw in it, that which is complete, that which is consistent, that which is sound. We mean the opposite to imperfect. As we know well what imperfection in religious service means, we know by the contrast what is meant by perfection. He then is perfect who does the work of the day perfectly—and we need not go beyond this to seek for perfection. (You need not go out of the *round* of the day [.]) We are perfect, if we do perfectly our duties as members of the Oratory. I insist on this, because I think it will simplify our views, and fix our exertions on a definite aim. If you ask me what you are to do in order to be perfect, I say—first—Do not lie in bed beyond the due time of rising—give your first thoughts to God—make a good meditation—say or hear Mass and communicate with devotion—make a good thanksgiving—say carefully all the prayers which you are bound to say—say Office attentively, do the work of the day, whatever it is, diligently and for God—make a good visit to the Blessed Sacrament. Say the Angelus devoutly—eat and drink to God's glory—say the Rosary well, be recollected—keep out bad thoughts. Make your evening mediation well—examine yourself duly. Go to bed in good time, and you are already perfect.[40]

This way of thinking is so simple and so ordinary, so—as St. Thérèse de Lisieux might say—so little. Yet it is so big too. Newman's view of holiness is as one might expect from one steeped in the *Disciplina Arcani* from ancient Alexandria, which was so influenced by and had such an influence over the monastic traditions of the desert fathers. Serenity, detachment, *apatheia*, purity of heart were the secondary ends of the monastic life of the desert fathers, which prepared them for the true goal of union with God in the heart. This is why Newman insists that "peace" and "calmness" are the true signs of holiness in all saints.[41] It might not be fully accurate to say Newman wanted Oratorians to be *hesychasts*, but then again there is certainly a close family resemblance between this type of mystical faith and what Newman was advocating for the Oratory.

40. Newman, *Newman the Oratorian*, 360.
41. Newman, *Newman the Oratorian*, 236, 356–57.

Conclusion

At the start, I quoted two lines from Newman. The first was from *Apologia*: "[I]f I am asked why I believe in a God, I answer that it is because I believe in myself..." Given what we have seen in this essay, the meaning of the line from the *Apologia* comes into focus—the deification theology Newman presupposes involves such a close intertwining of God's reality and the self's process of discovering its true identity in God that it almost compels this sort of assertion.

The second line quoted in the introduction was from the Oratory Paper No. 31: "Every one in this world has to play a part, the part which the great Lord and Master of all assigns him. This is my consolation: I must take my part whether it is high or low; as in the cast of characters in a drama." That seems more difficult to interpret, given Newman's strident objections to what he saw as the depersonalizing rigidity of some religious orders. Indeed, interpreting this passage becomes even more difficult if we continue reading beyond what we cited already. Newman continues, "If He [God] gives me that part which in fact He has given me; and made me Superior, and you my subjects, I must take mine, and you must take yours, without any concern what each of us may be in his own personal qualifications and his private spiritual history, in his own individuality in the sight of his Maker. We must each of us submit himself to God's will, and in each case the resignation, as it will gain for us His approval, so will it be attended doubtless with self mortification."[42] How can this talk of overriding one's "private spiritual history" and "own individuality" in the sight of God in favor of "resignation" and "self mortification" in service to the community match the strong emphasis on freedom and autonomy throughout the Oratory Papers?

We must recall Newman's declaration in Oratory Paper No. 1 from June 1846: "The one object to practice and promote [is]the loving adoration of the mysteries of Religion—especially that of the most Sacred Trinity."[43] As we have seen, the "mysteries of Religion" involve one in the mystical process of becoming God. If God is a Trinity of unique *hypostases* existing in *homoousios*, which is the unity of sharing perfect Love, then God is the absolute reality of personal uniqueness perpetually maintained in and through the deepest possible unity. If salvation is deification, then Christian life will be about living the paradox of becoming more and more personally unique in and through one's ever-deepening bond with the whole. Newman begins the Oratory Papers with

---

42. Newman, *Newman the Oratorian*, 368. See also his discussion of self-mortification and obedience on pages 403–8.

43. Newman, *Newman the Oratorian*, 149.

his insistence that the goal of the Oratorian life is to "practice and promote the loving adoration" of the mystery of the Trinitarian God. He then proceeds in subsequent papers to give full weight to the value of personal uniqueness in Oratory life. It makes sense, then, that in the later Oratory Papers he would arrive at the theme of perfect unity and community oneness.

Notice that the passage cited above about playing one's role in a drama comes up in one of the later Oratory Papers, No. 31 from February 1858, where Newman is discussing the question of the unique charism of the Oratory. In all religious communities, he avers, a "homogeneity of spirit is necessary" whether there are vows or not; each community must have "a particular spirit" unique to itself to function as "the principle of corporate unity . . ."[44] What Newman believes is unique to the Oratory's charism, as we have seen, is its emphasis on the individual's autonomy and uniqueness. Paradoxically enough, therefore, conformity to one's role in the Oratory is conformity to the process of becoming one's unique self, or becoming free. Why does this involve "resignation" and "self mortification," and why does Newman contrast it to each Oratorian's "private spiritual history" and "individuality in the sight of his Maker"?

If we think carefully about Newman's point about the simplicity of perfection, it seems reasonable to conclude that his message here is consistent with his concerns about the Spartan nature of the Society of Jesus, and about the slavery of monastic orders. Newman understood how, in a twisted and pharisaical psychodynamic, the soldier who submits to his commander becomes a glorious hero in his own mind, and a slave who labors with sweat becomes superior to the Master whose labor is no labor at all but only the ease and relaxation of commanding from the chair. It is this psychodynamic that must undergo mortification so that one is no longer the glorious heroic individual in the sight of the Master, earning so many merits in his eyes with the labors of one's private spirituality. Instead, Newman desires the Oratorians to resign themselves to the nonheroic and the nonglorious, which is of course not the same as the cowardly and disgraceful. The way of the Oratory is the little way of perfection, the simple way of holiness characterized above all not by the self-inflating intensity of achievement but by calmness, tranquility, and serenity. Living in the perfect unity of love means submitting to the demands of the community and its leaders without either self-abasement or self-aggrandizement, or, more accurately, without the perverse psychodynamic that seeks the latter through the former. If one lives the simple, quiet path

---

44. Newman, *Newman the Oratorian*, 370–71.

of openness to God in the depths of the self as one goes about the mundane business of submitting to the demands of loving others in ordinary life, Newman believed, one then finds one's truest identity. That identity is intrinsically connected to the role one plays in the "drama" of community life: God teaches us our identity from within, if only we get ourselves out of the way to listen long enough and attentively enough. Those who do so—and the Oratory was designed to facilitate doing so—learn their true "character" in the drama, learn their lines, their place in the whole. The community of the Oratory was intended to be a living sacrament of the Trinity, with free, willing self-surrender to others in love. Just as there is no compulsion or external coercion in God in Eternity, so to there can be none in people and communities that embody God on Earth.

Bibliography

Alexander, Christopher, Sara Ishikawa, and Murray Silverstein. *A Pattern Language: Towns, Buildings, Construction.* New York: Oxford University Press, 1977.

Allchin, A. M. "Anglican Spirituality," in *The Study of Anglicanism.* Edited by Stephen Sykes and John Booty, 313–24. Philadelphia: Fortress Press, 1988.

Amico, Charles R. "William Paley's Argument from Design and Newman's Critique," in *The Natural Knowability of God according to John Henry Newman with Special Reference to the Argument from Design in the Universe,* 38–56. Rome: Urbaniana, 1986.

Anatolios, Khaled. *Retrieving Nicaea: The Development and Meaning of Trinitarian Doctrine.* Foreword by Brian E. Daley, SJ. Grand Rapids: Baker, 2011.

Aquinas, St. Thomas. *Summa Theologica.* Translated by the Fathers of the English Dominican Province, 5 vols. Allen, TX: Christian Classics, 1981.

Augustine, *Confessions.* Translated by Henry Chadwick. Oxford: Oxford University Press, 1998.

Aumann, Jordan. *Spiritual Theology.* New York: Continuum, 2006.

von Balthasar, Hans Urs, and Joseph Ratzinger. *Mary: The Church at the Source.* Translated by Adrian Walker. San Francisco: Ignatius, 2005.

———. *Explorations in Theology I: The Word Made Flesh.* Translated by A. V. Littledale with Alexander Dru. San Francisco: Ignatius, 1989.

———. *The Theology of Karl Barth: Exposition and Interpretation.* Translated by Edward T. Oakes, SJ. San Francisco: Ignatius, 1992.

Barron, Robert. *The Priority of Christ: Toward a Postliberal Catholicism.* Grand Rapids: Brazos, 2007.

Barth, Karl. *Church Dogmatics* I/1. Translated by G. W. Bromiley, 2nd ed. Edinburgh: T. & T. Clark, 1975.

Bell, Rod. *Love Wins: A Book About Heaven, Hell and the Fate of Every Person Who Ever Lived.* New York: HarperOne, 2012.

Benedict XVI, "Address of His Holiness Benedict XVI to the Roman Curia," 22 December 2005. Accessed June 27, 2013, http://www.vatican.va/holy_father/benedict_xvi/speeches/2005/December/documents/hf_ben_xvi_spe_20051222_roman-curia_en.html.

———. "Christmas Address to the Roman Curia." Accessed May 20, 2013, http://www.vatican.va/holy_father/benedict_xvi/speeches/2005/december/documents/hf_ben_xvi_spe_20051222_roman-curia_en.html.

Berry, Wendell. *The Art of the Commonplace: The Agrarian Essays of Wendell Berry.* Edited by Norman Wirzba. Berkeley, CA: Counterpoint, 2003.

Birmingham Oratory Archives. Various Collections, Essay on Development. Fr. James Stanton to John Henry Newman, 17 August 1855.

Blehl, Vincent Ferrer. *The White Stone: The Spiritual Theology of John Henry Newman.* Petersham, MA: St. Bede's, 1993.

Bouyer, Louis. *Cardinal Newman: His Life and Spirituality.* New York: P. Kennedy, 1958.

———. *The Roman Socrates.* Translated by Michael Day. Westminster, MD: Newman, 1958.

———. *Dictionary of Theology.* Translated by Rev. Charles Underhill Quinn. Tournai, Belgium: Desclée, 1965.

Boyce, Philip, ed. *Mary: The Virgin Mary in the Life and Writings of John Henry Newman.* Grand Rapids: Eerdmans, 2001.

Breisach, Ernst. *Historiography: Ancient, Medieval, and Modern.* Chicago: University of Chicago Press, 1983.

Brown, David. *Through the Eyes of the Saints: A Pilgrimage Through History*. London: Continuum, 2005.

Brown, Peter. *The Cult of the Saints: Its Rise and Function in Latin Christianity*. Chicago: University of Chicago Press, 1981.

Buckley, Michael J. SJ. *At the Origins of Modern Atheism*. New Haven: Yale University Press, 1987.

———. "Spirituality and the Incarnate God," in *Spirituality for the 21st Century: Experiencing God in the Catholic Tradition*. Edited by Richard W. Miller III, 23–38. Ligouri, MO: Ligouri, 2006.

Butler, Joseph. *The Analogy of Religion: Natural and Revealed, to the Constitution and Course of Nature*. Edited by Joseph Cummings. New York: Cosimo, 2005.

Caldecott, Stratford. "Theories of Evolution." Accessed April 22, 2013, www.secondspring.co.uk/articles/Evolution.pdf, 1–12.

———. *Beauty for Truth's Sake: On the Re-Enchantment of Education*. Grand Rapids: Brazos, 2009.

The Catechism of the Catholic Church. San Francisco: Ignatius, 1994.

Chadwick, Owen. *Catholicism and History: The Opening of the Vatican Archives*. Cambridge: Cambridge University Press, 1978.

———. *From Bossuet to Newman*. Cambridge: Cambridge University Press, 1987.

Congar, Yves. *Vrai et fausse réforme dans l'Église*. Paris: Cerf, 1950.

Congregation for the Doctrine of the Faith. *Donum Veritatis*. Accessed June 20, 2013, http://www.vatican.va/roman_curia/congregations/cfaith/documents/rc_con_cfaith_doc_19900524_theologian-vocation_en.html.

Connolly, John R. "Newman's Notion of the Indwelling of the Holy Spirit in the *Parochial and Plan Sermons*," *Newman Studies Journal* 5, no. 1 (Spring 2008): 5–18.

———. *John Henry Newman: A View of Catholic Faith for the New Millennium*. Lanham, MD: Rowman & Littlefield, 2005.

Cross, F. L., and E. A. Livingstone, eds. *The Oxford Dictionary of the Christian Church*, 2nd rev. ed. Oxford: Oxford University Press, 1983.

Cross, Lawrence. "John Henry Newman: A Father of the Church?" *Newman Studies Journal* 3, no. 1 (Spring 2006): 5–11.

Cunningham, Lawrence S. *A Brief History of Saints*. Malden, MA: Blackwell, 2005.

Dawkins, Richard. *The Blind Watchmaker*. Harlow, UK: Longman & Scientific Technical, 1987.

Denzinger, Heinrich. *The Sources of Catholic Faith*. Translated by Roy J. Deferrari. Fitzwilliam, NH: Loreto, 2002.

Dessain, Charles Stephen. *John Henry Newman*. Stanford: Stanford University Press, 1971.

———. "Cardinal Newman and the Doctrine of Uncreated Grace," *Clergy Review* 47 (1962): 207–25; 269–88.

———. "Cardinal Newman and the Eastern Tradition," *Downside Review* 94 (1976): 83–98.

———. *Newman's Spiritual Themes*. Dublin: Veritas, 1977.

———. "The Biblical Basis of Newman's Ecumenical Theology," in *The Rediscovery of Newman: An Oxford Symposium*. Edited by John Coulson and A. M. Allchin, 100–22. London: Sheed & Ward, 1967.

———. *The Spirituality of John Henry Newman*. Minneapolis: Winston, 1980.

Dolan, Gerald. OFM, "The Gift of the Spirit According to Newman (1828–1839)," *Franciscan Studies* 30 (1970): 77–130.

Dulles, Avery Cardinal SJ. *Newman*. New York: Continuum, 2002.

———. Newman: The Anatomy of a Conversion," in *Newman and Conversion*. Edited by Ian Ker, 21–36. Notre Dame: University of Notre Dame Press, 1947.

Egan, Philip A. "John Henry Newman and Bernard Lonergan: A Note on the Development of Christian Doctrine," *Revista Portuguesa de Filosofia* 63 (2007): 1103–23.

Ekeh, Ono. "John Henry Newman on the Mystery of the Trinity," *Irish Theological Quarterly* 74 (2009): 202–23.

Emery, Giles OP. *The Trinitarian Theology of St. Thomas Aquinas*. Translated by Francesca Aran Murphy. Oxford: Oxford University Press, 2010.

Eusebius of Caesarea. *Eusebius: Ecclesiastical History*. Translated by Kirsopp Lake, 2 vols. Loeb Classical Library. London: Heinemann, 1926.

Faber, Frederick William. *The Spirit and Genius of St. Philip Neri*. London: Burns & Lambert, 1850.

Finucane, Daniel J. *Sensus Fidelium: The Use of a Concept in the Post-Vatican II Era*. San Francisco: International Scholars, 1996.

Fletcher, Patrick J. "Newman and Natural Theology," *Newman Studies Journal* 5, no. 2 (Fall 2008): 26–42.

Ford, John T. "John Henry Newman: Conversion as Inference," *Newman Studies Journal* 10, no. 1 (Spring 2013): 41–55.

———. "John Henry Newman: The Relationship Between Theology and Science," *Newman Studies Journal* 4, no. 2 (Fall 2007): 54–63.

Francis I, Pope. "Homily for inaugural Mass of Petrine Ministry." Accessed April 27, 2013, http://www.news.va/en/news/pope-homily-for-inaugural-mass-of-petrine-ministry.

———. "Apostolic Journey to Rio de Janeiro on the Occasion of the XXVIII World Youth Day," Sunday, July 28, 2013, accessed September 4, 2013, http://www.vatican.va/holy_father/francesco/speeches/2013/july/documents/papa-francesco_20130728_gmg-celam-rio_en.html.

Friedel, Francis. *The Mariology of Cardinal Newman*. New York: Benziger Brothers, 1928.

Gaillardetz, Richard, ed. *When the Magisterium Intervenes: The Magisterium and Theologians in Today's Church*. Collegeville, MN: Liturgical, 2012.

———, ed. "Reflections on Key Ecclesiological Issues Raised in the Elizabeth Johnson Case," in *When the Magisterium Intervenes: The Magisterium and Theologians in Today's Church*, 177–82. Collegeville, MN: Liturgical, 2012.

Gherardini, Brunero. *The Ecumenical Vatican Council II: A Much Needed Discussion*. Translated by Franciscans of the Immaculate. Frigento, Italy: Casa Mariana Editrice, 2011.

Gilley, Sheridan. "Newman and the Convert Mind," in *Newman and Conversion*. Edited by Ian Ker, 5–20. Notre Dame: University of Notre Dame Press, 1997.

———. *Newman and His Age*. London: Darton, Longman, & Todd, 1990.

Govaert, Lutgart. *Kardinal Newmans Mariologie und sein persönlicher Werdegang*. Salzburg und München: Universitätsverlag Anton Pustet, 1975.

Graef, Hilda. *God and Myself: The Spirituality of John Henry Newman*. London: Peter Davies, 1967.

Graham, Donald G. *From Eastertide to Ecclesia: John Henry Newman, the Holy Spirit, & the Church*. Milwaukee: Marquette University Press, 2011.

———. "Blessed Newman's Sacred Heart Theology and the 'intercommunion of hearts,'" *Downside Review* 129, no. 457 (2011): 14–37.

Greaves, R. W. "The Jerusalem Bishopric, 1841," *The English Historical Review* 64, no. 252 (July 1949): 328–52.

Gregoris, Nicholas. *"The Daughter of Eve Unfallen": Mary in the Theology and Spirituality of John Henry Newman.* Mount Pocono, PA: Newman House, 2003.

Grenz, Stanley. *Rediscovering the Triune God.* Minneapolis: Augsburg Fortress Press, 2004.

Groppe, Elizabeth Teresa. *Yves Congar's Theology of the Holy Spirit.* Oxford: Oxford University Press, 2004.

Hammond, Jay. "The Interplay of Hermeneutics and Heresy in the Process of Newman's Conversion from 1830-1845," in *Authority, Dogma and History.* Edited by Kenneth L. Parker and Michael Pahls, 45–76. Bethesda, MD: Academica, 2008.

Hill, William J. *The Three-Personed God: The Trinity as a Mystery of Salvation.* Washington, DC: Catholic University of America Press, 1982.

Hopkins, Gerard Manley. *Hopkins: Poems and Prose.* New York: Knopf, 1995.

Hughes, Gerald. "Conscience," in *The Cambridge Companion to John Henry Newman.* Edited by Ian Ker and Terrence Merrigan, 189–200. Cambridge: Cambridge University Press, 2009.

Isasi-Diaz, Ada Maria. *Mujerista Theology: A Theology for the Twenty-first Century.* Maryknoll, NY: Orbis, 1996.

Johnson, Elizabeth. *Friends of God and Prophets: A Feminist Theological Reading of the Communion of Saints.* New York: Continuum, 2003; reprint 1998.

Kasper, Walter. *Die Lehre von der Tradition in der Römischen Schule.* Freiburg im Breisgau: Herder, 1962.

Keating, James. "Newman: Theologian of Prayer," *Downside Review* 122 (January 2004): 1–18.

Kemp, Anthony. *The Estrangement of the Past: A Study in the Origins of Modern Historical Consciousness.* Oxford: Oxford University Press, 1991.

Kenrick, Francis P. "Article I—1. De Immaculato Deipare conceptu Caroli Passaglia commentarius. Romae, 1854, 1855, 3 Tomi, 4to.—2. *The Immaculate Conception of the Most Blessed Virgin Mary a Dogma of the Catholic Church*. By J. D. Bryant, M.D. Boston, 1855.—3. *L'Immaculée Conception de la Bienheureuse Vierge Marie considerée comme dogme de Foi*. Par Mgr. J. B. Malou, Évêque de Bruges. Bruxelles, 1856, 2 Tomes, 6 vols.," in *Brownson's Quarterly Review*, New York Series (October 1859): 4:417–37.

Ian Ker and Alan G. Hill, eds. *Newman after a Hundred Years*. Oxford: Clarendon, 1990.

———. "The Church as Communion," in *The Cambridge Companion to John Henry Newman*. Edited by Ian Ker and Terrence Merrigan, 137–55. Cambridge: Cambridge University Press, 2009.

———, ed. *Newman and Conversion*. Notre Dame: University of Notre Dame Press, 1997.

———. *John Henry Newman*. Oxford: Oxford University Press, 1988.

———. *Newman and the Fullness of Christianity*. Edinburgh: T. & T. Clark, 1993.

———. *Healing the Wound of Humanity: The Spirituality of John Henry Newman*. London: Darton, Longman & Todd, 1993.

Ker, Ian, and Terrence Merrigan, eds. *Newman and Faith*. Louvain: Peeters, 2004.

Kerr, Fergus. *Twentieth-Century Catholic Theologians: From Neoscholasticism to Nuptial Mysticism*. Oxford: Wiley-Blackwell, 2007.

King, Benjamin. *Newman and the Alexandrian Fathers*. Oxford: Oxford University Press, 2009.

———. "Newman and the Church Fathers: Writing Church History in the First Person," *Irish Theological Quarterly* 78, no. 2 (2013): 149–61.

Krieg, Robert. "Apostle's Creed," *The HarperCollins Encyclopedia of Catholicism*. Edited by Richard P. McBrien, 74–76. New York: HarperSanFrancisco, 1995.

La Delfa, Rino. "Christ and the Face of the One and Triune God in John Henry Newman," *Louvain Studies* 35 (2011): 266–78.

Lakeland, Paul. *Catholicism at the Crossroads: How the Laity Can Save the Church*. New York: Continuum, 2007.

Lamm, William R. SM. *The Spiritual Legacy of Newman*. Milwaukee: Bruce, 1934.

Lash, Nicholas. *Newman on Development: The Search for an Explanation in History*. Shepherdstown, WV: Patmos, 1975.

_____. *Newman and Development: The Search for an Explanation in History*. New York: Sheed & Ward, 1975.

Lonergan, Bernard. "Reality, Myth, Symbol," in *Myth, Symbol, and Reality*. Edited by Alan M. Olson, 31–37. Notre Dame: University of Notre Dame Press, 1980.

Mansel, Henry Longueville. *The Limits of Religious Thought*. London: John Murray, 1867.

Manning, Henry. Manning to unknown correspondent, 10 March 1846. Bodleian Library, Oxford, MS Eng. Lett.c. 662, fol. 68r.

_____. Manning to William Gladstone, Pitts Library, Emory University, Manning Papers, Box 1, Folder 22, Manning to Gladstone, 6 March 1846.

Martin, Ralph. *Will Many Be Saved?: What Vatican II Actually Teaches and Its Implications for the New Evangelization*. Grand Rapids: Eerdmans, 2012.

McCarren, Gerard. *"Tests" or "Notes"? A Critical Evaluation of the Criteria for Genuine Doctrinal Development in John Henry Newman's Essay on the Development of Christian Doctrine*. Ph.D. diss., Catholic University of America, 1998.

McCarthy, David Matzko. *Sharing God's Good Company: A Theology of the Communion of Saints*. Grand Rapids: Eerdmans, 2012.

McDonnell, Kilian. *The Baptism of Jesus in the Jordan: The Trinitarian and Cosmic Order of Salvation*. Collegeville, MN: Liturgical, 1996.

McGrath, Francis FMS, *John Henry Newman: Universal Revelation*. Tunbridge Wells, UK: Burns & Oates, 1997.

_____. *The Church of the Fathers*. Edited by Francis McGrath. Notre Dame: University of Notre Dame Press, 2002.

Merrigan, Terrence. *Clear Heads and Holy Hearts: The Religious and Theological Ideal of John Henry Newman*. Louvain: Peeters, 1991.

_____. "The Anthropology of Conversion: Newman and the Contemporary Theology of Religions," in *Newman and Conversion*. Edited by Ian T. Ker, 117–44. Edinburgh: T. & T. Clark, 1997.

_____. "Newman on Faith in the Trinity," in *Newman and Faith*. Edited by Ian Ker and Terrence Merrigan, 93–116. Louvain: Peeters, 2004.

_____. "Newman and Religions," *Louvain Studies* 35 (2011): 336–49.

Miller, Edward Jeremy. *John Henry Newman on the Idea of Church*. Shepherdstown, WV: Patmos, 1987.

_____. "Newman on the Tension between Religion and Science: Creationism, Evolution and Intelligent Design," *Newman Studies Journal* 7, no. 1 (Spring 2010): 5–19.

Milner, Joseph. *History of the Church of Christ*, 5 vols. London: T. Cadell and W. Davies, 1810.

Mongrain, Kevin. "The Eyes of Faith: Newman's Critique of Arguments from Design," *Newman Studies Journal* 6, no. 1 (Spring 2009): 68–86.

Morales, Jose. "Newman's Ideal of Holiness in This World," in *Christliche Heiligkeit als Lehre und Praxis nach John Henry Newman*. Edited by Gunter

Biemer and Heinrich Fries, 148–59. Sigmaringendorf: Regio-Verlag Glock und Lutz, 1988.

Morgan, Drew, CO. "John Henry Newman—Doctor of Conscience: Doctor of the Church?" *Newman Studies Journal* 4, no. 1 (Spring 2007): 5–23.

Mozley, Thomas. *Reminiscences: Chiefly of Oriel College and the Oxford Movement*, 2 vols. London: Longmans, Green, & Co., 1882.

Murray, Placid. *Newman the Oratorian: His Unpublished Oratory Papers*. Westminster, MD: Christian Classics, 1969.

Newton, Thomas. *Dissertations on the Prophecies*, 2 vols. London: F. C. and J. Rivington, 1803.

Newman, John Henry. *Apologia Pro Vita Sua*. Edited by David J. Delaura. New York: W. W. Norton, 1968.

_____. *Apologia Pro Vita Sua and Six Sermons*. Edited by Frank M. Turner. New Haven and London: Yale University Press, 2008.

_____. *Apologia Pro Vita Sua, Being A History of His Religious Opinions*. Edited by Martin J. Svaglic. Oxford: Clarendon, 1967.

_____. *Apologia Pro Vita Sua*. Edited by A. Dwight Culler. Boston: Houghton Mifflin, 1956.

_____. *Apologia Pro Vita Sua*. Edited by Phillip Hughes. New York: Image-Doubleday, 1956.

_____. *Apologia Pro Vita Sua*. London: Longman, 1864.

_____. *The Arians of the Fourth Century*. London: J. G. and F. Rivington, 1833.

_____. *The Arians of the Fourth Century*. Edited by Rowan Williams. Notre Dame: University of Notre Dame Press, 2001.

_____. *The Arians of the Fourth Century*. Westminster, MD: Christian Classics, 1968.

_____. *Autobiographical Writings*. Edited with Introduction by Henry Tristram. New York: Sheed & Ward, 1957.

_____. *An Essay in Aid of a Grammar of Assent*. Introduction by Nicholas Lash. Notre Dame: University of Notre Dame Press, 1979.

_____. *An Essay in Aid of a Grammar of Assent*. Oxford: Clarendon, 1985.

_____. *An Essay on the Development of Christian Doctrine*. London: James Toovey, 1845.

_____. *An Essay on the Development of Christian Doctrine*. New York, Longmans, Green, & Co., 1949.

_____. *An Essay on the Development of Christian Doctrine*. Notre Dame: University of Notre Dame Press, 1989.

_____. *Callista: A Tale of the Third Century*. London: Longmans, Green, 1922.

_____. *Certain Difficulties Felt by Anglicans in Catholic Teaching Considered*, vol. 2. London: Burns, Oates, & Co., 1875.

_____. *Church of the Fathers*. Edited by Francis McGrath. Notre Dame: University of Notre Dame Press, 2002.

_____. *Discourses Addressed to Mixed Congregations*. London: Longmans, Green, 1902.

_____. *Essays Critical and Historical*, vol. 1. London: Longmans, Green, & Co., 1907.

_____. *Faith and Prejudice and Other Unpublished Sermons*. New York: Sheed & Ward, 1956.

_____. *Fifteen Sermons Preached Before the University of Oxford*. Edited by James David Earnest and Gerard Tracey. Oxford: Oxford University Press, 2006.

_____. *Fifteen Sermons Preached Before the University of Oxford Between A.D. 1826 and 1843*. Notre Dame: University of Notre Dame Press, 1997.

_____. *Historical Sketches*, 3 vols. London: Longmans, Green, & Co., 1897.

_____. *The Idea of a University*. Edited by I. T. Ker. Oxford: Clarendon, 1976.

_____. *John Henry Newman Sermons 1824-1843, Volume 1: Sermons on the Liturgy and Sacraments and on Christ as Mediator*. Edited by Placid Murray, OSB. Oxford: Oxford University Press, 1991.

_____. *Lectures on the Doctrine of Justification*. London: Longmans, Green, 1900.

_____. *Lectures on the Doctrine of Justification*, 9th ed. London: Longmans, Green, 1908.

_____. *Lectures on the Prophetical Office of the Church*. London: J. G. and F. Rivington, 1837.

_____. *Lectures on the Present Position of Catholics in England*. Notre Dame: University of Notre Dame Press, 2000.

_____. *Letters and Diaries of John Henry Newman*. Edited by Stephen C. Dessain. London: Nelson, 1962/Oxford: Clarendon, 1961.

_____. "Letters on the Church of the Fathers, no. IX," *British Magazine* 6 (1834): 288–89.

_____. *Lives of English Saints*. Introduction by Arthur Wollaston Hutton. London: S. T. Freemantle & Picadilly, 1901.

_____. *Loss and Gain*. London: Longmans, Green, 1906.

_____. *Meditations and Devotions*. Edited by Rev. W. P. Neville. London: Longmans, Green, 1894.

_____. *Meditations and Devotions of the Late Cardinal Newman*. New York: Longmans, Green, & Co., 1907).

_____. *Newman the Oratorian: Oratory Papers (1846-1878)*. Edited by Placid Murray, OSB. Herefordshire, UK: Gracewing, 2004.

_____. *On Consulting the Faithful in Matters of Doctrine*. Edited by John Coulson. New York: Sheed & Ward, 1961.

_____. *Parochial and Plain Sermons*. San Francisco: Ignatius, 1997.

_____. *Prayers, Verses, and Devotions*. San Francisco: Ignatius, 1989.

_____. *Rise and Progress of Universities*. Introduction by Mary Katherine Tillman. Notre Dame: Gracewing, 2001.

_____. *Select Treatises of St. Athanasius in Controversy with the Arians*, 2 vols. 5th ed. London: Longmans, 1895.

_____. *Sermons Preached on Various Occasions*. Notre Dame: Gracewing, 2007.

_____. *The Via Media of the Anglican Church*. Edited by H. D. Weidner. Oxford: Clarendon, 1990.

_____. *Tracts for the Times*, 3 vols. New York: AMS, 1969.

_____. *Verses on Various Occasions*. London: Longmans, Green, 1903.

_____. Newton, Thomas. *Dissertations on the Prophecies*, 2 vols. London: F. C. and J. Rivington, 1803.

Nichols, Aidan. *The Shape of Catholic Theology*. Collegeville, MN: Liturgical, 1991.

Nockles, Peter. *The Oxford Movement in Context: Anglican Highchurchmanship, 1760-1857*. Cambridge: Cambridge University Press, 1994.

"'Nones' on the Rise." The Pew Forum on Religion & Public Life. Accessed June 19, 2013, http://www.pewforum.org/Unaffiliated/nones-on-the-rise.aspx.

O'Connor, Benjamin. "An Introduction to the Oxford Movement," in *Authority, Dogma, and History: The Role of Oxford Movement Converts in the Papal Infallibility Debates*. Edited by Kenneth L. Parker and Michael J. G. Pahls, 9–43. Bethesda, MD: Academica, 2009.

O'Donnell, Timothy Terrence. *Heart of the Redeemer: An Apologia for the Contemporary and Perennial Value of the Devotion to the Sacred Heart of Jesus.* San Francisco: Ignatius, 1989.

O'Malley, John W. "Vatican II: Did Anything Happen," in *Vatican II: Did Anything Happen?* Edited by David G. Schultenover, 52-93. London: Continuum, 2007.

Pahls, Michael J. "Development in the Service of Rectification: John Henry Newman's Understanding of the *Schola Theologorum*," in *Authority, Dogma, and History: The Role of the Oxford Movement Converts in the Papal Infallibility Debates.* Edited by Kenneth L. Parker and Michael Pahls, 195-211. Bethesda, MD: Academica, 2009.

Paley, William. *Natural Theology.* New York: Oxford University Press, 2006.

Pannenberg, Wolfhart. *Systematic Theology: Volume 1.* Grand Rapids: Eerdmans, 1991.

———. "Dogmatic Theses on the Doctrine of Revelation," in *Revelation as History.* Edited by Wolfhart Pannenberg. London: Macmillan, 1968.

Parker, Kenneth L. "Re-visioning the Past and Re-sourcing the Future: The Unresolved Historiographical Struggle in Roman Catholic Scholarship and Authoritative Teaching," *Studies in Church History*, 49 vols. Woodbridge, UK: Ecclesiastical History Society and Boydell, 2013, 49: 384-411.

———. "Francis Kenrick and Papal Infallibility: How Pastoral Experience in the American Missions Transformed a Roman Ultramontanist," in *Pluralism and Tradition: Essays in Honor of William Shea.* Edited by Kenneth Parker, Peter Huff, and Michael Pahls, 181-200. Lanham, MD: University Press of America, 2008.

———. "The Role of Estrangement in Conversion: The Case of John Henry Newman," in *Christianity and the Stranger: Historical Essay.* Edited by Francis Nichols, 193-99. Atlanta: Scholars, 1995.

Parker, Kenneth L., and Erick Moser, eds. *The Rise of Historical Consciousness among the Christian Churches*. Lanham, MD: University Press of America, 2012.

Parker, Kenneth L., and C. Michael Shea. "Johann Adam Möhler's Influence on John Henry Newman's Theory of Doctrinal Development: The Case for a Reappraisal," *Ephemerides Theologicae Lovanienses* 89, no. 1 (2013): 73–95.

Paul, Pope John II. "Address of the Holy Father to a Symposium on John Hus, 17 December 1999." Accessed June 27, 2013, http://www.vatican.va/holy_father/john_paul_ii/speeches/1999/december/documents/hf_jp-ii_spe_17121999_jan-hus_en.html.

_____. *Fides et Ratio*. Accessed May 10, 2013, http://www.vatican.va/holy_father/john_paul_ii/encyclicals/documents/hf_jp-ii_enc_15101998_fides-et-ratio_en.html.

Pereiro, James. *Ethos and the Oxford Movement: At the Heart of Tractarianism*. Oxford: Oxford University Press, 2008.

Perham, Michael. *The Communion of Saints*. London: Alcuin/SPCK, 1980.

Pius IX, Pope. *Singulari Quidem*, in *The Papal Encyclicals 1740-1878*. Edited by Claudia Carlen. Raleigh, NC: McGrath, 1981.

_____. *Ubi Primum*, in *The Papal Encyclicals, 1740-1878*. Edited by Claudia Carlen. Wilmington, NC: McGrath, 1981.

Pontifical Council for Culture and Pontifical Council for Interreligious Dialogue. *Jesus Christ, The Bearer of the Water of Life: A Christian Reflection on "The New Age"* (2003). Accessed April 27, 2013,
http://www.vatican.va/roman_curia/pontifical_councils/interelg/documents/rc_pc_interelg_doc_20030203_new-age_en.html#top.

Pramuk, Christopher. "'They Know Him by His Voice': Newman on the Imagination, Christology, and Theology of Religions," *Heythrop Journal* 48, no. 1 (2007): 61–85.

Pusey, Edward. *English Churchman* (1845), *Annals of the Tractarian Movement, from 1842 to 1860.* Edited by Edward George Kirwan Browne, 121–22. London: Charles Dolman, 1863.

Riancho, Magali Del Bueno. "Veni Sancte Spiritus: The Indwelling of the Holy Spirit in John Henry Newman's Theology." Paper presented at Loyola Marymount University, 2011.

Rahner, Karl. *The Trinity.* Translated by Joseph Donceel, with an introduction by Catherine Mowry LaCugna. New York: Crossroad, 1997.

———, and Henri Rondet. *Encyclopedia of Theology: The Concise Sacramentum Mundi* Tunbridge Wells, UK: Burns & Oates, 1975.

———. *Later Writings.* Translated by Karl-H. Kruger. Baltimore: Helicon, 1966.

———. *Theological Investigations*, vol. 5. Translated by Karl-H. Kruger. London: Darton, Longman, & Todd, 1966.

Ratzinger, Joseph Cardinal, with Vittorio Messori, *The Ratzinger Report: An Exclusive Interview on the State of the Church.* Translated by Salvator Attanasio and Graham Harrison. San Francisco: Ignatius, 1985.

———. *Einführung in das Christentum.* München: Kösel, 1968.

———. *Introduction to Christianity.* New York: Seabury, 1969.

———. "The Ecclesiology of the Second Vatican Council," *Communio* 13 (1986): 239–52.

———. "Homily for Beatification of Cardinal Newman," accessed August 14, 2013, http://www.speroforum.com/a/40077/Pope-Benedicts-homily-for-beatification-of-Cardinal-Newman.

Religions in Canada, *2001 Census: analysis series.* Accessed April 30, 2013, http://www12.statcan.gc.ca/english/census01/products/analytic/companion/rel/pdf/96F0030XIE2001015.pdf.

Routhier, Gilles. *La Réception d'un Concile.* Paris: Cerf, 1993.

Rush, Ormond. *The Reception of Doctrine: An Appropriation of Hans Robert Jauss' Reception Aesthetics and Literary Hermeneutics*. Rome: Gregorian University Press, 1997.

Saïd, Suzanne, and Monique Trédé. *A Short History of Greek Literature*. New York: Routledge, 1999.

Sardi, Vincenzo. *La Solenne Definizione del Dogma dell'Immacolato Concepimento di Maria Santissima*, 2 vols. Rome: Tipografia Vaticana, 1905.

Schaff, Philip. *What Is Church History?: A Vindication of the Idea of Historical Development*. Philadelphia: J. B. Lippincott & Co., 1846.

Schleiermacher, Friedrich. *On Religion: Speeches to Its Cultured Despisers*, Cambridge Texts in the History of Philosophy. Edited by Ricard Crouter. Cambridge: Cambridge University Press, 1996.

———. *The Christian Faith*, 2nd ed. Translated by H. R. Mackintosh and J. S. Stewart. Philadelphia: Fortress Press, 1928.

Schneiders, Sandra M. "Theology and Spirituality: Strangers, Rivals, or Partners?," *Horizons: Journal of the College Theology Society* 13 (1986): 253–74.

———. "Spirituality in the Academy," *Theological Studies* 50 (1989): 676–97.

Shea, C. Michael. "The Role of Newman's Theory of the Development of Christian Doctrine in the Events Leading to the Definition of Papal Infallibility at the First Vatican Council," in *Authority, Dogma, and History: The Role of the Oxford Movement Converts in the Papal Infallibility Debates*. Edited by Kenneth L. Parker and Michael Pahls, 77–94. Bethesda, MD: Academica, 2009.

———. "Newman's Early Legacy: Giovanni Perrone and Roman Readings of the *Essay on the Development of Christian Doctrine* 1845-1854." Unpublished Ph.D. dissertation, Saint Louis University, forthcoming 2014.

Sheehan, Peter F. *The Realization of the Divine Presence Through the Indwelling of the Trinity, According to John Henry Cardinal Newman.* Ph.D. Diss. Pontificium Athenaeum Angelicum, Rome, 1956.

Schmemann, Alexander. *For the Life of the World*, 2nd ed. Crestwood, NY: St. Vladimir's Seminary Press, 1973.

Second Vatican Council. *Decree on the Apostolate of the Laity, Apostolicam Actuositatem.* Washington, DC: National Catholic Welfare Conference, 1965.

_____. *Constitution on the Church, Lumen Gentium.* Washington, DC: National Catholic Welfare Council, 1964.

_____. *Lumen Gentium.* Accessed July 3, 2013, http://www.vatican.va/archive/hist_councils/ii_vatican_council/documents/vat-ii_const_19641121_lumen-gentium_en.html.

Short, Edward. *Newman and His Contemporaries.* New York: T. & T. Clark, 2011.

Shultenover, David, ed. *Vatican II: Did Anything Happen?* London: Continuum, 2007.

Strange, Roderick. "Newman and the Mystery of Christ," in *Newman After a Hundred Years.* Edited by Ian Ker and Alan G. Hill, 323-36. Oxford: Clarendon, 1985.

_____. "The Development of Newman's Marian Thought and Devotion," *One in Christ* 16, no. 1–2 (1980): 114–26.

"'Strong' Catholic Identity at a Four-Decade Low in U.S." The Pew Forum on Religion & Public Life. Accessed June 19, 2013, http://www.pewforum.org/Christian/Catholic/Strong-Catholic-Identity-at-a-Four-Decade-Low-in-US.aspx.

Suenens, Leon Joseph Cardinal. *Memories and Hope.* Translated by Elena French. Dublin: Veritas, 1992.

Synod of Bishops, *The New Evangelization for the Transmission of the Christian Faith, Synodus Episcoporum Bulletin,* XIII. Ordinary General Assembly, October 2012. Accessed July 20, 2013, http://www.vatican.va/news_services/press/sinodo/documents/bollettino_25_xiii-ordinaria-2012/02_inglese/b33_02.html.

Tanner, Norman SJ. *Decrees of the Ecumenical Councils,* 2 vols. Washington, DC: Georgetown University Press, 1990.

Taylor, Charles. *A Secular Age.* Cambridge, MA: Belknap, 2007.

Terence. *Andria, Et Heauton Timorumenos.* Edited by Andrew F. West. Charleston, SC: Nabu, 2011.

Thiel, John. "Creation, Contingency, and Sacramentality," *CTSA Proceedings* 67 (2012): 46–58.

Thomas, Stephen. *Newman and Heresy: The Anglican Years.* Cambridge: Cambridge University Press, 1991.

Tilley, Terrence. "Aggiornamento Adjourned," *Commonweal* (April 11, 2008): 35.

Tillman, Mary Katherine. "An Introduction to 'The Dream of Gerontius' by Cardinal John Henry Newman and Sir Edward Elgar," *Newman Studies Journal* 1, no. 1 (Spring 2004): 42–48.

Todd, John M. "The New Eve," *Worship* 27, no. 6 (1953): 273–78.

Tuner, Frank M. *John Henry Newman: The Challenge to Evangelical Religion.* New Haven: Yale University Press, 2002.

Türks, Paul. *Philip Neri: The Fire of Joy.* Translated by Daniel Utrecht. Edinburgh: T. & T. Clark, 1995.

Tutu, Desmond, and Douglas Abrams. *God Has a Dream: A Vision of Hope for Our Time.* New York: Image-Doubleday, 2005.

Vainio, Olli-Pekka. *Beyond Fideism: Negotiable Religious Identities.* Burlington, VT: Ashgate, 2010.

Vélez, Juan R. *Passion for Truth: The Life of John Henry Newman*. Charlotte, NC: Tan Books, 2012.

———. "Newman's Theology in the Dream of Gerontius," *New Blackfriars* 82, no. 967 (2001): 387–98.

Vorgrimler, Herbert, ed. *Commentary on the Documents of Vatican II*, 4 vols. New York: Herder & Herder, 1969.

Wainwright, Geoffrey. "Dispensations of Grace: Newman on the Sacramental Mediation of Salvation," in *Newman and Faith*. Edited by Ian Ker and Terrence Merrigan, 143–82. Louvain: Peeters, 2004.

Wakefield, Gordon S. "Anglican Spirituality," in *Christian Spirituality: Post-Reformation and Modern*. Edited by Louis Dupré and Don E. Saliers, 257–93. New York: Crossroad, 1993.

Ward, Wilfrid. *The Life of John Henry Newman: Based on His Private Journals and Correspondence*, 2 vols. New York: Longmans, Green, & Co., 1921.

Weigel, George. *Courage to Be Catholic: Crisis, Reform, and the Future of the Church*. New York: Basic Books, 2002.

Whapham, Theodore James. *The Term "Person" in the Trinitarian Theology of Wolfhart Pannenberg*. New York: Peter Lang, 2012.

Wilcox, Peter C. *John Henry Newman: Spiritual Director, 1845-1890*. Eugene, OR: Pickwick, 2013.

Wilkins, John. "Why I Became Catholic: A Witness to Vatican II," *Commonweal* 136 (February 27, 2009): 16–19.

Zeno, OFM, *John Henry Newman: His Inner Life*. San Francisco: Ignatius, 1987.

List of Authors

JOHN R. CONNOLLY:
John Connolly is an Emeritus Professor of Theological Studies at Loyola Marymount University (LMU) in Los Angeles, California. He retired in January 2011 after forty years of teaching at LMU. He is presently the President of the Newman Association of America. He also served as the co-moderator of a Newman Interest Group on Spirituality for the Catholic Theological Society of America. In addition to a number of articles on Newman, his most notable publication is his book, *John Henry Newman: A View of Catholic Faith for the New Millennium*, 2005.

JOHN T. FORD:
John T. Ford, CSC, a Professor of Theology and Religious Studies at the Catholic University of America, Washington, D.C., for the last ten years served as editor of *Newman Studies Journal,* and he is presently the area editor for Liberation Theology of *Religious Studies Review*. In addition to articles about Newman, he recently published *John Henry Newman: Spiritual Writings* (Orbis, 2012).

DONALD G. GRAHAM:
Donald Graham is Adjunct Professor of Systematic Theology at the Institute of Theology of St. Augustine's Seminary, which is a member of the Toronto School of Theology at the University of Toronto. He is also Academic Advisor on the Postgraduate Research Program in Catholic Studies at Maryvale Institute, Birmingham, UK. He has published on Newman's views of pneumatic Christology, development of doctrine, the Sacred Heart, and the Trinity. His recent book is *From Eastertide to Ecclesia: John Henry Newman, the Holy Spirit, & the Church* (Milwaukee: Marquette University Press, 2011).

BRIAN W. HUGHES:
Brian W. Hughes received his Ph.D. in systematic theology from Boston College, where he taught for a number of years in the Perspectives Program. Currently, he is Associate Professor of the Theology, Philosophy, and Pastoral Ministry Department at the University of Saint Mary, Leavenworth, Kansas.

In addition to writing articles about John Henry Newman, he is co-convener of the Newman Interest Group on Spirituality for the Catholic Theological Society of America. His recent book is *Saving Wisdom: Theology in the Christian University* (Eugene, OR: Pickwick, 2011).

RYAN MARR:
Ryan Marr received his B.A. in Theological Studies from John Brown University, Siloam Springs, Arkansas. He completed his M.Div. degree at Duke Divinity School in 2006. Presently, he is a doctoral candidate in the Historical Theology program at Saint Louis University. His research interests are Newman's ecclesiological writings and ecumenism.

KEVIN MONGRAIN:
Kevin Mongrain earned a Ph.D. in Religious Studies from Yale University in 1999. In addition to his research on John Henry Newman, he has published on the thought of Hans Urs von Balthasar and René Girard. Dr. Mongrain taught theology at St. Mary's University in San Antonio, Texas, and Great Books in the Program of Liberal Studies at the University of Notre Dame. He currently holds the Ryan Chair of Newman Studies at Duquesne University, and is the Executive Director of the National Institute for Newman Studies in Pittsburgh.

DANIELLE NUSSBERGER:
Danielle Nussberger received her Ph.D. in Systematic Theology from the University of Notre Dame. Currently, she is Assistant Professor of Systematic Theology at Marquette University in Milwaukee, Wisconsin, where she teaches courses on Trinitarian theology, Hans Urs von Balthasar, and suffering and redemption in the Christian tradition. In addition to publishing articles in the area of Newman studies, she has also written pieces on Hans Urs von Balthasar's theology of the saints and on Catholic feminist theology.

KENNETH L. PARKER:
Kenneth L. Parker received his Ph.D. in historical theology from the University of Cambridge and pursued postdoctoral studies at the University of Fribourg in Switzerland. Currently he is Associate Professor of Historical Theology at Saint Louis University in Saint Louis, Missouri. In addition to writing articles and essays on John Henry Newman, Parker has written or edited works on the early modern English Church, the rise of historical consciousness among the Christian churches, and the role of Oxford Movement

converts on the papal infallibility debates of the 1850s and 1860s. He is currently working on an annotated chronological bibliography of books Newman borrowed from the Oriel College Senior Library from 1824 to 1845.

THEODORE JAMES WHAPHAM:

Theodore James Whapham is Assistant Professor of Historical and Systematic Theology and Director of Master's Degree Programs at St. Thomas University's School of Theology and Ministry, Miami Gardens, Florida. He has made numerous scholarly contributions in the areas of Trinitarian Theology and Fundamental Theology. He is the author of *The Term "Person" in the Trinitarian Theology of Wolfhart Pannenberg* and the forthcoming volume *The Unity of Theology* from Fortress Press.

Index

Abrams, Douglas, 113, 220
Achilli, Giacinto, 16
Acton, Lord, 24
Adam, 34, 36, 37, 69, 87, 89, 94, 95,114–16, 118, 120, 122, 138, 151, 215
Alexandria, School of, 12, 59, 70, 85, 87–88, 193, 194, 197, 208
Ambrose, St., 20, 172, 181–83
Anatolios, Khaled, 84, 201
Anglican: bishopric, 19; Church, 1, 7, 32, 64, 69, 134,135, 157, 181, 214; divines, 27; orthodoxy, 62; spirituality, 2–3, 15, 18, 63, 65, 201, 221; Tractarian, 2, 9, 18, 23, 30, 174, 216; theology, 4, 42, 54, 61, 154; via media, 19, 23, 63–64, 69, 134, 135, 181, 214
anti–Christ, 58
apartheid, 113, 117
apatheia, 197
apocatastasis, 90
apologetics, 9, 25,
Apostles' Creed, 101, 172–73
Apostolicam Actuositatem, 162, 218
apprehension, real and notional, 100–01, 103, 106, 107
Aquinas, St. Thomas, 26, 79, 201, 205
Arian controversy, 60, 97, 179
Ascension, 90, 103, 108
asceticism, 5, 77
assent: real, xi, 1, 3–5, 9–10, 14, 26, 30, 37, 44–45, 47, 63, 82, 97–106, 108–09, 111, 131, 133, 137, 159, 165; notional, 4, 9, 44–45, 98–99, 103, 132, 143, 159, 165
Asterius, 84

Athanasius, St., 20, 84, 85, 92, 115, 132, 192, 214
Athenians, 191
Augustine, St., 13 14, 19–20, 24–25, 27–28, 30, 56–58, 90, 175, 178–79, 201, 223
Aumann, Jordan, 77, 201
autonomy, 86, 189, 198–99
authority, 55, 57, 61–62, 70–71, 139, 207, 214–15, 218; church, 2, 61, 66, 141, 164, 179; papal, 55, 57
Balthasar, Hans Urs von, 77, 90, 136, 201, 224
baptism, 3, 35–36, 38–40, 42, 43, 47–48, 87, 103, 117, 120, 157–59, 164, 175, 184, 209
Barberi, Dominic, 19
Barth, Karl, 90, 102–3, 201
Benedict, St., 105, 189
Bernard, St., 64
Biemer, Gunter, 155, 210
bishops, 6–7, 17, 56, 60, 63, 69, 72, 81, 140–41, 172, 174, 219
Blehl, Vincent, 7–8, 41, 46, 48, 77, 159, 202
body of Christ, 73, 95, 140, 143, 173, 175. See also church
Bouyer, Louis, 8, 21, 90, 169, 202
Boyce, Philip, 119, 131, 138, 202
Browne, Edward, 18, 216
Brownlow, William Robert, 83
Buckley, Michael J., 5, 81, 83, 203
Bull, George, 60
Butler, Joseph, 155, 203

Caldecott, Stratford, 83, 87, 203
Calvin, John, 23, 63, 90
Cambridge Platonists, 3

Caroline Divines, 62, 63, 65
Catholic Church, 1–2, 5, 17, 19–20, 24, 26, 27, 52, 67, 70–72, 85, 129, 162, 170, 203, 207
Catholic Social Teaching, 164
Catholic theologians, 52, 73, 130, 138, 143, 208; ecclesial vocation of, 137
Catholic University of Ireland, 171
Chenu, Marie-Dominique, 52
Christmas, 53, 91, 103, 108, 144, 148, 202
Christology, 87, 90, 94, 100, 216, 223
Chrysostom, St. John, 64, 92
Church, xi, 1–2, 4–7, 9, 11–15, 17–24, 26–27, 29, 32–34, 36, 38–40, 42–44, 47, 52–75, 77–78, 85–86, 88, 90, 92, 95, 101, 103, 105, 107, 108, 120, 129–32, 134–45, 156–57, 161–65, 168, 170, 173–79, 181–85, 188–89, 192–96, 201–04, 206–10, 212–15, 217–19, 221, 223, 224; Anglican, xi, 1, 7, 32, 64, 69, 134, 135, 157, 181, 214; of Alexandria, 193; body of Christ, 73, 95, 140, 143, 173, 175; and doctrinal truths, 66, 138; and dogma, 4, 55, 62, 65, 70–72, 77, 82, 88, 99, 139–140, 157, 202, 207, 214, 215, 217, 218; Priestly office of, 95, 134; Prophetical office of, xi, 7, 57, 64, 67–68, 134–36, 141, 213; Regal office of, 134–36, 141; primitive, 12, 66–69, 189, 192–94, 196; Roman Catholic, 1, 17, 19–20, 24, 26, 27, 67; Tridentine, 67, 70
church fathers, 9, 54–56, 62, 64, 138, 194, 208. *See also* Early Christian Writers
Church, R.W., 75
clergy, 15–16, 18, 26, 124, 139, 141, 192
Commonweal, 130, 220, 221
communion of saints, vii, 11–12, 46, 47, 123–124, 167–69, 171–77, 179–81, 183–85, 207, 209, 216; intercession of, 172, 173, 176, 180–181, 183
Confessions, 14, 178, 179, 201
Congar, Yves, 73, 203, 207
Congregation for the Doctrine of the Faith, 54, 78, 137, 203
Constantine, 173
conversion, vii, 3, 8, 9, 13–14, 16–28, 30, 49, 53–56, 69–70, 94, 96, 108, 135, 143, 148, 157, 171, 172, 205–08, 210, 215; Anglo-Catholic, 22; conversion stories, 13–14, 25, 28; Roman Catholic, 18; evangelical, 3, 22, 54, 56, 157; noetic, 9, 22–24, 29
conscience, 2, 23, 37, 78, 82, 100, 142, 163, 188, 207, 210
councils, 7, 59, 60, 79, 82, 87, 95, 135, 141–44, 216, 219; ecumenical, 59, 60, 79, 82, 95, 138, 143, 206, 219; Lateran IV, 78; Second Vatican, 1–2, 7, 11, 51, 53, 95, 129–31, 135, 141–44, 162–64, 217, 218; Trent, 51
creation, doctrine of, 10, 34, 36, 41, 57, 75, 80, 84–85, 87, 96, 101, 107, 110, 116, 164, 173, 220
creed, Athanasian, 101, 103, 106
Corpus Christi, 103, 108
Covenant, 39, 90, 114, 118, 122–23, 126, 176
cross, *see also* Jesus Christ, 103, 116, 121–22, 126
Culler, A. Dwight, 49, 155, 211
Cunningham, Lawrence, 173, 204
Cyril, St. of Alexandria, 87

Dalgairns, John Dobrée, 182
Darwin, Charles, 21, 82
David, ix, 15, 18, 43, 72, 103, 130, 144, 168, 171, 185, 203, 209, 211–12, 219
Dei Verbum, (Word of God), 51
deification, 3, 10, 12, 80, 108, 192–93, 198; *theosis* (θέωσης), 3, 192

deism, 83, 101
Del Bueno Riancho, Magali, 164, 204
Dessain, Charles Stephen, 8, 45, 77, 139, 149, 157, 171, 192, 204, 213
detachment, 5, 182, 197. *See also* spirituality
development, 1–2, 7, 9, 11, 16–17, 21–22, 29–30, 42, 44, 52–54, 56, 65–73, 75, 77, 84, 97, 99–101, 107–08, 115, 118, 124, 131, 133–34, 136, 138–39, 141, 154–55, 157, 201–02, 205, 209, 212, 215, 218–19, 223; doctrine of, 7, 66, 72, 223; theory of, 22, 52–54, 66–68, 70–72, 75, 130
Disciplina Arcani, 12, 60, 194, 196–97
doctrinal truths, 66, 138. *See also* church
dogma, 4, 22–23, 55, 62, 65, 70–72, 77, 82, 88, 95, 99, 103, 107, 139–40, 157, 202, 07, 214–15, 217–18. *See also* church
Dolan, Gerald, 165, 204
Döllinger, Ignaz von, 24
Dominic, St., 189
Donatism, 19
Donum Veritatis, (On The Ecclesial Vocation Of The Theologian), 137–38, 203
Dulles, Avery, SJ., 16, 40, 133–34
duties, of daily life (duties of the day), 1, 4–5, 8, 10–11, 26, 106, 145, 161–64, 170, 184, 196,

ecclesia discens, 139
ecclesia docens, 139
ecclesiology, 2, 53–54, 130, 134, 140, 184, 217
education, 2, 4, 7, 15, 86, 93, 95, 170–72, 203; liberal, 2; religious, 7
Ekeh, Ono, 102–03, 110, 205
Epiphany, 36, 103, 108
eschatological, 9, 122–23, 156, 174

Evangelicals, Evangelicalism, 18, 22–23, 32, 42
Eve, 8, 115, 118–20, 131, 138, 206, 220
Eucharist, 6, 10–11, 108, 114, 120–27, 175; as communion, 122; Lord's Supper, 122–23; Sacrifice, 114, 117, 121–26
Eusebius of Caesarea, 56, 205
Evil, 35, 41, 42, 116, 119, 138, 148, 151–54
experience, mystical 45, 168

Faber, William 24, 169, 171–72, 175, 180, 183, 205
faith, 1, 3–6, 9–11, 19, 23–24, 26, 30, 38–40, 42–46, 51–55, 57, 59–60, 63, 66–68, 71, 73, 77–78, 81–83, 97–98, 100–104, 106, 108–9, 111, 113, 116, 120, 125, 130–37, 140–44, 146–47, 151, 153, 156–58, 164–65, 167, 172, 174, 176, 178, 180, 185, 189, 193–194, 197, 203–4, 208, 210, 212, 218–19, 221, 223; deposit of, 60, 71, 13; faith and reason, 1, 133, 142
fanaticism, 150
Fathers of the church, 20
Ferguson, Craig 113
Fideism, 132, 220
Fides et Ratio (Faith and Reason), 26, 216
First Vatican Council, 71–72, 82, 101, 218
Forgiveness, 92, 113, 115, 121, 125–27
Francis, St., 13, 189
Friedel, Francis, 131, 206
Froude, Hurrell, 15, 23, 61
Froude, James Anthony, 15, 149

Gaillardetz, Richard, 138, 144, 206
Gherardini, Brunero, 143, 206
Gibbon, Edward, 55
Gilley, Sheridan, 24–26, 167, 206
Gladstone, William, 70, 206

God, 3–5, 7–9, 11–12, 24–25, 28–29, 32–45, 48, 57, 66, 68, 73–74, 76, 78–91, 93, 96, 98, 100–3, 105, 107–10, 113–27, 131, 133, 136–138, 141–43, 145–65, 167–68, 171–80, 182–85, 188, 191, 193–201, 203–9, 220; and *hypostases*, 198; Images of, 119, 179; and metaphor, 75, 79, 110, 178; and personhood, 90, 107, 110; argument from design, 82–82, 201; transcendence of, 84, 86, 105; and *philanthropia*, 84, 90

the Gospels, 66, 132

good, 35, 38, 41–42, 48, 67, 76, 78, 83, 85, 91, 119, 121, 138, 147, 149–52, 154, 168, 181–83, 185, 191, 197, 209

Govaert, Lutgart, 131, 206

grace, 10, 23, 30, 33–38, 40–45, 87, 92–95, 107, 113–16, 119–22, 124–27, 131, 138, 140, 156, 165, 175, 178–79, 191–92, 195, 204, 221; actual, 42–43; personal relationship, 45, 165, 177, 180, 184; sanctifying, 41–42, 119, 122

Graef, Hilda, 7, 8, 88, 148–150, 154–58, 206

Gregoris, Nicholas, 8, 131, 206

Grenz, Stanley, 101, 206

Hawkins, Edward, 22–23, 28

heaven, 15, 46–48, 79, 85, 89–92, 102, 114–15, 117–120, 122, 147–48, 158–159, 162, 165, 176, 196, 202

hell, 90–91, 119, 202

heresy, 20, 60–63, 70, 88, 136, 207, 220; Apollinarian, 88; Arian, 60, 97, 179; monophysite controversy, 19–20, 68

hermeneutic of reform, 53–54, 73–74

*Hesychasts,*197

Hick, John, 109

historical consciousness, 9, 51–53, 55, 57, 73, 207, 215, 224

Hippolytus, 172

holiness, *vii, ix,* 2–5, 7–11, 24, 35, 43–44, 47–49, 53, 77, 87, 92–93, 95, 113–17, 120, 123, 126, 145, 147–63, 165, 168, 175, 177–78, 183–84, 163, 194, 197, 199, 202, 210; as a process, 4, 9, 24, 48, 158; Christian perfection, 1, 48, 77, 105, 119, 161, 189, 195–97, 199; growth in, 35, 48; other-worldly holiness, 11, 145, 147–48, 150, 152, 154; social dimension, 4, 163; this worldly holiness, 11, 145, 154, 157, 159–63, 165

Holy See, 141

Homoousios, 198

Hooker, Richard, 64

Hopkins, Gerard Manley, 86, 207

humanism, Christian, 93, 95

human nature, 41, 88, 92–95, 108, 115, 147, 155, 158, 189; corruption of, 41; natural person, 41–42

Hume, David, 18

Hus, Jan, 52, 216

illative, 9, 17, 26; illative epistemology, 17; illative sense, 9; and reason, 26

illumination, 61, 158

imagination, vii, 3–4, 10, 57, 59, 93, 97, 99–101, 103–9, 111, 206

Immaculate Conception, 71, 119, 140, 207

Incarnation, 10–11, 46, 80, 84–85, 88–91, 108, 114–18, 120–21, 124–27, 146, 155

indwelling of the Holy Spirit, vii, ix, 3–4, 7, 9–10, 31–49, 105, 145, 154, 157–60, 163–65, 173, 184, 192, 203, 216; at baptism, 3, 35–36, 38–40, 42–43, 47–48, 87, 103, 117, 120, 157–59, 164, 175, 184, 209; a real change, 36, 41, 158; as a personal presence, 34, 171; as a real assent, 3–5, 10, 45, 98–106, 108–09, 111,

159, 165; Divine indwelling, 32, 43, 193; gift of, 33, 38, 41, 165, 204; God's presence, 11, 32–33, 108, 113, 145, 194; grace of the, 38, 119, 122, 165; Holy Ghost, 36–37, 79, 102, 174; indwelling of Christ, 32; indwelling of the Trinity, 32, 42, 218; new creation, 34, 41; realizing the presence of, 4, 7, 9, 44–45, 157; outside the Church, 38, 40, 47; effects unity, 46–47, 68, 173, 177, 199; within the Church, 6, 36, 40, 62

Ineffabilis Deus, 71

infallibility, 2, 62, 64, 71–72, 139, 214–15, 218, 224

inference, 13–14, 26, 205

Isasi–Diaz, Ada Maria, 164, 207

Jager, Abbé, 66

Jerusalem Bishopric, 19

Jesus Christ, 4, 21, 34. 37–38, 40, 43, 73, 82, 87, 95, 125, 137, 147, 178 ; marked by the presence of 10–11, 113–14, 119–21, 125; new Adam 87, 89, 94, 116, 120

Jesuits, 169–70, 182, 190–92. *See also* Society of Jesus

Job, 175, 181

John, St., 92, 148, 172, 181–83

Johnson, Elizabeth, 12, 73, 109, 138, 172, 177, 206, 207

joy, 46, 53, 81, 113, 116, 121, 123, 147, 148, 169, 174, 177, 220

Judaism, 38, 40, 42; Jews, 36, 38, 40, 42–43, 156; Jewish dispensation, 37; Jewish Law, 38; people of Israel, 38

Jüngel, Eberhard, 109

justice, 10, 88, 91, 111, 193

justification, xi, 23, 35, 37–40, 42–43, 67, 70, 87, 89, 103, 132, 157–58, 160, 192, 194–95, 213; by faith, 23, 67, 157

Keating, John, 158–59, 207

Keble, John, 14, 23, 27–29, 61, 155

Kenrick, Francis, 71– 72, 207, 215

Ker, Ian, 3, 8, 16, 24, 32, 77, 82, 97, 134, 139, 155–56, 162, 167, 173–74, 205–08, 210, 219, 221

King, Benjamin, 54, 70, 87

Kingdom of God, 107–108

Kingsley, Charles, 15–16, 28

Knox, Thomas Francis, 180, 182–83

LaCugna, Elizabeth Mowry, 103, 109, 216

laity, 1, 2, 7, 11, 47, 69, 129, 130, 139–44, 161–65, 209, 218; temporal vocation of, 162; and church, 2, 11, 47, 139–42, 144, 161,

Lakeland, Paul, 129, 209

Lamm, William, 7, 33, 43–44

Lash, Nichola,s, 27, 73, 209, 211

Last Judgment, 83, 91, 178, 196

Law, 15, 36–38, 42, 48 78, 91, 139, 163, 172, 179, 189–91, 197; Mosaic, 38

Lérin, Vincent of, 51–52, 63, 65–66, 69

liberalism, , 23,61

Liberation Theology, 163–64, 223

Lisieux, St. Thérèse de, 197

Littlemore, 19, 21, 70

Liturgy, 3, 103, 122–23, 125, 164, 175–76, 213

lo cotidiano, 164

love, 4, 9, 10, 44, 46, 48, 55, 78–80, 83–85, 90–91, 95, 100, 113, 115–17, 120, 124–25, 132, 134, 147, 151–52, 154, 160, 165, 168, 170–71, 174, 176–78, 199, 200, 202

Loyola, St. Ignatius, 95, 191

Lumen Gentium (Light of Peoples), 7, 135, 141, 164, 219

Luther, Martin, 58, 63

Macmillan's Magazine, 15

Magdalen, St. Mary, 92, 131

magisterium, 6, 135, 137–38, 143, 145, 206
de Maistre, Joseph, 70
Manning, Henry Edward (Cardinal), 65–68, 70–71, 181, 209
Mansel, Henry, 98, 209
Marcellus, St., 172
Mariology vii, 11, 129, 130–31, 133–43, 206; Marian mode of interpretation, 11, 131, 142–143
Mary, 4, 8, 10, 41, 76, 114, 117–19, 120–21, 123, 125–27, 131–38, 140–44, 155, 201–02, 206–07; Blessed Virgin, 71, 130–31, 138, 140, 140, 142, 207; Christ's Mother, 118–19; Mother of God, 117, 136; new Eve, 118, 120, 220; pattern of faith, 11, 130–32, 135, 137, 142–43, 144; Queen of Heaven, 119; *Theotokos*, 119
Mayers, Walter, 18
McCarthy, David Matzko, 168, 185, 209
McFague, Sallie, 109
Merrigan, Terrance, 25, 82, 91, 97, 99, 156, 174, 207–08, 210, 221
Messori, Vittorio, 129, 217
Meynell, Charles, 98
Miller, Edward, 139, 210
Milner, Joseph, 54–57, 61, 210
modalism, 110
Möhler, Johann Adam, 69–71, 215
Monasticism 5, 104, 189–90, 197, 199
Monk, Maria, 16
monotheism, 101, 107
Morales, Jose, 155, 160–62, 210
More, Henry, 3
Morgan, Drew, 75, 210
Moriarty, Bishop David, 72
Mozley, James, 70
Mozley, Thomas, 15. 211
Murray, Placid, O.S.B., 1, 122, 161, 181, 183, 187–88, 191, 211

natural theology, 82–83, 205, 215. *See also* theology
Nazianzen, St. Gregory, 92
Neri, St. Philip, 11, 92, 167–69, 171–72, 180, 183–84, 189, 205
Neoscholasticism, 52, 73, 208
Newman, Francis, 149
Newman, John Henry: beatification of, 2, 7, 8, 217; on accomplishments, 149, 152–54; works of: *Apologia Pro Vita Sua*, xi, 2, 8, 14–15, 30, 49, 54, 82, 103, 155, 169, 188, 211; *Arians of the Fourth Century*, 47, 59–60, 115, 192–93; *Autobiographical Writings*, 23, 28, 55, 148, 211; *Difficulties Felt by Anglicans*, 87, 131, 212; *Essay on Development*, 21–22, 30, 53, 70, 72–73, 134, 136, 202; *Grammar of Assent*, 1, 4, 10, 14, 26, 30, 47, 82, 97–101, 105, 211–12; *Historical Sketches*, 63, 160, 212; *John Henry Newman Sermons, 1824–1843*, 122–24, 213; *Letters and Diaries*, 7, 19, 26, 59, 65, 72–73, 75, 87, 98, 139, 142, 149, 171–72, 179–83, 192, 213; *Lectures on the Doctrine of Justification*, 87, 158, 192, 194–95, 213; *Loss and Gain*, 16, 213; *Meditations and Devotions*, 30–31, 33, 44, 76, 157, 182, 213; *On Consulting the Faithful*, 2, 17, 139, 213; *Parochial and Plain Sermons*, 2, 9, 13, 31–48, 39, 41, 47, 79–80, 88–89, 92, 94, 115–18, 121, 123, 139, 146–47, 150, 152–54, 156–65, 173–74, 176–75, 185, 192, 195, 213; *Present Position of Catholics in England*, 16, 142, 213; *Sermons Preached on Various Occasions*, 13, 89, 165, 213; *Tracts for the Times* 32, 62, 216; *University Sermons*, 1; *Via Media of the Anglican Church*, 19, 64, 134–35, 181, 214;

Newman Studies Journal, ix, 25–26, 31, 78, 173, 192, 203–05, 210, 220, 223
Newman, Thomas, 62, 70, 88
New Evangelization, 81, 83, 91, 96, 209, 219
Newton, Thomas, 55, 58, 62, 70, 88, 211, 214
Nicene Creed, 60
Nichols, Aidan, 138, 214
Noah, 176
Northcote, Spencer, 96

O'Malley, John W., 144, 214
ontology, 107
oppression, 164
Oratory, 53, 172, 181, 187, 202
Oratorian, 1, 4, 12, 161, 169–70, 172, 180–85, 187–99, 211, 213
Oriel College, 15, 22, 55, 211
Orthodoxy, 60–62, 71, 88, 136
Oxford, 15, 19, 23, 25, 45, 52, 61, 65, 75, 79, 82–83, 150
Oxford Movement, 15, 23, 27–28, 32, 37, 55, 59, 62, 64–65, 69–70, 157, 224
Oxford University, 3, 11, 17, 19, 22, 26, 47, 58, 73, 86, 101, 130–31, 137, 201, 204–5, 207–8, 212–13, 215–16
Pahls, Michael J., 55, 62, 72, 40, 207, 214–215, 218
Paine, Thomas, 18, 22
Paley, William, 82
Pannenberg, Wolfhart, 97, 106–10, 215, 221, 225
Pantheism, 83, 101
papacy, 2, 55, 57, 62, 134. *See also* popes
Perrone, Giovanni, 71–72, 218
personalism, 82
Petavius, Dionysius, 60
Petrarch, 58
Pirminius, St., 172
polytheism, 110

Poole, Sr. Imelda, 183
popes, 71,73,129; as Anti–Christ, 58; Benedict XVI, 53–55, 143–44, 189, 202, 217; John XXIII, 73; John Paul II, 26, 252; Leo XIII, 52; Paul VI, 129; Pius V, 71, 73; Pius IX, 7, 53, 140–141, 216
poverty, 151, 163–64; the poor, 113, 163
Pramuk, Christopher, 100, 101, 216
prayer, 2–3, 5–6, 10, 13, 18, 24, 35, 44, 48, 76, 95, 103–08, 120, 148–49, 156, 158–59, 163, 172, 175–76, 184, 193, 197, 207, 213; as communion with God, 3, 159; mental prayer (meditation), 44, 48, 158–59, 163, 156, 197, 221
predestination, 90–91
Protestants, Protestantism, 19, 23, 55, 62–65, 70, 90, 173
purgatory, 91–92
Pusey, Edward, 23–24, 17, 29, 55, 131, 136, 138, 216

racism,164
Rahner, Karl 90, 102–03, 137, 216
The Rambler, 140
rationalism, 18, 22–23, 55, 132–36; and Enlightenment 18, 22, 55, 81, 83, 86, 132,
Ratzinger, Joseph. 2, 51–54, 73, 129–30, 136, 201, 202
reason, 1, 7, 12, 26, 28, 65, 83, 93, 100–01, 115, 119, 132–34, 142–43, 147, 163, 177
reception, vii, 7, 11, 19, 24, 36, 90, 127, 129–31, 136, 138–39, 142, 144, 217; spirituality of, 7, 11, 129–31, 136, 138, 142, 144
redemption, 35, 80, 84, 88, 91, 109, 115, 117, 123–25
Reformation, 3, 55, 58–59, 62–65, 67–68, 221

regeneration, 34–36, 38–39, 42–43, 46–47, 157–58
religion, 10, 14, 25, 33, 35, 47–48, 53, 61, 63, 66, 81, 83, 90, 91, 98, 100–01, 133–34, 142, 154–56, 160, 167–68, 188–89, 193–96, 198, 203, 210, 214, 216–17, 219–20; natural, 33, 193; revealed, 47, 91, 133
repentance, 48, 117
resurrection, 115, 117, 119, 122, 126
revelation, 4, 9, 10, 38, 45, 47, 58, 71, 77, 83, 89, 91, 101–2, 107–8, 110,131–32, 134–35, 137, 146, 156, 193, 210, 215; Christian, 45; Universal, 47, 91, 210
Rickards, Samuel, 64
Righteousness, 35–37, 157–58, 164, 195; Imputed, 35–37, 157–58; real, 35–37, 195,
Rogers, Frederic (Lord Blachford), 75
Roman Catholicism, 9, 16, 19–20, 22–23, 26–27, 30, 53–55, 62–65, 70, 131, 145
Roman Curia, 53, 87, 137,144, 202–03, 216
Romanism, 30, 64, 70
Romanticism, 87
Roncalli, Angelo, 73. *See also* Pope John XXIII
Rose, Hugh James 99
Routhier, Gilles 130, 217
Rufinus, St. 172
rule of faith, 66
Rush, Ormond, 130, 217
Russell, Charles William, 23

sacraments, 3–4, 23–24, 42, 122, 135, 156, 165, 174–75, 213
sacramental principle, 11, 145, 154–56, 160
saints, vii, 4, 11–12, 15, 20, 46–47, 58, 76, 78, 91–93, 95, 122–24, 126, 141, 156, 158, 167–69, 171–85, 196–97, 203–4, 207, 209, 213, 216, 224. *See also* communion of saints
Saint Mary, 41, 92, 131, 223,
salvation, 4, 12, 21, 33, 35–36, 39, 76, 79, 85–87, 89–91, 94, 107, 114, 118, 124–26, 131, 136–38, 151, 156, 162, 165, 179, 185, 192, 194–95, 198, 207, 209, 221
salvation history, 36, 85
sanctification, 10, 35, 76, 93, 108, 123, 194
Satan, 48, 57–58, 61
Saul, 13–14, 28
Savanarola, Giacomo, 169
Schaff, Philip, 70–71, 218
Schleiermacher, F.D.E., 90, 98, 101, 106, 218
Schneiders, Sandra, 5, 53–54, 105–06, 218
schola theologorum, 138–39, 215
Schultenover, David G., 144, 214
science, 82–83, 86, 98, 151, 205, 210
scholastic, 103
Scriptures, 4, 66, 152; New Testament, 13, 39, 45, 103, 137; Old Testament, 38, 114
Second Vatican Council, 1–2, 7, 11, 51, 53, 95, 129–31, 135, 141–44, 162–64, 217– 18
secularism, 81, 86, 93, 162, 165, 219
sensus fidelium, 7, 139, 141, 144, 205
Sheehan, Peter, 42, 218
sin, 4, 13, 35, 37, 40–42, 47, 119; actual, 35; original, 35, 40–41, 4, 119; proneness to, 41–42; sinfulness, 115–16
Singulari Quidem, 53, 216
skepticism, 55, 132, 136
Smith, John, 3
Society of Jesus, 190, 192, 199. *See also* Jesuits
Spartans, 169, 190
*Spiritual Exercises,*105

spirituality, vii, ix, 2–12, 14, 18, 21, 23, 31–32, 43, 45, 51, 53–53, 63, 65, 76–78, 81, 85–89, 96–97, 99, 101, 103–09, 111, 113–14, 125, 129–31, 137, 145, 148–49, 157, 161, 167, 177, 184–85, 187–89, 191, 193, 195, 197, 199, 201–04, 206, 208, 218, 221, 223, 224; ascent, 5; and descent, 5; a spiritual life, 44; and brokenness, 114, 117, 125; and detachment, 5, 182, 197; as self–offering, 123–24; incarnational, vii, 10–11, 113–14, 125, 184; Marian dimension, 136–37; puritanical, 148; spiritual development, 44, 124; spiritual direction, 9, 45
St. John, Ambrose, 20, 172, 181–83
Strange, Roderick, 87–88, 97, 118, 219
subordinationism, 110
Suenens, Cardinal Leon Joseph, 137, 219
supernatural, 33, 77, 92, 141, 191
surrender, 117, 200
sympathy, vii, 10, 75–96, 184

Talbot, Msgr., 7, 140
Taylor, Jeremy, 64
temporal advantages, 152, 154
Terence, 93–94, 220
Theodoret, St., 173
Theology, vii, 4–5, 7–11, 21, 23–25, 29, 32, 42–43, 45, 54, 57, 73, 75–79, 81–83, 85–87, 89–93, 95–98, 100–01, 104–07, 109–11, 114, 131–33, 135–36, 138, 141, 144, 157, 159, 164, 168, 172, 175, 178, 188, 192–93, 198, 201–02, 204–07, 209–10, 214–18, 220–221, 223–25; natural, 82–83, 205, 215; patristic, 14, 53, 55, 57, 59–60, 64, 84, 114, 118, 120–21, 172, 177, 192
Theological inquiry, 83, 133, 135
theopoiēsis (θεοποιεσης) 192, 194

theory of development, 22, 52–54, 66–68, 70–72, 75, 130
Thirty–nine Articles, 59
Tilley, Terrence, 130, 144, 220
Tract 90, 19, 23, 29, 69
Tractarian movement, 18, 216; Tractarianism, 32, 65, 143, 216
Tradition, 3–5, 12, 22–23, 51–53, 57, 60–65, 69–73, 78, 83, 135, 138–39, 143–44, 172, 192, 203–4, 207, 215, 224
Trinity, vii, 4, 10, 12, 32–33, 42–43, 76, 78–79, 88–89, 96–111, 194, 198, 200, 205, 207, 210, 216, 218, 223; *circumincessio,* 79–81; doctrine of, 97–98, 101–4, 106–11; communio, 2, 53, 79, 217; divine persons, 4, 32–33, 79–80, 110; subsistent relations, 79; subordinationism, 94
Trinity College, 148–49
truth, 15, 23, 25, 34, 43–33, 46,51–52, 56–57, 59–60, 62–63, 65–66, 69, 72–74, 77, 79–80, 82, 88, 91–92, 95, 98–99, 109, 113, 117, 130–34, 136, 138–39, 141–42, 170–171, 175, 190, 193, 195–96, 220; Christian, 52, 56–57, 59–60, 65–66, 69, 132
Tutu, Archbishop Desmond, 113–14, 117, 125, 220

Ubi Primum,(On Discipline for Religious), 140–41, 216
Ullathorne, Bishop William Bernard, 72, 140
Unitarianism, 195

Vaino, Olli–Pekka, 132, 220
Vanhoozer, Kevin, 109
Vatican Archives, 52, 203
Vélez, Juan, 25, 90, 220
Vico, Giovanni Battista, 51

Wainwright, Geoffrey, 156, 221

Ward, Wilfrid, 7, 23, 45, 55, 73, 96, 110, 132, 139–40, 148, 204, 209, 211–13, 221
Weigel, George, 135, 221
Whately, Richard, 22–23, 28
Whichcote, Benjamin, 3
Wilberforce, W., 148
Wilcox, Peter, 30, 221
Wilkins, John, 130, 221
Wiseman, Bishop Nicholas, 19, 171, 172
Wood, Samuel Francis, 65–68
world, vii, ix, 2, 4–7, 9–11, 15, 19, 23, 40, 47, 77, 83, 85, 87, 91, 93, 95, 99, 101, 108, 113–14, 116–26, 137–38, 140–41, 145–65, 167, 175–76, 182, 184, 188, 196, 198, 205, 210, 218; invisible, 11, 145–49, 151–56, 158–60, 162, 165; visible, 11, 145–48, 151, 153–56, 158–61, 165
Wyclif, John, 57–58

Xavier, St. Francis, 169

Zeno, Dr., 45, 159, 167, 221

www.ingramcontent.com/pod-product-compliance
Lightning Source LLC
Chambersburg PA
CBHW071156070526
44584CB00019B/2809